TURGENEV'S LITERARY REMINISCENCES

IVAN TURGENEV

———◆———

LITERARY REMINISCENCES

AND AUTOBIOGRAPHICAL FRAGMENTS

TRANSLATED WITH AN INTRODUCTION BY

David Magarshack

AND AN ESSAY ON TURGENEV BY

Edmund Wilson

Ivan R. Dee, Publisher

CHICAGO

Library of Congress Cataloging-in-Publication Data:
Turgenev, Ivan Sergeevich, 1818–1883.
 [Literaturnye i zhiteiskie vospominaniia. English]
 Literary reminiscences and autobiographical fragments / by Ivan Turgenev ; translated with an introduction by David Margarshack ; with an essay on Turgenev by Edmund Wilson.
  p. cm.
 Originally published: New York : Farrar, Straus and Cadahy, 1958.
 ISBN 1-56663-405-9 (alk. paper)
 1. Turgenev, Ivan Sergeevich, 1818–1883. 2. Authors, Russian--19th century--Biography. I. Margarshack, David. II. Title.

 PG3431.L5 E5 2001
 2001028947--dc21

2001028947

CONTENTS

TURGENEV'S LITERARY REMINISCENCES

Turgenev and the Life-Giving Drop

by Edmund Wilson

I

THE MAIDEN NAME OF TURGENEV'S MOTHER was Varvara Petrovna Lutovinova. The family knew little of their ancestry before the beginning of the eighteenth century, but they had since then accumulated a fortune by methods which sometimes amounted to plunder. The family history was full of scandals. When Varvara Petrovna was a little girl, her mother married again and took her to live with her stepfather, a drunken country squire, who beat her and humiliated her in ways that she could not bear to talk about. Varvara's mother was hardly gentler: she made favorites of the daughters of her husband and did nothing to defend her own daughter. Turgenev gave the following account of her to one of his German friends: "The quick-tempered old woman was stricken with paralysis, and spent all her time sitting almost motionless in an armchair. One day she got very cross with the little serf boy who was in attendance on her, and in a fierce fit of anger seized a log and hit him over the head with such force that he fell unconscious on the floor. This sight produced a most unpleasant impression on her: she bent down, picked the little boy up, put him beside her on the big armchair, placed a pillow on his bleeding head, and, sitting down on it, suffocated him." The daughter was unattractive but extremely strong-willed, and she knew that she would inherit the family property. When Varvara Petrovna was sixteen, her stepfather tried to rape her, and she ran away, on foot and half dressed, to the house of an uncle twenty miles away. The uncle took her in, but the atmosphere of the household was not friendly. He kept her under rigorous discipline, and she resented this. By the time she was twenty-six, the relations between them had become so embittered that he threatened to put her out and wanted to disinherit her, but before he had a chance to remake his will, he died of a heart attack.

Varvara Petrovna now found herself mistress of an enormous property—a number of separate estates, tenanted by thousands of serfs (Turgenev's friend Pavel Annenkov says that she possessed five thousand in the Government of Orel alone)—whom she ruled with a brutality which rivalled that from which she herself had suffered. She identified herself with the Tsar and referred to her peasants as "subjects." She was not only tyrannical but ogreish. For the slightest deviation from her orders, and sometimes on trumped-up pretexts, she would have her people flogged or ship them off to Siberia—though from this latter fate they were sometimes rescued by neighbors, who took them on their own estates, while Varvara Petrovna's household pretended that her sentences had been carried out. She would not allow her maids to have children, because children interfered with their duties, and they threw their babies into a pond. When two of her favorite servants were married to one another, by her orders and without being consulted, she permitted the wife to have children but made her keep them so far away that the mistress could not hear them crying, in a place to which it was rarely possible for the mother to get to see them. On her removal to Moscow for the winter, the mistress forbade this woman to bring her children along, and when she learned that the girl had dared to disobey, she made a terrible scene, which a member of the household has described: "Varvara Petrovna, hoarse with rage, threw herself out of bed, with one hand seized Agatha by the throat, and with the other it seemed as if she tried to tear her mouth to pieces . . . but immediately let go, and almost falling into the nearest armchair, she had an attack of nerves." She gave orders that the children should be sent back to the country, but they were hidden in a servant's room, where they lived locked up all winter, never allowed to go out, for fear the mistress would see them. On one occasion, when the keeper of the linen was having a celebration of her "name day," enlivened, as a matter of course and as Varvara Petrovna well knew, by a liberal consumption of vodka, the mistress played on her servants a morbid and ferocious practical joke. She declared herself to be dying and summoned the fifty members of her household and office staffs to pass before her bedside. Pretending to be only half conscious, she noted which servants did not appear and which had a smell of vodka. Then she quickly recovered, demanded tea and decreed that all these culprits should be punished: "Rascals, drunkards! You were all drunk. You were glad that your mistress was dying! . . . You were drinking and celebrating a name day with your mistress dying!"

There is, of course, in all this the terrible need of a woman who has never been loved to make herself felt by others. She had married a young cavalry officer, of an older and more honorable family, which, however, was going bankrupt. He was handsome and attractive to women, and he had found Miss Lutovinova so repellent that it had been only by his father's going down on his knees and begging him to rescue the family estate, which would otherwise be sold at auction, that he had been persuaded to marry her. He gave Varvara three sons—Ivan and his older brother Nikolai and a younger boy, who died at seventeen—but was continually unfaithful to her. He was allowed by her no power in the household, and he did nothing to protect the children, whom their mother sometimes thrashed every day, for reasons which in some cases were never explained to them. He died when he was forty-one and when Ivan was sixteen. Thereafter, Varvara Petrovna carried on up to the time of her death, when Ivan was thirty-two, a systematic persecution of her children. She had nothing but contempt for writers, and she never forgave Ivan for his interest in literature, which she considered no career for a Turgenev. But by refusing to give him an allowance, she forced him to earn money by his pen and so to become a professional writer, to get published and to prove his competence, earlier, perhaps, than might otherwise have happened. By the time he had inherited property, he had written *A Sportman's Sketches* and had proved himself already a master of both story-telling and Russian prose.

The content of Ivan's early work is mostly in one way or another a product of his mother's personality. In the stories Turgenev wrote before 1847, when the series of *Sketches* was begun, there is an alternation of two main themes. The salient one is a force of evil so powerful and so audacious that no resistance to it is possible—a force that, as long as his mother was living, appeared in a masculine form. The queer scoundrels of *The Duellist* and *Three Portraits**—the latter perhaps an episode from the family history, in which the Lutovinovs appear as Luchinovs—seduce and mishandle women and provoke their more decent rivals to duels in which the latter get killed. In the one-act play *The Indiscretion,* of 1843, which begins as an amusing comedy, you have the same implacable villain, who bullies and ends by murdering the heroine. This comes as a surprise to the reader, who expects her to extricate herself, and makes the otherwise adroit little piece

---

* Except for the spelling of proper names, I have usually given Turgenev's titles in the versions of Constance Garnett, unsatisfactory though these sometimes are. I have, however, used *Fathers and Sons* instead of *Fathers and Children* in order to make this title consistent with the translation Mr. Magarshack prefers.

impossible, one would think, for the stage. Turgenev even added an epigraph, consisting of two lines of dialogue, in which it is shown that this scoundrel was not merely never brought to justice but that he lived to become a respected official.

The complementary theme to this—in *Andrey Kolosov* and *Petushkov*—is the timid or inadequate man who lets the woman down. In *Andrey Kolosov* you have something of both. Andrey wins and drops poor Varya in a selfish, cold-blooded way, and the narrator, who worships Andrey—in slavish imitation of his hero—after winning her, drops her, too. Here we find in Turgenev's first story a situation that is to run through all his work and to have its great development in *Fathers and Sons:* two friends, one ruthless, one shy, who become involved with the same woman. In the case of *A Sportsman's Sketches,* the whole impact of the book is a protest against the antiquated system of serfholding that Varvara Petrovna stood for: without explicit sympathy for the serfs or overt condemnation of the masters, the latter are played off against the former. In this book, Turgenev invented what was really a new genre. He had been able to learn from Pushkin, whom he took for his master, the trick of evading the censorship by telling a story in such a way as to make it convey its moral without any explicit statement, and he was the first Western writer of fiction to perfect the modern art of implying social criticism through a narrative that is presented objectively, organized economically, and beautifully polished in style. The stories of Mérimée—many of them written before Turgenev's—are distinguished by similar qualities, but so were the short stories of Pushkin and those of Lermontov's *A Hero of Our Time.* The following dates will give some idea of the way in which this form was developed: Pushkin's *Tales of Belkin,* 1831; Mérimée's *Mosaïque,* 1833; Lermontov's *A Hero of Our Time,* 1840; *Andrey Kolosov* (Turgenev's first prose short story), 1844; Mérimée's *Carmen,* 1845; the first of *A Sportsman's Sketches,* 1847. But no

7

prose tale before Turgenev attempts, through sheer technical precision, not merely to tell a story but also to hit on the head a social and moral nail. *Madame Bovary* was not begun till 1851 and not published till 1857. *A Sportsman's Sketches* appeared as a book in 1852.

Varvara Petrovna Turgeneva ignored Ivan's stories as they came out in periodicals, and in her last years she worked herself up into paroxysms of hatred against both her sons. Nikolai had outraged his mother by marrying her German *femme de chambre*, and Varvara refused to receive his wife. The most she would do to recognize that a marriage had taken place was to direct that her little grandchildren be led past the window of her house in order that she might have a look at them. She had at last, however, been induced to give her acceptance of the marriage on condition that Nikolai should resign from his civil-service job in St. Petersburg and come to live in Moscow and manage her property from there. She promised to buy him a house, but after he had picked one out and signed an agreement for it, she did not supply the money, and left him with his furniture on the pavement and his family still in the capital. It was weeks before she made it possible for him to complete the sale of the house, and then, when he had moved to Moscow, she compelled him to spend every day with her from eleven o'clock in the morning to three or four in the afternoon, and would not supply him with further funds, so that, once he had spent what he had got for the sale of his St. Petersburg place, he had no way of keeping up his establishment. Ivan was living in Paris. It had made him so unhappy to stay at Spasskoye (the estate on which his mother chose to live), on account of her crushing cruelty and his powerlessness to do anything about it—since she received his appeals with indignant scorn—that he preferred to go away and forget her. She attempted to make him return by withholding even the small sums of money she had grudgingly granted before, and when he would not, she vicariously revenged herself. Turgenev had had a daughter by a seamstress who worked for Varvara Petrovna. The little girl was now seven. Varvara Petrovna, on leaving Moscow, where she went for the winter months, took the child away from her mother and sent her to work in the kitchen. On occasions when she was entertaining guests, she would sometimes have the little girl cleaned up and more presentably dressed and brought in to be exhibited to visitors. She would ask them whom they thought she resembled, and when they at once said Ivan Sergeyevich, she would send her back to the kitchen to become the butt of the servants.

Nikolai and Ivan at last decided to have a showdown with their mother. They appealed to her to give them small incomes, so that at least they could know what to count on. She received this request with calm and proceeded to present them with "deeds of gift," which purported to make over to them two of her other estates but which were actually of no value whatever, since she had not had them legally drawn, and had, in the meantime, as they learned, sent orders that all the corn in both places be sold, and the money forwarded to her, so that there would not be a ruble to be got from them or even a grain left for sowing. She mocked her two sons in a nasty scene, handing them the worthless papers and demanding that they thank her for them. "No one," wrote Pavel Annenkov, "could equal her in the art of insulting a man, of humiliating him and making him unhappy, while preserving decorum and calm and maintaining her own dignity." Nikolai kissed her hand and left the room, but Ivan simply got up and went. The next day his mother challenged him; why had he not thanked her? "Do you mean to say you are still dissatisfied with me?" We have an account of what followed from a member of the household who overheard it:

"Listen, Mamma," began Ivan Sergeyevich at last, "let us drop this conversation. Ah, why do you want to renew it?"

"And why do you not want to speak out?"

"Mamma, once more, I beg you, let us drop it—I know how to be silent, but I cannot lie and pretend. Do what you will, I cannot. Do not force me to speak—it is too distressing."

"I don't know what you mean by 'distressing,' " continued Varvara Petrovna harshly, "but I am offended. I do everything for you, and then you are dissatisfied with me!"

"Do not do anything for us. We don't ask you for anything now. Please leave the subject alone—we shall continue to live as we have lived."

"Not as you have lived! You have some property now," Varvara Petrovna continued to urge severely.

"Now, why; tell me why do you say such a thing?" At last Ivan Sergeyevich lost patience. "We had nothing yesterday and we have nothing today, and you know it very well!"

"Why nothing!" cried Varvara Petrovna. "Your brother has a house and an estate, and you have an estate."

"A house! And you know that my brother is too honest to look upon that house as his own. He cannot fulfill the conditions on which you gave it to him. You demand that he shall live in it, but you won't give him anything to live on. He has nothing."

"What? He has an estate."

"He has no such thing! You haven't given us anything, and you won't. Your deeds of gift, as you call them, are not valid; you can take from us tomorrow what you have given us today. Yes, and why all this bother? The estates are yours. Everything is yours. Simply tell us that you don't want to give us anything, and you will not hear a word from us. But why this farce?"

"You are mad!" cried Varvara Petrovna. "You forget to whom you are speaking!"

"But I never wanted to speak. I wanted to be silent. Do you think it was easy for me to say this? I asked you to drop it," and there was such distress in his voice that it seemed as if tears were choking him.

"I am sorry for my brother," he continued, after a short silence. "Why have you ruined him? You allowed him to marry, compelled him to give up the service and remove here with his family. Before this he did manage to live, he lived by his own labor, he didn't ask you for anything, and he was comparatively com-

fortable then. But here, from the day he came, you have condemned him to a life of misery—you are always tormenting him
in one way or another."

"How do you mean? Tell me how?" Varvara Petrovna was
aroused.

"In every way!" Ivan Sergeyevich was desperate and could not
help shouting. "Do you not tyrannize over everybody? Who can
breathe freely near you?"—and he strode up and down the room.
"I feel that I ought not to be saying this—I beg of you, let us
stop!"

"So that is your gratitude for all . . ."

"Again, Mamma, again, you will not understand that we are
not children, and that your behavior is insulting! You are afraid
of giving us anything! You think that it would lessen your power
over us! We have always been dutiful sons, but you have no faith
in anything or anybody. You believe only in your own power!
And what has that given you? The right to tyrannize over everybody!"

"So you think that I am wicked?"

"You are not wicked, but I do not know what is going on in
your mind, why you should behave in this way. Do examine yourself and remember what you have done."

"What, exactly? To whom have I done wrong?"

"To whom? Who is happy with you? Remember only Polyakov
and Agatha [the two servants whose children had been suppressed]
—all whom you persecute, exile. They would all love you, all be
ready to lay down their lives for you, if—but you make them all
miserable. Yes, and I myself would give half my life if I did not
know all this and did not have to say it. They are all afraid of
you, and they could love you. . . ."

"Nobody loves me! Nobody has ever loved me! Even my children are against me!"

"Do not say that, Mamma: we are all ready, your children first
of all. . . ."

"I haven't any children!" suddenly shouted Varvara Petrovna.
"Go away!"

"Mamma!" Ivan Sergeyevich ran to her.

"Go!" repeated Varvara Petrovna still more loudly, and with

this word she herself left the room, slamming the door behind her.

The next morning she was handed a letter in which Nikolai announced that Ivan and he were about to move in on their father's estate, the village of Turgenevo. They had obtained a legal authorization and believed that their mother could not dislodge them. Ivan attempted to see her, but, when told that he had presented himself, she "went to her writing table, seized Ivan Sergeyevich's youthful portrait, and threw it on the floor. The glass was smashed to pieces, and the portrait flew against the opposite wall. When the maid came in and wanted to pick it up, Varvara Petrovna cried, 'Leave it,' and so the portrait lay there from the beginning of June to the beginning of the next spring." It should be noted that Ivan was her favorite son, and that she had never been able to forgive him his infatuation with Pauline Viardot, the celebrated Spanish singer, his lifelong admiration and at one time mistress. He now rescued his daughter from the household and sent her to stay with Mme. Viardot, and he never saw his mother again. He and Nikolai moved into Turgenevo, which was only a few miles from Spasskoye. One day, when his mother was absent, Nikolai brought his wife over and showed her around Spasskoye, which she had not seen. When Varvara Petrovna learned of this, she slashed Polyakov in the face with a riding whip, then collapsed and passed into a decline, from which she never recovered. When she was dying, Ivan was summoned, but she had died before he arrived. "May the Lord save us from such a death," he wrote to Pauline Viardot. "She was merely trying to stupefy herself. A short time before she died, she ordered her orchestra to play dance music in the next room. One ought to speak of the dead with pity and respect, so I shall not say anything further. But since I must tell you what I know and feel, I shall mention one thing more: my mother thought of nothing else in her last months except (I'm ashamed to say) of ruining us—my brother and me. In her last letter to the manager of her estates, she gave him clear and precise orders to sell everything for a song—if need be, to burn everything! . . . And yet I feel that it could have been so easy for her to have made us love her." And later, when he had read her diary: "What a woman, my dear friend, what a woman! I could not close my eyes all night. May the Lord forgive her for everything! But what a life! Truly I am deeply shocked. Yes, yes, we must be good and just, if only in order not to die as she died."

This story is told by David Magarshack in his recent biography, *Turgenev, a Life*—to which I am here much indebted—and in *The Turgenev Family*, by Varvara Zhitova, which, though published first in Russia in 1884, just after Turgenev's death, has only recently been translated into English. Varvara Zhitova was a child of poor parents, who had been adopted by Varvara Petrovna a few days after her birth. Her picture of the Turgenev household is already bad enough, but it is made even worse when we learn from a letter of Ivan's to Pauline Viardot, written after his mother's death, that the adopted daughter was one of two "hangers-on" who had to be "removed from the house, where they were constantly creating discord . . . a regular Mme. Lafarge, false, sly, malicious and heartless. It would be impossible to tell you all the bad things that that little viper has done." He partly, however, blames her bad character on the influence of his mother. It had apparently been one of Varvara Petrovna's tricks to play the adopted Varvara off against her slighted sons, yet at the same time she was always furious when there was any suggestion that the girl was becoming a favorite with the servants.

Turgenev, entertaining the children of a friend, once made up the following story:

"A poor child had sick parents and did not know how to cure them, which gave him a great deal of unhappiness. One day somebody said to him, 'Somewhere there exists a cave, and in that cave every year on a certain day a drop of water oozes down from the roof—a miraculous drop of life-giving water. Whoever drinks this drop of water will receive the gift of being able to heal both the diseases of the body and the pains of the soul.' So a year passed, and then another year—I don't know exactly how long, but the child at last found the cave, and went inside. It had been hollowed out in the rock, and the stones of its vault were cracked. As soon as he had gone inside, the poor child was seized with fright; all around him crawled snakes and reptiles, each more horrible and repulsive than the other, which looked at him with evil eyes. But the brave boy did not want to go back without having got the drop, so he waited to watch for the moment when he would see it ooze out of the rock. After waiting a long time, very frightened, he perceived at last, on the roof, a something wet that glistened. Little by little, this liquid pearl grew round and was forming a drop as transparent as a tear. But hardly had the drop formed than all the reptiles strained up from below it and opened their jaws to catch it. At that moment, the drop, which was just about to form, disappeared back into the vault. The child mustered his patience and continued to wait. And again the reptiles and serpents stretched themselves up on their tails, and, almost grazing the little boy's face, they opened their jaws toward the vault. But the child was no longer afraid. It seemed to him at every moment that the snakes were going to throw themselves on him, to plunge their fangs into his flesh or to wrap themselves about him to strangle him. But he never forgot his purpose; he, too, stood with open mouth. And a miracle occurred! The drop of life fell between his lips—he swallowed it. The snakes all began to hiss, and they made an infernal racket, but, unwillingly, they had to give way and allow the boy to pass; they were forced to confine themselves to piercing him with envious looks. And it turned out that it had not been for nothing that the child had drunk the life-giving drop. It made him a great savant; he was able to cure his parents and came to be a famous man."

Here Turgenev stopped.

"What happened then?" asked the children.

"What more do you want?" he said. "Surely that's enough for today. I'll tell you something more tomorrow. But you must give me time to think."

II

And what was the rest of the story? Let us see what happened to the brave little boy who got away with the life-giving drop.

He did not, we may note as important, much care to revisit the cave. There was already, on the Lutovinov side, a tradition of horror behind the Turgenevs. Once, Varvara Petrovna took the adopted Varvara to look in on her stepfather's place, which now belonged to her. The house, in which nobody lived, was almost in ruins. Some of the windows were broken, and the frames of the portraits, which were never cleaned, had become quite black. They walked through a long, dark and narrow hall and turned off into another corridor, where they were faced by a door boarded up with planks. There was, however, an old-fashioned latch, toward which the girl put out her hand. Varvara Petrovna snatched it away: "Don't touch it! You mustn't! Those rooms are accursed!" "I shall never forget her accent and look, so much fear, hate and fury they expressed." It had been her stepfather's apartment, and it had revived some intolerable memory. It is quite evident that Ivan felt hardly less reluctance to return to the Spasskoye household. He had inherited eleven estates, including Spasskoye—in all, about thirty thousand acres. He had immediately liberated his household serfs, and he had tried to persuade his peasants to pay him rent for their land instead of compensating him by work on his. He was arrested in 1852, and exiled to his country place, for

15

having written an article on Gogol's death, in which he had called Gogol "great." (It was as impossible for Nicholas I as for Stalin to brook the magnification of any other Russian, and Turgenev was already *mal vu* on account of *A Sportsman's Sketches.*) He was thus obliged at this time to spend sixteen continuous months at Spasskoye, and he had later to return at intervals in order to keep track of his properties, yet one feels that he was never much at home there, and—except in his literary treatment of them—not close to the people and their work. He sees them casually; he shuts himself up to write; he is much addicted to hunting. The supervision of his huge property is a task with which he cannot grapple, and he installs an uncle as manager. Ivan spends as much time as possible in St. Petersburg or Western Europe. But the uncle proves extremely incompetent, and Turgenev has to go back from time to time to straighten matters out. On one occasion—in 1867, seventeen years after his mother's death—the complaints of his uncle at his absence compel him to return to Russia, but he can hardly drag himself to Spasskoye. The situation is all the more trying because by this time Turgenev has decided to have the uncle replaced. His letters to Pauline Viardot have the sound of a journey to the Dark Tower on the part of a reluctant Childe Roland who is equipped with no resonant slug horn to challenge the evil spirits. In St. Petersburg, business delays him from making the trip to Moscow. In Moscow, he expects to return to Baden in less than four weeks: "I am leaving tomorrow for Spasskoye. . . . I hope to be back in a week." But the train can take him only sixty miles. "We are in Russia at the time of year when, due to the melting snow, all communications cease." By the time he has travelled two or three miles by sleigh over roads that are full of appalling holes, he has developed "a violent cough, which is continually getting worse. . . . I passed a sleepless night in a wretched inn room, with my pulse at a hundred a minute and a cough that was cracking my chest, and at seven o'clock in the morning I was obliged, in that miserable condition, to subject myself again to the torture of the washout holes and to get back, more dead than alive, to the railroad line and Moscow. . . . If my uncle would only be reasonable and let things be arranged by mail!" In Moscow, he partly recovers: "Tomorrow I set forth again on the assault of Sebastopol." But he doesn't; three days later he is still in Moscow, with the iron ball of the journey still fastened, as he says, to his legs; and this iron ball turns into gout, which keeps him in Moscow till spring. "I have received not a letter but a novel from my uncle, who treats me as if I were a murderer because I don't come to Spasskoye. . . . My new manager has found everything literally in chaos—there are debts that I didn't expect." Turgenev never got to Spasskoye; he returned to St. Petersburg in April.

Two years after his mother's death, Turgenev wrote two short stories—*Mumu* and *The Wayside Inn* (1852), in which, for the first time in his fiction, he deals with his mother directly. The first of these was based, he said, on actual happenings, and Varvara Petrovna appears in person as a tyrannical and cruel landowner who compels a deaf-mute serf to drown a little pet dog which he has earlier rescued from drowning and which is the only thing he has to love. The bitterness of the mistress at not being loved herself figures here as a motive, and we appreciate the story more if we have some independent knowledge of Varvara Petrovna's life: she has tried to make friends with the little dog, which has refused to come to her when called and then snarls at her when she tries to pat it. In the other story, the callous woman landowner is combined with the Force of Evil—unconquerable and inexpugnable—embodied in a masculine character. This demon in human form works on the lady's cupidity to induce her to sell him an inn that has been occupied and run for years by one of her most trusted serfs. This serf has had every reason to assume he could trust his mistress, but the scoundrel has moved in on him, seduced his wife and brought her to a point of infatuation at which she is ready, at his orders, to steal her husband's savings. The villain conceals his real plan, pretending he needs the money for another purpose, and when he uses it to buy the inn and turn her husband out, she is horrified at what she has done, whereupon he turns her out, too. He prospers and is lucky enough to sell the inn just before it burns down. His victim, who has lost his wife and his living, is driven to fall back on religion and spends the rest of his life in pilgrimages.

There is so little overt bitterness in Turgenev, and to his contemporaries his life seemed so easy, that they were likely to be puzzled by his pessimism. It moved Henry James to complain of his "atmosphere of unrelieved sadness. We go from one tale to the other in the hope of finding something cheerful, but we only wander into fresh agglomerations of gloom." And, what is more striking, even Mérimée—at the moment when he has just written *Lokis!*—begs Turgenev not to be so painful: *"Faites-nous donc une histoire qui ne finisse pas trop mal. Vous abusez depuis quelque temps de notre sensibilité."* But the stories of Mérimée, some of them practical jokes, are shockers. Turgenev's show the permanent stamp of an oppressive, a completely hopeless and a permanently harrowing experience.

He could not have talked very much of the uglier aspects of his early life, for no one appears to have thought of accounting in terms of this for the themes and the mood of his fiction. Nor could even his great Russian contemporaries, Tolstoy and Dostoevsky, when they reproach him for his love of the West, for his indifference to affairs in Russia, have quite understood the terrible weight, the lasting effect of Spasskoye—its implications for the whole of Turgenev's thought. Dostoevsky was a congenitally dislocated man; his family had gone to pieces even before his parvenu father had been murdered by his own peasants. Tolstoy had been an orphan, exhilaratingly self-dependent; he had inherited his estate at nineteen, with no hateful family memories, and during the years of his rather wild freedom and his service in the Crimean War, it had been kept for him as a home by an affectionate aunt whom he loved. When he married, he founded a family that was something completely his own. His property of Yasnaya Polyana was a romance he was always inventing, as he had invented—out of old family papers and legends—the idyll of *War and Peace*. And even in his latest phase of pretending to abdicate his status of landowner, nobleman and popular writer, he was reserving for himself *le beau rôle*. But Spasskoye for Turgenev was a block of his past; he had grown up in it, been maimed by it, escaped from it. In jeering at him for making himself comfortable abroad and shirking his duties to Russia, his contemporaries were mistaken in several ways—not least in regard to the degree of his comfort. As he had never been at home in Spasskoye, so he was never really to feel at home anywhere, and even in the freedom of Europe—as Mr. Magarshack and others have noted—he reëstablished Varvara Petrovna in the person of Pauline Viardot, a formidable Spanish gypsy—like his mother, not handsome, though magnetic—who carried her household with a very high hand and cost Turgenev a good deal of suffering. What was fatal in her hold on Turgenev was that she not only possessed a strong character but combined with it a remarkable voice, which enabled him to regard her as a great artist. Her manager was her husband, and Turgenev had adored her and paid court to her for years without her allowing him to become her lover. He did, however, eventually succeed—Viardot was twenty years older than she—and, in a more or less harmonious *ménage à trois,* he became a kind of member of the family. He lived, in fact, with Viardot on terms that seem to have been almost fraternal. A great deal of his time was spent in the house of the Viardots or near them, but his daughter, who had been put in the care of Pauline, coming eventually to understand her father's position in the household, strongly reacted against it and her, and refused to remain with the family. Pauline, in the long run, was unfaithful to Turgenev with Ary Scheffer, at a time when he was painting her portrait, and Turgenev, finding out about this, broke with her. The next year she gave birth to a son, and the situation became even more painful—because, if the boy was his, Turgenev wanted to see him, but he could not be sure that he was and tormented himself with the suspicion that Pauline's love affair with Scheffer had already been going on for some time before he discovered it.

Turgenev resented his slavery, and in the story called *A Correspondence*—as Mr. Magarshack suggests—he is evidently caricaturing himself as an idiotic lover and Pauline as a stupid ballerina: "From the very first moment I saw her . . . I belonged to her entirely, just as a dog belongs to his master; and if now that I am dying I have ceased to, that is only because she has thrown me down. To tell the truth, she never paid much attention to me." In his letters to her, you feel his awe of her, and that he is writing of his thoughts and imaginings to someone who will not listen and who he knows will not listen. Many of Turgenev's friends did not like Pauline Viardot and deplored his devotion to her, but if one does not know anything about her except in connection with Turgenev, it is difficult to estimate how far the unpleasant impression one has of her is due to Turgenev himself. Here is one outside piece of testimony—by Heine, in an article on the music season in Paris in 1844: "One regrets, at the Opéra Bouffe, the absence of Pauline Viardot, or, as we like to call her, La Garcia. There is nobody to replace her, and nobody can replace her. This is no nightingale, who has only the talent of her species and admirably sobs and trills her regular spring routine; nor is she a rose—she is ugly, yet ugly in a way that is noble—beautiful I might almost say, and which has sometimes stirred to enthusiasm the great lion painter Lacroix [evidently Delacroix]! La Garcia recalls, in fact, not so much the civilized beauty and the domesticated face of our European homeland as the terrible splendor of an exotic wilderness, and at moments of her impassioned performances, especially when she opens wide her great mouth with its dazzling white teeth, and smiles with such cruel sweetness and such delightful ferocity, you feel as if the monstrous plants and animals of India or Africa were about to appear before your eyes."

If one were to put together all of Turgenev's stories of the unappeasable Evil Force, and if one were to read only these, one might think him a one-theme writer—like Poe or Nerval or Bierce, the victim of a neurotic obsession. Actually, however, these stories make little impression on the ordinary reader. The reason for this is that the Evil Power with which Turgenev is dealing here is, in a sense, no part of Turgenev himself but something that has been forced on his unwilling attention. With Dostoevsky, the Devil is inside him, and we are made to enter as much into the perverse and malignant characters as into the saintly ones. But though Turgenev can describe from inside many varieties of masculine weakness, he is unable to identify himself with any kind of aggressive malice. Already, in his early stories— and even more in the later ones, which have an element of the supernatural—the demons always come from outside. The villain of *The Wayside Inn* walks in on the family he will ruin from a world that is never described and is never accounted for; in the end, he disappears. The story is presented entirely from the point of view of his victim.

Turgenev, in his personal relations, had nothing of morbid suspicion; he was likely to believe in people to the point of gullibility, and when their treachery or dishonesty was proved to him, he would refuse to have anything more to do with them. Short of this, he gave money, in France, to every Russian who asked him for it, and one finds in *Tourguéneff Inconnu,* by a Russian friend, Michel Delines, some curious stories about this. Two young men, just arrived from Russia and representing themselves as Nihilists who had served prison terms for their writings, were taken up and aided by Turgenev. "One would have thought that the appearance of these two young men was of a kind that might have excited the mistrust of a student of faces, but they elicited, on the part of the novelist, only benevolent feelings; he was convinced that he was dealing with honest fellows." Later, apropos of an article in which Turgenev had expressed his political opinions, one of these young men sent Delines a letter of vulgar abuse of Turgenev and declared that he would never have anything more to do with him; yet, still later, he persuaded Delines to borrow for him some money from Turgenev, without mentioning for whom it was wanted—he would pay it back in a month. Then, instead of paying it back, he went to Turgenev and told him that he had owed Delines two hundred francs and that the latter had repaid himself by collecting this amount from Turgenev. When he was told that he had behaved dishonestly, the young fellow only sneered.

Delines at once wrote to Turgenev to straighten the matter out and let him know about the abusive letter. Turgenev asked to see it, and when he had read it turned pale and was silent. "Gradually his face lit up and he said to me with a reassured air, as if with the satisfaction of a man who has just made a discovery: 'I was mistaken about that young man, but now I can predict with certainty what his future career will be . . . [he] will become a collaborator with Katkov [the editor of a reactionary paper], he will desert the Nihilists, with whom he is now allied, and he will cover them with mud; after my death, he will write about me and pretend to have been my intimate friend!' . . . I began to protest at this, but with an angry gesture he interrupted. He was feeling the impatience of the artist who is not allowed time to finish his sketch. 'Wait, wait,' he said. 'I haven't finished. He will not die a natural death. He will be killed by a woman. He's a coward before the strong, and bold, very bold, against the weak. Women will have a good deal to suffer from him. But someday he'll fall into the hands of one of those strong and resolute Russian women, and she will blow his brains out.' " As for the other young Russian, continued Turgenev—" 'He, too!' I cried with amazement." Turgenev went on to explain that he had got his young man a subsidy to pursue his chemistry studies, "because he promised me that he would then return to Russia to apply his science to agriculture, and to teach the peasants new methods. But now that he has finished his studies, he thinks about nothing but getting rich and regards a humble schoolmaster's duties as far beneath him. . . . Oh, you'll see that he'll raise hob with the muzhiks; he'll turn moneylender and rob our peasants of their last bit of earth; he'll become the terror of the village, and he'll be murdered in the end by a muzhik." The first of these men, adds Delines, did abandon his Nihilist associates and bring accusations against them, did write for a reactionary paper and did publish a memoir of Turgenev. He did exploit women, and brought one of them to misery and madness; he had not, at the date of this writing, as yet been murdered by one. The other man did not return to Russia but became a planter in Africa, and was said to be a very harsh master. It was thus from observation of others that Turgenev had learned how such people behaved; his own character gave no key to their conduct, and it never at first occurred to him that there was anything sinister about them.

But in observation Turgenev is always extremely strong. He is the expert detached observer rather than the searching psychologist of the phenomena of Russian life, and when he tries to go inside his characters he is likely to be less satisfactory than when he is telling you merely what they say and do, how they look and what one feels about them. It is curious, in view of this, that he should so much complain, in his criticism of Tolstoy, of the ineptitude of the latter's account of what is going on in his character's minds. It was surely one of Tolstoy's most conspicuous gifts that he could put himself in the place of other people; it seems scarcely even a question of "psychology" but a matter of living in another's skin. Whereas, when Turgenev is telling what his hero or heroine is thinking, what ordeals they are going through, he sometimes becomes—what is rare with him—a little bit labored and boring. His characters perhaps come out best when they are presenting themselves to other people—as in such masterpieces of irony as *A Correspondence* and *Faust,* in which the two ignoble men, in their letters, unconsciously reveal to the reader what they do not know about themselves.

What people show themselves to be in relation to other people is Turgenev's particular forte, and he is for this reason especially successful in the invention of social types. This is now the direction that his work is to take. He is embarked by the middle eighteen-fifties on a deliberate and scrupulous study of the social situation in Russia. The cool, clear and balanced intellect that was central to the character of Turgenev was expanding and taking over after the panics and the repressions of Spasskoye. Turgenev, in his early stories, had usually concentrated on a single character or on his ever-recurrent two friends—one rather well-off and timid, the other rougher and bolder, a pair who almost count as a unit. This pair—with the accompanying girl, in whom, as a rule, they share—begin, with *The Two Friends* of 1853, to represent more than the intimacy of a personal relationship. Here the youth who is more cultivated and sensitive marries a much less well-educated wife, who charms him at first and then bores him. He escapes to St. Petersburg, promising to come back soon, but then goes on to Germany and then to France, and in Paris, to which he comes as a greenhorn, he is killed by a Frenchman in a stupid duel. The cruder but more enterprising friend takes over the uneducated wife, and they live together in perfect contentment. A social dilemma emerges: shall a cultivated Russian landowner remain at home and be bored or shall he go to the West, where he does not belong, and which may very well prove fatal to him? But in the next story—*A Quiet Backwater* of 1854— Turgenev's world opens out. We have here, for the first time in his fiction—though it had earlier appeared in his plays— the Turgenev country house, with its full cast of characters. The men—as is so common in Turgenev—let the women down, but the St. Petersburg petty snob, the genial swaggerer who comes to nothing, the correct unimaginative man of property are all intended here to be typical, as are the proud and serious girl, who, finding no one worthy of her, throws herself into a pond, and her jolly attractive friend, who has to content herself with a pretentious but shoddy Pole; and the weakness of the men in comparison with the women is here made, by implication, to illustrate a theory of Turgenev's as to the relative stamina of the sexes in Russia. This is followed the next year—after three of his weak-hero stories: *A Correspondence, Faust, Yakov Pasynkov*—by Turgenev's first novel, *Rudin*. The character of Rudin was partly suggested by Turgenev's friend Mikhail Bakunin, and Rudin is evidently impotent, as Bakunin is known to have been. He, too, disappoints the heroine.

These basic themes—the two friends, the inadequate man and the demanding woman—are present in the novels that follow, and they are always now made to figure as motifs in a large social picture. The more farouche and tough-minded of the two friends comes to the front as a new kind of hero: the Bulgarian patriot Insarov, who is awaiting, in *On the Eve,* the moment to go back to Bulgaria and fight for his country against the Turks; the humbly born young medical student Bazarov of *Fathers and Sons,* who, in performing an autopsy on a peasant in the primitive community where his parents live, cuts his finger and, having no means of cauterizing it, gets it infected and dies of blood poisoning. But Turgenev's recurrent characters appear in a variety of guises. The women who demoralize or outclass the

men may be selfish coquettes, like Irina in *Smoke* and Maria
Nikolaevna in *The Torrents of Spring,* or noble zealots, like
Elena in *On the Eve* and Marianna in *Virgin Soil.* These latter
—along with Maria Pavlovna of *A Quiet Backwater*—are likely to
be monsters of pride, and one remembers that one of the last en-
tries that Turgenev read in his mother's diary was, "My mother!
my children! Forgive me! And you, Lord, forgive me, also, for
pride, that deadly sin, was always my sin." *On the Eve* is a significant example of the author's familiar pattern, for, though
Insarov is tenacious and dedicated, he is tubercular and not up to
his mission, and thus weak in relation to Elena, who runs the
poor patriot ragged in insisting that he take her to Bulgaria as
truly as Irina does Litvinov in breaking up his relations with his
fiancée and then backing down on elopement. It is Elena who
gets to Bulgaria; Insarov expires in Venice. But these principals
have foils and opponents. The characters about them multiply;
whole new milieux appear.

A brilliant satirical element now comes to life in Turgenev's
work: the expatriate Russians at the beginning of *Smoke,* all
rallying around their empty great man and alternately, among
themselves, denouncing and fraternizing; the wonderfully carica-
tured family of Sipyagin in *Virgin Soil,* an official in smart society, who is ostensibly and smilingly liberal but in a pinch un-
relentingly conservative. Each of these books is designed to throw
light on some general situation and to suggest certain conclusions
about it. *A House of Gentlefolk* (1858) develops on a larger scale
the theme of the as yet unbridgeable gulf between Russia and
Western culture: Lavretsky, who has been studying agriculture
abroad, finds conditions at home too primitive for him to have
any field for his science, and his unreliable wife, who has been
making a fool of him in Paris and whom he has left and believes
to be dead, turns up to prevent him from marrying the serious
little girl at home. Elena, in *On the Eve* (1860), cannot find any

Russian she respects and runs away with a foreign insurrectionist. Bazarov, in *Fathers and Sons* (1861), has really been training himself for a technical and classless society that does not as yet exist, and in the meantime he cannot survive in the contemporary Russian world, where he is bound to be out of place and which has no faith but science to offer him. In *Smoke* (1867), again, as in *A Quiet Backwater*, the simple old Russian virtues, enduring though a little dull, are betrayed by international sophistication; and in *Virgin Soil*, Turgenev's last novel (1876), the radicals of the Populist movement, who have been trying to "go to the people," are shown to be as powerless to make contact with it as the landowner Lavretsky has been with his up-to-date methods of agriculture or as the medical student Bazarov, who has sprung from it but is quite out of touch with it.

Turgenev—in the teeth of the Populists, the mystical Slavophils and the official reactionaries—remained firmly a "Westernizer." He never ceased to compare Russia with Europe, to see it in the perspective of history, to estimate Russian possibilities in terms of the preliminary conditions that had made Western institutions possible. He was not in the least susceptible to the visionary excitements of his countrymen: he tried to look at everything in Russia with the same self-possession and realism that one brings to a foreign country, and to judge it with the same common sense. Turgenev was always proud to believe that he had contributed— through *A Sportsman's Sketches*, by which Alexander II was supposed to have been influenced—to the emancipation of the serfs, but in politics he was not optimistic. He could never lose sight of the discrepancies, the disparities so impossible to reconcile, that he was occupied with dramatizing in his novels. He did not approve of Russian feudalism, so he was hated by all the conservatives, but he could not believe in the imminence of a genuine revolution, since he could not make out any forces that were as yet far enough developed to put a revolution through, so he antagonized the more advanced Leftists. He was publicly opposed to violence and declared that he looked to the government to introduce the needed reforms, yet in his work insubmissive violence does certainly play a role. In a later edition of *Rudin,* six years after its first publication, he made his hero die on the barricades, but in Paris, in 1848; in *On the Eve,* we have an intransigent rebel, but a rebel against the Turks in Bulgaria, who has no involvement in Russia and who has, in consequence, seemed to Russians a more or less unconvincing character. Turgenev's last novel, *Virgin Soil,* however, is all about revolutionaries at home. He still believes at this point that the Populist agitation is premature, and he makes one of his characters predict that there will be no revolution for thirty years. This was said as of 1876, and twenty-nine years later the 1905 revolution occurred, to be followed twelve years afterwards by the Kerensky revolution, so Turgenev was not far out.

In the meantime, Turgenev had no religion, so he could not bedazzle himself with the light of Russian Christianity, by means of which Tolstoy and Dostoevsky were able to console themselves and which led them to condemn him so readily as a frivolous man of the world. No delusion and no emotion could fantasticate his strong conviction of the wretched situation of Russia or obscure his lucid perception that the remedy would be a long time coming. He was taken in by fraudulent idealists; he was stirred to bursts of sympathy by real ones. He was constantly under fire from both sides, and he sometimes answered his opponents back. He had always, on the one hand, to be careful of arousing the censorship and, on the other, to resist the clichés that his editors tried to impose on him. But through his casual blowings of hot and cold, his professions of belief in reforms from above and his secret contributions to radical papers; through his sometimes hysterical encounters with Tolstoy and Dostoevsky, his glowing amours and his slumps of gloom, his shuttling between Russia and Europe—like the man in his strange story *Phantoms,* who flies back and forth between them without ever being satisfied with either—he sticks to his objective judgment, his line of realistic criticism, his resolve to stand free of movements, to rise above personalities, to recognize all points of view that have any sincerity or dignity, to show Russia how to know herself. In this he is truly heroic, and the time has come now to thank him for an effort that in Turgenev's own day would seem to have been sometimes most thankless—since he had constantly to offend his countrymen and since foreigners who admired his writings could have had no idea of the pressures that Turgenev was obliged to withstand or even of the significance of what he wrote. It is as if his sense of justice, his magnanimity, his instinct to see things in their proper proportions had been prodded to especial stubbornness, in the household of Varvara Petrovna, by injustice, vindictiveness and outrageous pretensions. And if Pushkin, "my idol, my teacher, my unattainable model," had taught him how to pack social meaning into the simple presentation of incident, it is probable that the Germany of Goethe (another of his admirations), the Germany of his student days, had inspired him with the high conception of the writer's responsibility that was to win him his peculiar authority, an authority all the more striking because many of his countrymen would not admit it. It is, in any case, true that by Turgenev's time—as Annenkov tells us in an eloquent passage—the imaginative writer, since he could comment on society as other people could not do, had come to play a rôle of unique importance.

Turgenev explains his ideals as a writer and defends the integrity of his literary career in a preface—composed at the end of his life for the collected edition of 1880—which seems to me particularly worth quoting since it has not been included by either Isabel Hapgood or Constance Garnett in their complete translations of Turgenev's fiction. He has been, he here tells us, reproached "with abandoning my former direction, with apostasy, etc. To me, on the contrary, it seems that I might be reproached more properly for having stuck to my position too consistently and, as it were, having followed my direction in too single-minded a way. The author of *Rudin,* written in 1855, and the author of *Virgin Soil,* written in 1876, are obviously one and the same man. I have been aiming, from beginning to end, in the measure of my strength and intelligence, dispassionately and conscientiously to describe and incarnate in appropriate types both what Shakespeare calls 'the body and pressure of time' and the quickly-changing physiognomy of Russians of the cultured class, which has served chiefly as the subject of my observations." He runs through the series of his novels and shows that his critics, in the long run, have more or less cancelled one another out, and he triumphantly ends by telling of the reactions to *Virgin Soil:* first people had said that Turgenev had been living so long out of Russia that he knew nothing about what was going on there and that no such persons existed as the woman revolutionary Marianna; then, hardly a month later, there had been a sensational arrest of a group of revolutionaries which included eighteen women, and Turgenev was immediately accused of having been affiliated with them, since otherwise how could he have known about them? He goes on, in an admirable paragraph, to point out the then current confusion of Russian literary criticism, which cries up the ideal of the "unconscious creator," the "poet" who "thinks in images" and always chooses subjects from "real life," yet who actually, nevertheless, is likely to treat his subjects with a perceptible political bias. You may deal with nature, they say, you may deal with the life of the people; but the moment that he, Turgenev, ventures to touch on the muddled, the psychologically complicated, the morbid, that lies below the surface of society, they shout at him: "Stop! That won't do—that is speculation,

preconceived ideas; that is politics! the work of a publicist!"
Yet are not such phenomena as these as susceptible of being represented "in images" as those of external nature? "You assert,"
Turgenev answers these critics, "that the publicist and the poet
have different tasks. Not at all: in both cases their tasks may be
exactly the same; but the publicist regards them with a publicist's eyes, the poet with the eyes of a poet. In the department of
art, the question how? is more important than the question what?
The fact that what you will not accept—in images, mind you: in
images—exists in the soul of the writer is no reason for impugn-
ing his intention. . . . Believe me, a genuine talent never serves
any alien ends, and it finds satisfaction in itself; its content is
supplied by the life about it—it is a concentrated reflection of
this; and it is as little capable of a panegyric as it is of a pasquin-
ade. The point is that that kind of thing is beneath it. To sub-
ordinate oneself to a given thesis or to carry out a program—this
is possible only for those who cannot do anything different and
better." * A wariness of the censorship here no doubt somewhat
shrouds the contours of Turgenev's actual thought: surely something is smuggled in when he slips into his argument the statement that the tasks of the publicist and the poet may be exactly
the same; yet the novels that Turgenev is defending have themselves been given their shape by the censorship. Their technique
is a further extension of that of *A Sportsman's Sketches:* the
noncommittal which is none the less committal. Turgenev got a
good deal farther with the challenging social problems of Russia
than either Tolstoy or Dostoevsky. Yet he satisfied the same kind
of aesthetic ideal as Mérimée, Flaubert and their school. It was
an art that was continued by Chekhov, who observed "the life
about him" with equal detachment and had even less of hope
for the immediate future.

---

* A fuller translation of this passage will be found on page 90 of Mr. Magarshack's introduction.

But now that we know the immediate future, both Turgenev and Chekhov are relevant to the present situation of Russia, because many of the old elements and problems are still there in the Soviet Union, and a reading of these two great Russian writers will do much to dissolve the mirages that the Soviets have projected for the rest of the world and that seem to float still before the Russians themselves. It may be worth while to note here some passages in Turgenev's novels which have acquired a special interest in the light of what has happened since.

One of the most amusing characters in *Smoke* is a man named Sozont Ivanich Potugin, whom Litvinov meets in Baden and with whom he has long conversations. Potugin is worried and depressed about Russia and disgusted with the delusions of his countrymen. They boast about "Russian inventiveness," but the Russians "have invented nothing"; they boast of their architecture, art and music, when none of these really exists (this did not long remain true of music); they even boast that nobody in Russia starves. In an earlier conversation, Litvinov has asked Potugin about another expatriate in Baden, whose prestige seems to be immense, though Litvinov does not find him interesting and cannot, in fact, get anything out of him:

"Tell me—how do you account for the unquestionable influence of Gubaryov on everybody around him? He's neither gifted nor able, is he?"

"No, of course not; he has no abilities."

"Is it character, then?"

"He hasn't got that either: what he does have is a strong will. We Slavs in general, as everyone knows, are not much endowed with that virtue, and when it does appear, we give up before it. Mr. Gubaryov wanted to be a leader, so everybody acknowledges him as one. What can you do about it?! The government has freed us from our dependence on serfdom, and we are grateful to it for that, but the habits of slavery are rooted too deep in us; we shan't get away from them so easily. In everything and everywhere, we have to have a master. This master is usually some active person, though sometimes some so-called tendency takes possession of us—just at present, for instance, we have all bound ourselves over to the natural sciences. But why—convinced by what sort of reasoning—we do give ourselves into bondage, that's the mysterious thing; it's evidently just in our nature to. The great point is that we must have a master. Well, we get one—which means he belongs to us, and we spit upon everything else! We're just naturally underlings! And the pride of being underlings and the underlings' abasement! Then a new master comes along—away with the old. Before it was Jacob, now it is Sidor; give Jacob a box on the ear and fall at the feet of Sidor! Remember how many such tricks we have played! We talk about non-compliance as if it were a peculiar characteristic of ours, but we don't make our refusals as a free man does, laying about him with his sword; we make them like a lackey, hitting out with his fists—and what is worse, if you please, this lackey does his thrashing by his own master's orders. And yet, my good sir, at the same time we're soft; it's not difficult to get us into one's hands. And that's how Mr. Gubaryov has achieved his present domination; he keeps chiselling and chiselling at the same spot and finally he chisels through. People become aware that a man has a high opinion of himself, that a man believes in himself, that he gives orders—that's the main thing, he gives orders; consequently, he is bound to be right, and one is compelled to obey him. All our schismatics, our Ony-phrites and Akulinites, established themselves in just this way: the man who takes the staff is the corporal."

Such leaders have nowhere to lead the people, and in the meantime the Slavophils bemuse themselves with a groundless belief in the "masses":

"According to them [the Slavophils], everything is always *going to be*. Nothing ever takes place in the present, and Russia through ten whole centuries has failed to produce anything of her own —not in government or jurisprudence or in science or in art or even in the crafts. . . . But wait a bit, be patient a bit: everything is going to come. And why should it be going to come?—if I may be so curious as to ask. Why, they answer, because we edu-

33

cated folks are trash; but the people—oh, that great people! Do you see that peasant's overcoat?—that's where everything is going to come from. All the other idols have been destroyed: let's believe in the peasant's overcoat. But suppose the overcoat fails us? No, it will not fail us—read Kokhanovskaya and roll up your eyes. [Kokhanovskaya was a woman novelist who wrote about rural life.] Really, if I were a painter, this is the picture I'd paint. An educated man would be standing before a muzhik and making a low obeisance: 'Cure me, little father muzhik,' he says. 'I'm deathly ill.' But the muzhik, in turn, bows low to the educated man: 'Teach me, little father master,' he says: 'I'm dying of ignorance.' "

The leader who was actually to impose himself on the demoralized Russia of fifty years later had more character and brains than Gubaryov, but his faith in the peasant's overcoat went somewhat beyond what was warranted. Turgenev—as Mr. Irving Howe has noted in a paper on him—anticipated the solid side of the Bolsheviks, something of the character of Lenin, as Dostoevsky, in *The Devils,** anticipated the fanatical side. Solomin, the factory manager of *Virgin Soil,* with his long-range view of Russia, who realizes the natural docility and the ignorance of peasants and workers and tries to make a beginning of training them by instituting a workers' school, goes on to a coöperative factory of his own when his hastier would-be allies have come to grief through precipitate action. "He's a really splendid fellow," someone says of him, "and the great thing about him is that he doesn't pretend to be any quick healer of our social ills. Why, pray, are we Russians the way we are? We're always waiting for something: something or somebody, we tell ourselves, is going to come along and fix everything up in a moment, heal all our sores, pull out all our diseases as if they were aching teeth. Who will that magician be? Darwinism? Country life? Arkhip Perepentev? A foreign war? Whatever you like! Only, little father, do please pull out

---

* *The Possessed* in Constance Garnett's translation.

the tooth! ! It's all laziness, flabbiness, inadequacy. But Solomin's not like that, no—he's not going to pull any teeth—he's really a splendid fellow!"

But they did expect Lenin to pull the tooth, and they continued to imagine he had pulled it long after their leader was dead, a victim of the monstrous discrepancies that Turgenev had insisted on facing. What the Russians were getting instead of Lenin was something that was at first very close to another of Turgenev's characters—the secretary of the Senate, Kurnatovsky, who appears in *On the Eve*. Elena is writing to Insarov, the Bulgarian patriot whom she loves. Her father has asked Kurnatovsky to dinner with the idea of having Elena marry him, and she describes him in a letter to her lover. He is short, she tells Insarov, with flat wide lips and hair cropped close, and he wears a constant smile—as it were, official, as if smiling in this way were a duty.

He conducts himself very simply, conducts himself with precision, and everything about him is precise: he walks, laughs, and eats as if he were performing a duty. . . . There is something iron in him, and dull and empty at the same time—and honorable; they say that he *is* very honorable. . . . He almost gave up his civil servant's job to take charge of a big factory. . . . He said he knew nothing about art, as if he meant to imply that he thought art unnecessary, but that a well-conducted government might, of course, permit it. Rather indifferent, however, to Petersburg and the *comme il faut:* he once even referred to himself as a proletarian. "We're common workmen!" he said. I thought to myself: If Dmitri Insarov had said that, I shouldn't have liked it, but let this fellow talk, let him boast! With me he was very polite; but it seemed to me that I was talking with a very very patronizing superior. When he wishes to praise someone, he says that So-and-So has principles—that is his favorite word. He must, I am sure, be very self-confident, industrious and capable to the point of self-sacrifice (you see I am quite impartial); that is, of the sacrifice of his own interests, but he is certainly a great despot. Woe to anyone who falls into his hands. At dinner they started talking about bribes.

"I know," he said, "that in many cases the man who takes a bribe is quite innocent; he couldn't have acted otherwise. But, if he's caught, we have to break him just the same."

"Break the innocent!"

"Yes—for the sake of principle."

"What principle?" Shubin asked. Kurnatovsky seemed to be surprised or to find himself at a loss, and replied, "That needs no explanation."

On the subject of Russian mendacity—one of the most serious national failings, which has been carried, since Turgenev's time, in the Soviet propaganda and purges, to such incredible lengths —Turgenev has a great deal to say, for it was evidently much on his mind. Henry James, who knew him in Paris, reports with characteristic litotes his dwelling on the subject in conversation. Of the failings of the Russian character Turgenev, he says, "was keenly conscious, and I once heard him express himself with an energy that did him honor and a frankness that even surprised me (considering that it was of his countrymen that he spoke) in regard to a weakness for which a man whose love of veracity was his strongest feeling would have least toleration." And lying is one of the vices against which Potugin rails: "One day, with my dog and gun, I was making my way through a forest . . . I am aiming for a bog in which there are supposed to be snipe. I look about me, and there, sitting in the meadow in front of his little house, I see a timber merchant's clerk, as fresh and as plump as a filbert. He's sitting there and grinning—about what I don't know. So I asked him, 'Where is that bog around here—are there any snipe in it?' 'Please, please,' he replied at once, as if I had given him a ruble: 'Fortunately for us, a bog of the very first quality; and as for gamebirds of every kind—why, good God!—in wonderful plenty you'll find them.' I proceeded on my way, but not only did I find no game, even the bog had been long dried up. Now, will you please tell me: why does the Russian lie? Why does the political economist lie?—and even about gamebirds?" Of Solomin and Marianna in *Virgin Soil,* he writes: "A man who told the truth—that was the great thing! That was what had made such an impression on her. Something which is very well known but not altogether understood is the fact that, although the Russians are the most incorrigible liars in the whole world, there is nothing they respect so much as the truth—to nothing do they respond so readily." There is an entry in the Goncourt Journal which may be added as a supplement to this: "He [Turgenev] said that, music apart, of all the peoples of Europe the Germans had the least correct response to art [the assumption evidently is that the Germans are scrupulous in other ways], and that the kind of little false and stupid conventionality which made us [the French] reject a book seemed to them the amenity of perfection applied to the truth of things. He added that, on the contrary, the Russians, who are a lying people, as is natural for a people who have long been slaves, liked truth and reality in art." In view of all this, it is striking that his respect for a friend of his youth, Nikolai Stankevich, was partly inspired by his feeling that the latter had cured him of lying. Even Tolstoy, who so liked to bait him, paid a tribute to Turgenev's exceptional truthfulness.

It is impressive to see how the authority of Turgenev was felt by the non-Russian world. Taine praised him, and George Sand wrote to him, apropos of *A Sportman's Sketches,* "*Maître, nous devons aller tous à votre école.*" For Mérimée, the courtier of Napoleon III, forlornly dying of asthma and the imminent collapse of the Second Empire, Turgenev, who had helped him with his Russian studies and with whom he had corresponded for years, seems to figure at this point in his life as a kind of last moral support in the serious practice of letters. Mérimée is always hoping that Turgenev will come to see him—as is Flaubert, in his different way also so dreary, in the provincial isolation of

Croisset, breaking his back, in his final years, over the desolating and thankless ironies of *Bouvard et Pécuchet*. "Courage!" Turgenev had written him, from Weimar, when his friend had been disappointed by the reception of *L'Education Sentimentale*. "After all, you are Flaubert!," and he tried to make him known in Russia by translating his *Hérodias* and *La Légende de Saint Julien l'Hospitalier*. Conversely, he sent to Flaubert a French translation of *War and Peace*, which was one of the last books the latter read, and passed on to Tolstoy the high praise of it—accompanied by certain reservations—in a letter that Flaubert had written him. Turgenev knew most of the important writers who were making of the novel, in that period, the great literary form of the nineteenth century, and he followed the work of all of them. He arranged to have Zola and Maupassant translated into Russian, and he was a pillar of the Goncourt dinners. The Goncourts admired him up to the moment when, after his death, Edmond discovered from a memoir by a friend of Turgenev's, Isaac Pavlovsky, that Turgenev had not really cared much for their novels. For Henry James—like Turgenev himself, never much at home among the French and dissatisfied with the ideals of French fiction—he provided the model of a more humane art not inferior in formal distinction, as well as an encouragement to James to develop his own point of view and to deal with his own people, who, like the Russians, were so little known in Europe and did not fit into the European categories. Even in England, Turgenev's name was known by the sixties. On a visit there in 1858, he was invited, at Mérimée's suggestion, to a banquet of the Royal Literary Fund, and, in aid of a similar Russian fund, founded the following year, he wrote a description of it, in which he dwelt on the effectiveness of the English in making such organizations work. He paid his respects to Carlyle, who had found *Mumu* very affecting but who rather surprised Turgenev by laughing immoderately when the visitor was telling him that he suffered from spots before his eyes and had once, on a hunting trip, mistaken one of these for a rabbit; and to Thackeray, who had never heard of him and who also roared with laughter when, after inviting his visitor to recite for him something in Russian, he was unable to restrain himself, at the outlandish sound to his English ears of one of Pushkin's loveliest lyrics. For Renan, who delivered, at the Gare du Nord, a speech over Turgenev's coffin, when his body was being sent back to Russia, Turgenev was a mind like his own, which comprehended the most diverse points of view and which contemplated their ultimate harmony:

The repellent aspects of things do not exist for him. Everything in him becomes reconciled: the most opposed parties unite to admire him and to praise him. In the region to which he transports us, the words that rouse the vulgar lose their venom. Genius achieves in a day what would otherwise require centuries. He creates a higher atmosphere of peace, in which those who were formerly adversaries discover themselves in reality to have been collaborators; he opens the era of the great amnesty, in which those who have fought in the arena of progress clasp hands as they sleep side by side.

This conception by Renan of Turgenev must, I think, derive from a passage in the latter's lecture on Hamlet and Don Quixote, which, though still little known in English, had been early translated in France. Though very characteristic of Renan, it does not really quite fit Turgenev. It was easy enough for Renan to look ahead to the ultimate resolution of conflicts; he was accustomed to dealing with movements that belonged to the remote past. The conflicts in Turgenev are not truly—or only rarely—resolved, any more than the forces they represent were resolved in his contemporary Russia. The Paris of the mid-nineteenth century was quite ignorant of Russian affairs, and for this reason the Russian Turgenev was largely invisible to it; what it knew was the distinguished visitor, the good Russian giant of the Goncourts, the correct and well-balanced and modest friend, the cultivated foreigner who spoke all the languages yet who always was somewhat exotic, and so could charm without discommoding. Turgenev thus came to present in his Western and in his Russian connections two distinct and contrasting faces. For George Moore and Henry James, his stories are beautiful idylls: the Irishman and the American adore his high-souled young women, and they sympathize with his weak young men; they admire the descriptions of forest and field as if they were Corot landscapes, and the peasants, with the fantasy of their folk tales, the devotion of their touching attachments, are a people, almost like the pixies, that appropriately inhabit these landscapes. Turgenev must, of course, have been aware of this, and he exhibited a great deal of skill in managing his double life. This is a problem that has to be dealt with by every Russian exile. The Russian assumes, as a matter of course, that no foreigner can really know Russia, since one cannot imagine it correctly in any terms supplied by the West, and nobody but a Russian, he thinks—not entirely without justification—can have the freedom of the Russian language. But the Russians, wherever they are living, carry with them the Russian world, to which, when they gather together, all the other worlds become peripheral. That this world is unlike the West, that it poses unique problems, that the people of their half-primitive country are innumerable and the country is vast, and that those Russians who are properly civilized are immeasurably more versatile and brilliant and learned than the intelligentzia of any other nation— all these considerations are bonds of solidarity and sources of pride. Yet when Russians come together and talk, nobody else can hear them, and even if the outsider *could* hear them, he would not in the least understand. Their movements, their groupings, their feudings, their scandals, their benefit performances and their domestic vicissitudes, discussed passionately wherever there are Russians—among whom every word or event seems communi-

cated instantaneously throughout the whole Russian circle—pass
unnoticed by the foreigners about them. But to this alien world
the Russian—unlike the average Englishman, Frenchman or
German—deliberately adapts himself; he speaks its language, gets
the hang of its attitudes; and the usual educated Russian is so
easy to get along with, so amusing and so good a story-teller, so
apparently outspoken and spontaneous, though at times perhaps
a little evasive, that the foreigner has no way of gauging the immense amount of reserve behind this. Turgenev was a typical
example. What Turgenev's friends in the West could hardly have
guessed about him was that each of his delightful novels, which,
in form and in sensibility, could stand up beside anything of the
kind that the West itself had produced, was, from the moment it
appeared in Russia, an occasion for passion and polemics, that for
Turgenev himself to return meant attacks and entreaties and rup-
tures, putting his head in a hornet's nest, as well as an opportunity for sudden reprisals by the government.

We are struck by this piquant contrast between these two faces
of Turgenev when we compare his letters to foreigners—rather
formal, in perfect taste, always respectful to the recipient and his
country—with his letters to his Russian friends. The voice of the
Turgenev who at thirty-eight addresses the twenty-eight-year-old
Tolstoy seems to proceed from a different person: "I shall never
cease to love you and to value your friendship, though—probably
through my fault—each of us, in the presence of the other, will
be bound for a long time yet to feel a certain embarrassment. . . .
Whence this embarrassment arises . . . I believe you yourself understand. You are the only person in the world with whom I have
misunderstandings, and this comes precisely from the fact that I
have wanted not to limit myself to simple friendly relations—I
have wanted to go further and deeper, but I have been doing this
in an indiscreet way: I hooked on to you, made demands on you,
and then, becoming aware that I had made a mistake, relin-

quished you, it may be, too hastily; that is what has caused this 'gulf' between us." And he goes on to analyze the situation. He is worrying, in another letter, about Tolstoy's opinion of his work: "I know you did not care for my last story [*Asya*], and you were not alone; many of my best friends are not enthusiastic about it; I am sure you are quite right; and yet I wrote it at white heat, almost in tears—so we never know what we are doing." In Paris, he complains to Tolstoy of the French, a line that was likely to please him: "I have met only one nice girl—and she is a Russian; only one intelligent man—he is a Jew. I don't really care much about the French; they may be splendid soldiers and administrators—but in their heads there is only one alley, along which they poke always the same ideas, ideas they have accepted once for all. Everything that isn't their own seems to them outlandish and silly: '*Ah, le lecteur français ne saurait admettre cela!*' Once he has said these words, the Frenchman cannot even imagine that it is possible for you to make any reply—well, let us leave them to God!" To another Russian friend, Turgenev expresses himself with equal frankness on the subject of *Anna Karenina*. What has here put Turgenev's back up is the issue raised by Tolstoy in his novel between good old honest Russian Moscow and wickedly Westernizing St. Petersburg—which is one of those matters of perennial interest to Russians, since the competition between these two centers has gone on even under the Soviets and was involved in the rivalry of Kirov with Stalin, of which the non-Russian is hardly aware. "I haven't yet," Turgenev writes, "read the last instalment of *Anna Karenina*, but I can see with regret the direction that this whole novel is taking. However great the talent of L. Tolstoy, he will not be able to extricate himself from the Moscow bog into which he has got himself. Orthodoxy, the gentry, Slavophilism, gossip, Arbat [a then aristocratic section of Moscow], Katkov [the reactionary editor], Antonina Bludova [who had a Slavophil salon in Moscow], bad manners, conceitedness, feudal customs, officerdom, hostility to everything foreign, sour cabbage soup and absence of soap—chaos, in a word. And in this chaos so gifted a man must perish. That's the way it always is in Russia." One feels here, on Turgenev's part, a certain impulse to assign to Tolstoy the destiny of a frustrated Turgenev character, to bury him in the old Russian swamp that Turgenev had come out of and dreaded.

Turgenev's relations with Tolstoy as well as with Dostoevsky were intensely dramatic and comic. In the case of both his great contemporaries, when, on visits to that Western Europe which they made such a point of disdaining, they had lost all their money gambling—Dostoevsky lost even his watch—Turgenev would lend them money. Dostoevsky rewarded him for this by denouncing him on every occasion, but, fleeing, two years later, from his creditors and making a stay in Baden, at the time when Turgenev was living there, Dostoevsky reasoned with himself that just because he had not paid Turgenev back he ought not to fail to call on him. Dostoevsky, in his account of this interview, an anonymous memorandum of which he wanted to have put in the official archives, reported that Turgenev had been outrageous; that the bad reception of *Smoke* had caused him to inveigh against Russia, declaring that if the Russians were totally destroyed, it would be no loss to human thought; that "we must grovel before the Germans" and that he now regarded himself as a German. Dostoevsky had advised him, he said, to acquire a telescope so that he could see what was going on in Russia. It is not implausible that Turgenev should have let himself go à la Potugin of *Smoke* and declared, as Dostoevsky reported, that "there was but one universal and inevitable road—that of civilization, and that any attempt at a policy of Russianism and independence was pigheaded stupidity and folly." But Turgenev does not elsewhere appear as a slavish admirer of the Germans, and in his own account of this interview—sent to Petersburg when he learned of the memorandum—he asserts that Dostoevsky's visit had lasted no longer than an hour, in the course of which he had bitterly attacked the Germans and had stormed against Turgenev and *Smoke* in tirades to which Turgenev "had had hardly the time or the wish to reply." He regarded Dostoevsky, he says, on account of his epileptic attacks and for "other reasons," as "not in full control of his intellectual faculties" and had "behaved with him as he would with a sick man." Dostoevsky was again gambling madly and as usual ruining himself. A few years later (Turgenev's loan still not repaid), he put his creditor into *The Devils* as the exquisite and silly Karmazinov. But at last, in 1874, nine years after the loan had been made, hearing that Turgenev had returned to Russia, Dostoevsky sent him the money. His explanation for not having done so before was that he had not been able to remember whether it was fifty or a thundred thalers—Dostoevsky had asked for a hundred but Turgenev had given him only fifty—and that it had been only a few days before, when he had come upon a letter from Turgenev, that he had learned the correct amount.

With Tolstoy, who was also opposed to Turgenev's Westernizing policy, Turgenev had a disagreeable quarrel in the course of a conversation in which he was telling with complacency of the new English governess he had found for his daughter. Turgenev the next morning sent apologies, but he misdirected his letter and soon received from his friend a challenge—not, Tolstoy fiercely declared, to the usual literary duel of the kind that concludes with the adversaries drinking champagne together; they would have to shoot it out with rifles. Turgenev apologized again, but later heard that Tolstoy was circulating the story and calling Turgenev a coward. Turgenev now challenged Tolstoy, but said that he was just going abroad and couldn't be bothered to fight him till he came back to Russia again. Tolstoy in his turn now apologized, and seventeen years later, when he had publicly become a Christain, wrote Turgenev proposing a reconciliation. Turgenev went to visit him in the country—their estates were not far apart—but said afterwards that he felt rather nervous when he beat the new saint at chess. Immediately after this, when Turgenev was in Paris, he received from Tolstoy a letter in which the latter tried to pick a quarrel with him, expressing doubts of Turgenev's "sincerity." Later, in 1881, when Turgenev was visiting Spasskoye again, Tolstoy, at one o'clock in the morning, suddenly descended upon him, dressed in a peasant's costume, and put on such a performance of Christian humility that Turgenev was rather impressed. What, Turgenev said, showed that Tolstoy was actually making some progress as a Christian was that, instead of laying down the law, he allowed his opponent to do some of the talking. When Turgenev returned this visit, there was a birthday party in progress. Turgenev took off his coat and danced the cancan with a twelve-year-old girl. Tolstoy noted in his diary: "Turgenev—the cancan. Sad."

Turgenev did sometimes lose his temper; with Russians he was rather touchy. Is it entirely Dostoevsky's parody—ascribed to the absurd Karmazinov—that makes the elegiac *Enough* sound perhaps a little petulant and mawkish? And yet it is impossible not to feel, as Mr. Magarshack suggests, that Turgenev, the atheist, was a good deal more successful at practicing the Christian virtues than either the holy man of Yasnaya Polyana or the creator of Alyosha Karamazov.

One result of assimilating Turgenev to the school of writers, either French or influenced by the French, of the late nineteenth and early twentieth centuries—to Mérimée, Flaubert, Maupassant, George Moore, Henry James, Joseph Conrad—has been that it has not hitherto been thought worth while to translate his non-fictional writings, which are mainly concerned with Russian affairs.

It was no doubt assumed at the time of Turgenev's great foreign reputation that the men and the movements with which these writings dealt were quite unknown in the West and that they would not be of interest abroad. Yet Turgenev's explanation of his literary aims—such as the preface already quoted—would, for example, have been salutary reading for our writers of the "Art is a weapon" thirties, when Russia had become so much more real to us but was sending us inferior literary products. And the *Literary Reminiscences* of Turgenev—which, in Mr. Magarshack's translation, appear now for the first time in English—is certainly of Turgenev's best, comparable in beauty and interest to Yeats's *The Trembling of the Veil,* which in some ways it rather resembles. In the case of the common run of such books of literary memories, we are mainly impressed by the author's having managed to see at close range so many distinguished people without finding anything interesting to report of them; but a Yeats or a Turgenev is able—as in the latter's two brief glimpses of Pushkin—to make of a remark or an anecdote the revelation of a whole personality. The dominating figure in these memoirs is Vissarion Gregorovich Belinsky, the great Russian critic of the eighteen-forties, who, seven years older than Turgenev, took an interest in his work from the first and with whom he became close friends. At a time when the young Turgenev paraded his affectations and was often considered an ass, Belinsky discerned his sincerity in his earliest published work, a long poem called *Parasha,* and, despite Belinsky's humble origin, his harsh manners, his limited learning and his ignorance of the world, Turgenev came not only to admire him but even to find inspiration in his candor and moral nobility, his passionate interest in letters (which was finely asethetic as well as moral), his vigorous and earnest efforts for the development of a great literature in Russia, at a time when, as Turgenev says, the Tsar was doing everything possible to discourage not merely literature but even higher education. To call on his friend, he remembered —in that atmosphere of spies and suppression—was enough to set one up for the day. This intimacy with Belinsky was undoubtedly one of the most important influences of Turgenev's life. It is obviously reflected in his fiction in the eternally recurring motif of the two contrasting friends—though, in the years before he knew Belinsky, he had already had a somewhat similar friendship with another intellectual, Nikolai Stankevich, already mentioned above, which makes one think that he must have been predisposed to this kind of relationship. Stankevich died in 1840, and Turgenev first met Belinsky in 1842, and the first of the stories that exploit this theme—*Andrey Kolosov*—was written in 1844. Later on, the description of Yakov Pasynkov in the story of that name is so similar to the description of Belinsky in the *Reminiscences* that it is evident that the latter had sat for Yakov, who dies of an injury to the lung, as both Belinsky and Stankevich died of tuberculosis. Now, *Yakov Pasynkov* is also a kind of preliminary study for the large-scale *Fathers and Sons*, and when we come to *Fathers and Sons*, we find that it is dedicated to the memory of Belinsky—who had died thirteen years before—and that its hero, like Belinsky himself, is the son of a poor army doctor and has a pitiful premature death. Turgenev had spent two months with his friend, not long before the latter's death in 1848, in a hotel at a German spa, where it was hoped that his health might improve. Turgenev pointed out to Pavlovsky that Bazarov, of *Fathers and Sons*, was blond, "like all my sympathetic heroes," like "Belinsky, Herzen and others." (It is also worth noting that the *Literary Reminiscences* contains Turgenev's account of the execution of the French murderer Troppmann, as great a piece of writing in its way— prosaic, circumstantial and somber—as any of Turgenev's stories.)

III

The work of Turgenev has, of course, no scope that is comparable to Tolstoy's or Dostoevsky's, but the ten volumes collected by him for his edition of 1883 (he omitted his early poems) represent a literary achievement of the concentratedly "artistic" kind that has few equals in nineteenth-century fiction. There are moments, to be sure, in Turgenev novels—*On the Eve* and *Virgin Soil*—when they become a little thin or unreal, but none can be called a failure, and one cannot find a single weak piece, unless one becomes impatient with *Enough*, in the whole four volumes of stories. No fiction writer can be read through with a steadier admiration. Greater novelists are more uneven: they betray our belief with extravagances; they bore or they fall into bathos; they combine poetic vision with rubbish. But Turgenev hardly even skirts these failings, and he is never mediocre; his texture is as distinguished as his temperament.

This texture barely survives in translation. Turgenev is a master of language; he is interested in words in a way that the other great nineteenth-century Russian novelists—with the exception of Gogol—are not. His writing is dense and substantial, yet it never marks time, always moves. The translations of Constance Garnett are full of omissions and errors; the translations of Isabel Hapgood do not omit, but are also full of errors and often extremely clumsy. Neither lady seems ever to have thought of taking the indispensable precaution of reading her version to a Russian holding the Russian text, who would at once have spotted the dropped-out negatives and the cases of one word mistaken for another. The translations of Turgenev into French —though some are by Mérimée and Turgenev himself—have a tendency to strip him down to something much barer and poorer. The task of translating this writer does present some impossible problems. "What an amazing language!" wrote Chekhov on re-reading the story called *The Dog*. But this language will not reach the foreigner. How to render the tight little work of art that Turgenev has made of *The Dog*, narrated by an ex-hussar, with his colloquialisms, his pungent sayings, his terseness and his droll turns? And the problems of translating Turgenev are to some extent the problems of translating poetry. There is a passage in *The Torrents of Spring*—a tour de force of onomatopoeia—that imitates in a single sentence the whispering of leaves, the buzzing of bees and the droning of a solitary dove. This is probably a conscious attempt to rival the well-known passage in Virgil's First Eclogue and Tennyson's imitation of it:

> *The moan of doves in immemorial elms,*
> *And murmuring of innumerable bees.*

But it would take another master to reproduce Turgenev's effects, just as it took a Tennyson to reproduce those of Virgil, and a Turgenev to compete with these.

Since I am going to go on in this section to call attention to the principal themes that run all through Turgenev's work and to relate them to his personal experience, I must emphasize here the solidity and the range of Turgenev's writings. It is only in the later stories which deal with the supernatural that these underlying themes emerge as obsessions or hallucinations. They are otherwise usually embodied in narratives, objectively presented, in which the backgrounds are always varied and in which even the individuals who belong to a constantly recurring type are always studied in a special context and differentiated from one another. Turgenev is not one of the great inventors, as his two colleagues and Dickens are, but in his tighter, more deliberate art he is perhaps the most satisfactory of the company to which he belongs, for he never oppresses, as Flaubert does, by his monotony and his flattening of human feeling, or fatigues, as

Henry James sometimes does when his wheels of abstraction are grinding, or makes us nervous, as Conrad may do, through his effortfulness and occasional awkwardness in working in a language not native to him with materials that are sometimes alien. The material of Turgenev is all his own, and his handling of it is masterly. The detail is always amusing, always characteristic; every word, every reference, every touch of description has naturalness as well as point; the minor characters, the landscapes, the milieux are all given a full succulent flavor. The genre pictures—the funeral supper at the end of *An Unhappy Girl,* the transference of the property in *A Lear of the Steppes*—are wonderfully organized and set in motion, though such exhilaration of movement as Tolstoy is able to generate in such episodes as the hunt in *War and Peace* and the races in *Anna Karenina* is quite beyond Turgenev's powers, as is the cumulative fun and excitement of the town celebration in Dostoevsky's *The Devils.* But neither can fill in a surface, can fit language to subject like Turgenev. The weather is never the same; the descriptions of the countryside are quite concrete, and full, like Tennyson's, of exact observation of how cloud and sunlight and snow and rain, trees, flowers, insects, birds and wild animals, dogs, horses and cats behave, yet they are also stained by the mood of the person who is made to perceive them. There are moments, though not very many, when the affinity between natural phenomena and the emotion of the character exposed to them is allowed to become a little melodramatic in the old-fashioned romantic way— the volcanic sunset in *Faust* when the heroine is herself on the verge of eruption—but in general Turgenev is protected from the dangers of the "romantic fallacy" by his realistic habit of mind.

Let me here, also, call attention to a story that seems to me a masterpiece and that sounds a different note from those I shall discuss later: *The History of Lieutenant Ergunov,* of 1867. This Lieutenant is a heavy and clumsy and extremely naïve young man

who is highly susceptible to women and who regards himself as
something of a dandy. Stationed in a provincial town, he becomes
involved with a household that purports to consist of an elderly
woman living with two nieces. They are of mongrel and dubious
origins; one of them, who calls herself Colibri, is semi-Oriental,
exotic. The Lieutenant never discovers that the two girls are
prostitutes and that their bully is lurking in the background. His
suspicions are not even aroused when he has dropped off to sleep
on a couch one day and been awakened by the efforts of one of
the girls—he is carrying government money—to detach from his
belt his wallet. He becomes so fascinated by Colibri that it is no
trouble at all for her to drug him. They rob him, bash in his
head and, assuming he is safely dead, throw his body down a
ravine. It is only his exceptional vigor that enables him in time
to recover from this. The thieves have, of course, made their get-
away, but he presently receives a long letter from the girl who
tried to steal his wallet, in which she tells him that though she
has "a bad morality" and is "flighty," she is not really "a villainess." She is terribly sorry about the whole thing; the others had
induced her to lend herself to luring him to the house and then
sent her away for the day. "The old villainess *was not* my aunt."
She begs him to answer, but he never does. Ergunov all the rest
of his life tells the story at least once a month.

It is typical of Turgenev's art that the anecdote in itself, as
I have sketched it, cannot convey Turgenev's point. Nothing
could be more different than a story, say, by Maupassant. There
are no tricks of the professional raconteur, no sudden surprise at
the end. We follow a steady narrative, built up with convincing
detail. It closes calmly enough with Ergunov's shaking his head
and sighing, "That's what it is to be young," and displaying his
terrible scar, which reaches from ear to ear. And it is only when
we have finished the story that we grasp the whole implication of
the triumph of good faith and respect for the innocent over the

brutal violation of human relations. Ergunov is the side of Turgenev himself that never could believe at first that the people who exploited him were not honest. It is a question in *Lieutenant Ergunov* not of one of the author's obsessive themes but of a feeling that, for all his demons, all his ogresses and their helpless victims, continues to assert itself almost to the end of his work —Gemma's letter of forgiveness to Sanin, in the later *Torrents of Spring*, reversing the roles of the sexes in *Ergunov*, embodies the same moral—and a feeling that he shares with the creator of Myshkin as well as with the creator of Pierre. This instinct sets the standards for Turgenev's mind, and it is the basis of his peculiar nobility. It is the essence of the life-giving drop that he has rescued from the cave of the reptiles.

But this story is almost unique. The positive force of honesty, even the survival of innocence—though they sometimes occur in the novels: Solomin in *Virgin Soil*, Tatyana and her aunt in *Smoke*—are excessively rare in these tales. There are examples of religious dedication—*A Living Relic* in *A Sportsman's Sketches*, *A Strange Story*, *A Desperate Character*—but, especially in the last two of these, you feel that they are simply cases, included with the other cases, of the unhealthiness of Russian life. In general, the ogresses and devils continue to have the best of it, and the timid and snobbish young men continue to disappoint the proud women. To return to the series where we dropped it—in 1857, ten years before *Lieutenant Ergunov*— this has happened to the heroine of *Asya* and to Gemma of *The Torrents of Spring*, and is to happen to the heroine of *An Unhappy Girl* (two of these the illegitimate daughters of gentlemen and one the daughter of an Italian confectioner). It is only in *First Love* that the girl under a social shadow is allowed to have a passionate love affair, and I am sure that it is partly to this, the exceptional element of sex interest, that the story owes its especial popularity—along with, for the same reason, *The Torrents of*

Spring—among Turgenev's shorter fictions. Yet note that it is not the young boy but his father who enjoys Zinaida's love, and that Turgenev explained that the story was based on an experience of his own youth. The figure of Turgenev's father plays no such role in his work as that of Varvara Petrovna, but the aloof and dashing father of the narrator of *First Love,* who fascinates Zinaida and slashes her arm with his riding crop, evidently has something to do with the diabolic brother of *The Song of Triumphant Love,* who mesmerizes and rapes his sister-in-law. If the heroes in Turgenev are inhibited from going to bed with the women and do so only, still with inhibitions, when—as in *Smoke* or *The Torrents of Spring*—they, the men, are themselves seduced, the man who prevails over women is likely to treat them with violence and to become an embodiment of the Evil Force.

In the meantime, Varvara Petrovna is reappearing in *Her Ladyship's Private Office* (originally intended as a chapter in an early attempt at a novel, but first published in the *Literary Reminiscences*), and in *Punin and Baburin,* and the Lutovinova grandmother who killed the little serf boy turns up as a variation of the Varvara Petrovna character in Agrippina Ivanovna of *The Brigadier.* The masculine Force of Evil, after lying in abeyance since *The Wayside Inn* of 1852, reappears five years later in *A Tour in the Forest,* and it is here for the first time invested —at least in the minds of the peasants of the story—with supernatural implications. This piece was added by Turgenev to a new edition of *A Sportsman's Sketches* published in 1860, but afterwards presented by the author—in his collected edition of 1865—in its chronological place. For it does not belong with the *Sketches*—it is more philosophical and more complex; it shows the development of Turgenev's art. I agree with Dmitri Mirsky in his admiration for *A Tour in the Forest*—with its wonderful descriptions of pine forests, its feeling for the non-human life of trees that both embraces and isolates human beings, that oppresses at the same time it calms. And in the forest the demon is found—Efrem, a bad peasant who fears nobody, who stops at nothing and whom his neighbors can do nothing about. He makes his living through robbery and brings up his son as a thief. It is no use to arrest him and put him in jail. The only good thing one can say of him is that he usually will not injure anyone who comes from his own settlement. Sometimes he will shout from a distance if he sees a fellow-villager, "Keep away, brother! I'm a killer! The forest demon is on me!" "But why do you mind what he says?" the narrator asks the man who is telling the story. "Can't the lot of you deal with a single man?" "That seems to be the way it is." "But he's not a magician, is he?" "Who knows?" And the forester goes on to tell of the chanter in the church who had thrashed Efrem in the dark when he did not know who he was, but then, when he recognized him, had fallen on his knees before him. Efrem had punished the chanter by putting a spell upon him and causing him to waste away. "That chanter must be an idiot." "Do you think so?" the peasant replies. Once an order goes out to catch Efrem. They have a smart chief of police, and he leads ten men into the forest. Efrem comes out to meet them. "Grab him! Tie him up!" someone cries. But Efrem, looking hideous and frightful, breaks off a big club from a tree and threatens them. "On your knees!" he commands them, and they all fall down on their knees. They have had to get a new chief of police. "But why did they all obey him?" "Why? That's the way it is." But though Efrem connects himself with the *leshi*, the forest goblin, and though, on one of his marauding exploits, he successfully masquerades as a devil, the element he represents has not yet come to wear the aspect of something quite outside the natural world. He is identified also with the bear; the foresters regard him as a kind of bear. And Turgenev here succeeds in assigning him to a role in a partly comprehensible world. When the narrator first came into the forest, he fell to brooding, in a moment of solitude, on the profound disappointment that had been his life. He has always been expecting happiness, and he has never been able to find it (Turgenev had just broken with Pauline Viardot at the time this story was written). On his second day in the forest, he and his peasant guides run into a forest fire deliberately started by Efrem—apparently, out of sheer *Schrecklichkeit*. The foresters console themselves in noting that it is only the kind of fire that runs along the ground and so does not burn the trees. They retreat from the flames to rest. The narrator lies under a tree and watches a dragonfly, who is also taking a rest on a branch. He reflects that it is wrong to complain. What is normal is to live like this insect in a state of tranquil equilibrium: whatever rises above or sinks below this level is automatically rejected by nature. If one suffers through one's own fault or others', one can only keep silent about it. The bad peasant—in his own way normal, as normal as his brother the bear—seems now to fade into the background as a part of the order of nature. The revery is interrupted: "What's the matter with you, Egor," cries one of his guides to the other. "What are you brooding about?" He explains to the narrator that Egor has just lost his last cow. As Egor drives them off in silence, " 'There,' I thought to myself, 'is a man who knows how not to complain.' " We are as far from the conception here of the inimical nature of Vigny —"*Tu ne recevras pas un cri d'amour de moi!*"—as from the sympathetic Nature of the "romantic fallacy." There are here no romantic poses, no rhetorical affirmations or negations. There is not even any attempt to develop a clear point of view: only a moment of experience, two days in the woods, human consciousness and animal life and the life of strong vegetation.

In reading *A Tour in the Forest*, it occurs to one that this indigenous demon, against whom the people of the forest feel themselves utterly helpless, against whom they can have no redress, represents a constant factor in Russian life, an ever-recurring phenomenon of history: the bad master whom one cannot resist, Ivan the Terrible, Peter the Great, Stalin. The masculine Force of Evil reappears in *An Unhappy Girl* (1868) as Susanna's horrible stepfather, and in *A Lear of the Steppes* (1870) you have one male and two female villains, all more or less unaccounted for. In *Lear*, the two daughters of old Kharlov, who destroy him, no doubt dominate the son-in-law, but there is nothing to explain why both of them should have risen to such positions of power save the example of Varvara Petrovna, on whose character they present variations. Maria Nikolaevna in *The Torrents of Spring* —another strong and cunning peasant—is a still further variation. And thereafter, as Turgenev nears sixty, both the female and the male evil powers not only cease to wear the aspect of noxious products of the social system or even of elements of animal nature; they become supernatural beings, who prey upon and take possession, who swoop in on us from outside our known world. This development on Turgenev's part synchronizes—despite the fact that during the seventies he wrote, in *Virgin Soil*, his most ambitious social novel—with a haunting and growing sense of the nullity of human life and the futility of his own endeavors. This feeling first breaks out in *Enough* of 1864. The title of *Smoke* is inspired by it: "He sat alone in the train," he writes of Litvinov at the end of this book. "There was nobody to disturb him. 'Smoke, smoke!' he several times said to himself [he is watching the smoke of the train]. And suddenly everything seemed to him smoke, everything, life itself, Russian life—everything human, especially everything Russian. It was all smoke and steam—he thought—everything seems constantly changing; always new shapes; appearances fly after appearances; but actually it is always the same and the same; everything is hurrying away, everything is speeding off somewhere—and everything vanishes without a trace, without ever achieving anything; a different wind has blown, and everything has been driven in the opposite direction, and there you have again the same ceaseless agitation, the same movement that results in nothing." In the late *Poems in Prose* (1878–82), this despondency has reached its nadir. You have, for example, the devastating dialogue between the Jungfrau and the Finsteraarhorn, which, waking or drowsing in the course of their millennia, see the human race, far below them, come to life, stir about for a little, and eventually die out like vermin. And at the same time the Force of Evil seems to rush in to fill this vacuum. These *Senilia,* as he calls them, are full of nightmares —the nightmare of the giant insect that fatally stings the young man, the nightmare of the end of the world, in which people in a country house are surrounded and swallowed up by a raging and icy sea.

These nightmares have begun in *Phantoms* of 1863, and this is followed, thirteen years later, by *The Dream*. The element of the supernatural first appears in *The Dog* of 1866. This very curious story associates itself with *Knock! . . . Knock! . . . Knock! . . . ,* which follows it in 1870. Both deal with mysterious destinies, one fortunate, the other unfortunate—a suggestion of which is also to be found in *The Torrents of Spring* of 1871. In *The Dog,* the Force of Evil wears the aspect of the gigantic mad dog which persisently attacks the hero and from which he is only saved by his heaven-sent protector: a setter which has come to him first as an invisible but audible presence. The canine guardian angel is again, like the Lieutenant's innocence, a form of the life-giving drop. But this angel in the subsequent stories grows weaker and at last gives way before the Demon of Evil: the diabolic baron of *The Dream;* the priest's son, possessed by the Devil, of *Father Alexey's Story;* the sinister Renaissance sorcerer of *The Song of Triumphant Love*. I do not agree with Mirsky that the realistic setting of these stories prevents them from being successful. They *are* certainly less compelling than the diabolic tales of Gogol, from which they may partly derive, for the reason that the world of Gogol, being always distorted and turbid, is more favorable for this kind of horror, but they are nonetheless creepy enough and can hold their own with any such fantasies. The fault that one would find with them is rather that they are not merely horrible but hopeless. The forces that battle with the goblins are too feeble; they do not have a chance of success. Compare Gogol's vampire story *Viy* with Turgenev's *Clara Milich,* which fundamentally it somewhat resembles. It is not only that the rude village church in which the young student of Gogol keeps his terrible vigil with the girl in the coffin is closer to peasant folklore than the "small wooden house" in Moscow where Turgenev's student lives with his aunt and has his rendezvous with the dead Clara; Gogol's hero arouses more sympathy, puts up a better fight than Turgenev's, who is actually, like Sanin in *The Torrents,* more attracted than frightened by the vampire.

This story—of 1882, the last that Turgenev published—is, in any case, the culmination of the whole morbid side of his work. Clara Milich is a talented young girl as to whom people cannot be sure whether she will turn out "a Rachel or a Viardot." She is not really beautiful; she has a swarthy complexion, coarse hair and a mustache on her upper lip. She is very much the gypsy type; one would imagine she was bad-tempered and capricious —a passionate, self-willed nature, hardly even particularly intelligent. "What tragic eyes!" someone says. Clara fixes upon the student Yakov, a somewhat feminine and frail young man, with whom she has hardly exchanged words at a party, and she sends him a mysterious and urgent message begging him to meet her in a certain street. When she meets him, she tells him, with tears in her eyes, that she feels a great need to talk with him but does not know how to go about it, and he behaves in such a priggish way—he thinks her not respectable, too forward—that she gibes at him and runs away. He soon hears that she has committed suicide. Performing in a provincial theatre, she had drunk poison just before going on and had played the first act with unusual feeling and warmth, then, the moment the curtain fell, had dropped writhing in convulsions to the floor. "What strength of will! What character!" people said. Yakov fears that he is to blame, and he looks up her family and reads her diary and finds that —for reasons not clear—she had counted on him to "decide her destiny," and had then written, "No! no! no!," in evident disillusionment and despair. Clara begins to haunt him in dreams and hallucinations (she is rather like the female spirit who carries Turgenev around in *Phantoms*). At one of their meetings he kisses her—he feels her burning nearness and her cold moist lips —and he wakes his aunt with a cry. What can come of such a love? he wonders. When he remembers that kiss from the dead, a wonderful sensation of cold runs quickly and sweetly through all his limbs. "Such a kiss," he says to himself, "not even Romeo and Juliet exchanged. But the next time I shall hold out better. . . . I shall possess her." The next time he throws himself upon her: "You have conquered! Take me!" he cries. His aunt finds him on his knees, with his head on the armchair where the ghost had been sitting. In a delirium, he declares he is Romeo, who has just taken the poison, and he dies with a smile on his face.

Spasskoye, the prison of his childhood, is closing in on Turgenev, but though his progress in nightmare has brought him to surrender to Clara Milich, he finds courage, in his strange last story, to strike back at the Evil Force. Turgenev in his earlier phase had hoped, as has already been said, that the feudal social system of Russia might be reformed from above by the Tsar. It is the Bulgarians, not the Russians, to whom, in *On the Eve*, Elena devotes her life. Bazarov, in *Fathers and Sons*, though he does not believe in institutions, is by no means a revolutionist. But the implication of *Punin and Baburin* is certainly revolutionary. Even after *Fathers and Sons*, the theme of the two friends persists, but in this story of 1874 the stronger of the pair is no longer a Nihilist: he is a republican who is sent to Siberia. The story ends, however, with the good news of the emancipation of the serfs. In *The Watch,* which follows *Punin and Baburin* in 1875, the two friends appear again, with the same Bazarov-Arcady relationship. In this ingenious parable, the narrator is given a watch by his godfather, a corrupt official who has lost his job but who still always powders his hair (it is the beginning of the nineteenth century). He is delighted by the present at first, but a cousin, whose father had been sent to Siberia for "agitational activities and Jacobin views," carefully examines the watch, declares that it is old and no good, and, learning that it was given the boy by his godfather, tells him that he should accept no gifts from such a man. The narrator worships the cousin, and the rest of the story consists of his efforts to get rid of the watch by burying it or giving it away. But he always—under pressure of his family or of his own insurmountable pride in it—is compelled to get it back again. What does this watch represent? The antiquated social system? The corruption of old Russia? The father and the godfather are crooks; the watch, though the boy does not realize it, has evidently been stolen. It is only at last expelled from their lives when the tough-minded Jacobin cousin hurls it into the river at the cost of falling in himself and of almost getting drowned. *Virgin Soil* (1876), as we have seen, is occupied entirely with a revolutionary subject. Though the agitational activities of the Populists are regarded as premature and shown here as coming to grief, it is implied at the end that the movement is quietly going on and may eventually result in something. And among the *Poems in Prose,* there is one, *The Threshold* (1878), that Turgenev did not publish and that was not known till after his death, when a Populist paper printed it, which was inspired by the attempt of Vera Zasulich to assassinate General Trepov: " 'O you who want to cross that threshold, do you know what awaits you there?' 'I do,' the young girl replies. 'Cold, hunger, hatred, ridicule, scorn, insult, jail, illness, and death itself.' 'I know it.' . . . The young girl crossed the threshold, and behind her fell a heavy curtain. 'Fool!' snarled someone after her. The answer came from somewhere: 'Saint!' "

"I once," Pavlovsky reports that Turgenev used to say in his latter years, "believed that the reforms would come from above; now I am entirely disillusioned. I should have joined the youth movement if I had not been so old and if I could have believed in the results of a movement that came from below. The new social type whose existence I have put on record, the literate peasant who reads the papers and despises and robs the other peasants, is a hundred times worse than the old-fashioned landlord."

In *Old Portraits* (1881), a cruel and unscrupulous landowner takes advantage of a technicality to reclaim from another landowner a serf who has spent twenty years as the latter's devoted servant. The serf promises to kill his new master, bides his time for a favorable moment, and then splits his head with a hatchet. Two weeks before Turgenev's death, in 1883, he carried this theme further. He was dying of cancer of the spine and in such pain that a little later, when Maupassant came to see him, he begged him to bring him a revolver. But he managed to compose one more story, which he dictated to Pauline Viardot in a mixture of French, German and Italian, and asked her to put into French. When she asked him whether he would not rather use Russian, he replied, with tears in his eyes, that he did not feel strong enough to bother about style as he would have to do if he phrased it in Russian. The title of this story—which in the Soviet edition of Turgenev will be found in a Russian translation—was originally *Une Fin*. Here the Russian landowning gentry, whose emergence from a barbarism of brigands has been shown retrospectively in *A House of Gentlefolk* and whose origins recur as a horror in the

Stenka Razin episode of *Phantoms* (Stenka's Cossacks had drowned in the Volga a seventeenth-century Turgenev), returns to its original brutality in a now degenerate form. Talagaev— *talagai* means an obstinate lout—belongs to an old country family, of which he is very proud. His father was famous for his hunting, for his turnouts with silver trimmings, and for once having ordered his coachman to blindfold the eyes of a horse and plunge into an ice-covered river. This father and his generation have squandered the family money, and the surviving Talagaev, though reduced to peddling poultry, makes a point of keeping up his appearance so as not to be taken for a peasant, a sacristan or a merchant: "Why shouldn't I go in for trade? What if I do belong to the gentry? What if my ancestor did wear the brocaded gold cap that was given him by Tamburlaine?" When an innkeeper refuses to buy, he insults him and shoots off a gun that he carries—"Do you think it's not loaded?" he jeers—and goes away singing *Stenka Razin* in a voice "neither pleasing nor true." "He wants to be a bandit," one of the men at the inn mutters, "but he can't even sing the bandits' song!" Having lost caste with his own social group, he succeeds in luring away from home, with the promise that he will show her the Kremlin, the fifteen-year-old daughter of a neighbor of good standing but small property, and makes the usual insolent scene when her father comes to take her back. When we next see Talagaev, he has just been detected in cheating a peasant on a horse deal and is mobbed in the market place. At last, in a bitter snowstorm, when the narrator is battling the weather on his way to dine with a neighbor and has been suggesting to his coachman that the latter might well marry the girl whom Talagaev has tried to abduct (a bridging of the social gulf which the coachman cannot accept: "Oh, but she's a lady," he says), the horses shy suddenly away from something dark in the road. It is the body of Talagaev, lying in a pool of blood, his forehead split with a hatchet and a thick rope around his neck. The narrator remembers having said once in the presence of the murdered man that it was sad to think he might end his life in a brawl, and that Talagaev had answered, "Oh, no, my good sir! The Talagaevs don't die like that!" So the Evil Force of Turgenev is again given a social role and—never defeated before—is finally brought to a reckoning.

The last important event of Turgenev's literary life was his well-known letter to Tolstoy, written not long before his death, in which he tells his uncomfortable friend how glad he is to have been his contemporary and urges him to return to literature. It is a good deal more moving than anything on record in his letters to Pauline Viardot. He had had a *rapprochement* with her when she was aging and had lost her voice, and she had joined Turgenev in Baden. Unable any longer to sing, she now began to compose and teach singing. Her ambition was to have a music school and a concert hall of her own, and Turgenev actually built her one. He wrote the librettos for the operas in which her pupils performed and himself pumped the bellows for the organ. He even acted comic parts in these operas. When a Russian friend tried to remonstrate, he only answered that Anton Rubinstein and Clara Schumann had thought so highly of *Le Dernier Sorcier* that they had advised Mme. Viardot to orchestrate it, but he wrote to a German friend, "I must confess, however, that when I lay stretched out on the floor in the part of the Pasha and saw a cold sarcastic smile of disgust play on the haughty lips of your Crown Princess, something went cold inside me. You know how little I care for my dignity, but even I could not help thinking that things had gone a little too far." Undoubtedly a latent resentment is expressed, in *The Torrents of Spring*, through the picture of the bondage of Sanin to the terrible Maria Nikolaevna, the daughter of a millionaire peasant, who combines irresistible attraction with merciless love of power. In the delirium of his last days, he called Pauline Lady Macbeth and railed against her for having denied him the happiness of married life. On one occasion, when she entered the room, he—symbolically—threw his inkwell at her. (One of her few recorded comments on Turgenev was that he was *"le plus triste des hommes."*) Later he sank into a coma and emerged from it only to say, *"Venez plus près . . . plus près. Le moment est venu de prendre congé . . . comme les tsars russes. . . . Voici la reine des reines. Que de bien elle a fait!"*

His body was transported to Russia and buried, by his orders, beside Belinsky's.

INTRODUCTION

———◆———

I

TURGENEV CONCEIVED the idea of writing his literary reminiscences at a time when his great reputation as a progressive writer seemed to have suffered a blow from which it would never recover. It was on him rather than on Dostoevsky that the mantle of Gogol had fallen, for it was he who with his *A Sportsman's Sketches* and other stories continued the work Gogol had begun of awakening the conscience of the educated classes in Russia to the evils of a political régime based on serfdom. At the beginning of his career as a writer Turgenev was closely connected with the progressive movement in Russia and, particularly, with its more revolutionary wing headed by the critic Vissarion Belinsky and afterwards by the poet and publicist Nikolai Nekrasov. It was Nekrasov who, with the financial help of well-to-do Ivan Panayev, short story writer, journalist and memoirist, bought Pushkin's literary quarterly *The Contemporary* from Professor Peter Pletnyov in 1847 and converted it into one of the most popular progressive monthlies of its time. Turgenev's first stories and novels were published in *The Contemporary,* and it was not till the appearance on the scene in 1857 of the young critic Nikolai Dobrolyubov, "the literary Robespierre," as Turgenev nicknamed him, that the rift between Turgenev and *The Contemporary* began. Dobrolyubov, who died at the age of twenty-six in 1861, was, like Nikolai Chernyshevsky, his close collaborator on *The Contemporary,* the son of a priest. Both of them were educated at religious seminaries and it is quite likely that the rigidity of their views was largely due to their religious education. At any rate, it was their uncompromising opposition to everything that did not agree with their own utilitarian conceptions of society and the world and their blind fanaticism that found expression in their hatred of the aesthetic values of the older generation which appalled Turgenev and made him break his connection with *The Contemporary.* At the time (1858–60) Turgenev was the most popular novelist in Russia and his defection from *The Contemporary* could not but be resented by Nekrasov on financial grounds alone. The two of them, who, as Turgenev declared in his "poem-in-prose" in which he described his last meeting with the dying Nekrasov, had been such "intimate friends," parted "as enemies." Indeed, Nekrasov did nothing to curb the violence of the attacks to which Turgenev began to be subjected by Dobrolyubov. The reasons why Dobrolyubov invariably treated Turgenev with contempt were not only political. Much as Dobrolyubov may have despised Turgenev's moderate liberal views, he despised even more the aristocrat in Turgenev, paying back in their coin the contempt in which, as Turgenev himself declared, the Russian landed gentry held the priestly class to which Dobrolyubov belonged. What must have been even more galling to Turgenev was that Dobrolyubov did not hesitate to hold up to public derision not only him but also Pauline Viardot, the famous singer to whom he had been so slavishly devoted all his life. Thus Dobrolyubov described Turgenev in *The Whistle,* the comic supplement to *The*

Contemporary edited by him, as "a fashionable novelist who is trailing in the wake of a female singer and arranging ovations for her in provincial theatres abroad." *The Whistle's* invective, incidentally, conferred on its editor the soubriquet of "whistler," which soon acquired a wider political significance and was used as a substitute for an unprincipled "revolutionary," in which sense it is used by Turgenev in his literary reminiscences.

After Dobrolyubov's death the attacks on Turgenev by *The Contemporary* were renewed with even greater intensity and fury. The pretext for them was the publication in the spring of 1862 of *Fathers and Sons*, Turgenev's greatest masterpiece, in whose hero Bazarov the editors of *The Contemporary* pretended to see a vicious caricature of Dobrolyubov. The publication of his next novel, *Smoke*, four years later, brought a renewal of these attacks. This time it was not only the left but also the right that joined in abusing Turgenev, who was now paying for the uncanny way in which he seemed to anticipate the political trends in his country and gave them artistic expression in his stories and novels. His enemies in the Russian literary circles went even so far as to insinuate that Turgenev, one of the finest Russian prose writers, had forgotten how to write Russian because of his long absence abroad and wrote his two last novels in French and had them translated into Russian. Turgenev had actually to issue a strongly worded denial of it.

Hurt and bewildered by the storm of condemnation in which his last two novels had been received and appalled at the length to which his enemies would go to abuse and humiliate him, Turgenev decided that the best way to reply to these attacks was to write a series of autobiographical reminiscences which would not only prove his lifelong adherence to liberal ideas, but would also allow him to reply to his critics in the only effective way possible, that is to say, by explaining his views on the art of writing, the place of the writer in society, and what the writer's attitude to the controversial problems of his day should be. Turgenev discussed the publication of these reminiscences with his publisher during one of his flying visits to Russia in 1868 in connection with the proposed publication of a complete edition of his works. The first five "autobiographical fragments" (as Turgenev described them), namely *Instead of an Introduction, A Literary Party at Pletnyov's, Reminiscences of Belinsky, Gogol* and *Apropos of "Fathers and Sons"* were, in fact, published under the title of *Literary Reminiscences* in the 1869 edition of Turgenev's works. They contain Turgenev's literary credo. Since the attacks he resented most came from his old friends on *The Contemporary,* it was only right and proper that the central piece of his rejoinder to them should be his description of his friendship with Belinsky, the man they all revered as their master. The rest of the eight "fragments" have more of an autobiographical than a literary significance. Two of them, *A Trip to Albano and Frascati* and *My Mates Sent Me,* were added in 1874, and the four others, *The Man in the Grey Spectacles, The Execution of Tropmann, About Nightingales* and *Pégas* in 1880. The last two, *The Quail* (omitted from the *Reminiscences* in some editions of Turgenev's works) and *A Fire at Sea,* were first published in 1883.

In his short introduction Turgenev makes a special point of replying to the rumour that he was no longer able to write his works in Russian by pointing out that his long sojourn abroad and his loyalty to Western ideas did not prevent him from "vividly feeling and zealously guarding the purity of the Russian tongue," and that but for the fact that he had gone abroad at the beginning of his literary career he would never have written *A Sportsman's Sketches.* He further reminds his countrymen that one of the reasons why he had left Russia in the first place was his hatred of serfdom and all it stood for and his conviction that from abroad he would be able to attack it more effectively. He was looking back over a period of twenty-five years and his brief but

violent enthusiasm for Hegelian philosophy appeared too childish and inconsequential to him to merit any mention except for
the four men who had studied it with him in Berlin: Nikolai
Stankevich, the leading light of the small group of young Moscow Hegelians, a man of a quite saintly disposition who died
shortly afterwards; the tempestuous Mikhail Bakunin, who took
over from Stankevich in Moscow and who was eventually to become the founder of the anarchist movement; Nikolai Frolov, the
least important of the four, a geographer and translator of Hum-
boldt's *Cosmos;* and Timofey Granovsky, immortalized by Dostoevsky as Stepan Verkhovensky in *The Devils,* a Westerner like
Turgenev, whose public lectures in Moscow, where he was professor of history at the university, were to become one of the great
social and political events of Moscow life.

II

The literary party at Pletnyov's at which the eighteen-year-old
Turgenev was present (one of the regular "Wednesdays" to which
Pletnyov invited all sorts of writers to exchange views and discuss
the latest literary news) in a way symbolizes the state of Russian
literature towards the end of the eighteen thirties. The Augustan
period of Russian poetry was on the way out with Alexander
Pushkin. The new "natural" (as Belinsky called it) literary movement, whose initiator was Gogol, had suffered its first defeat with
the almost universal attacks on Gogol's play, *The Government
Inspector,* and Gogol himself had left the country in disgust to
settle in Rome where he was to write *Dead Souls,* his other great
masterpiece. Meanwhile, mediocrity, clamant, conceited and intol-
erant, as all mediocrity is, as well as jingoistic, reigned supreme,
patted on the back by authority and protected by it from the
slightest breath of criticism. The writers present at the literary

party described by Turgenev were, with two exceptions, a good example of the low level of Russian literary talent of those days. The exceptions were, of course, Turgenev himself, still only vaguely conscious of his great destiny, and Alexey Koltsov, a genuine folk poet, born in a merchant's family in Voronezh, who had to spend most of his life travelling all over the country buying and selling cattle. He was a self-taught man who had never quite learned to write grammatically or to spell correctly. He was "discovered" by Stankevich during one of his business visits to Moscow. On Stankevich's recommendation several of his poems were published in different periodicals, and the Voronezh cattle-dealer became famous. "In Koltsov's songs," Alexander Herzen wrote, "a new world was opened up, sad, unhappy, by no means ridiculous but rather indescribably moving in its naive simplicity and in its resigned destitution. The forgotten Russia, poor Russia, peasant Russia—it is her voice that was heard in his poetry. . . . The time had come when Cinderella entered the ballroom. . . ." But, as can be seen from Turgenev's brilliant pen portrait of the poet, Cinderella-Koltsov did not feel particularly happy at the ball, that is, at Pletnyov's party among the other writers who were members of the nobility and not of the despised merchant class. He was only twenty-eight at the time and five years later he died of consumption.

Pletnyov himself was forty-five in 1837. As a young man he had dabbled in poetry, but he had soon realized his inadequacy as a poet ("his verse," Pushkin had observed, "is as pale as a corpse") and devoted himself to the study of literature and critical writing. He was a great friend of Gogol's and the only one of his friends who wholeheartedly approved of the views expressed in *The Selected Passages from the Correspondence with my Friends*. He outlived most of the guests at his party, dying at the age of seventy-three in 1865.

The oldest writer at the party was General Ivan Skobelev, a

crusty fifty-nine-year-old soldier, who had had two fingers of his right hand shot off and a third smashed in the Napoleonic campaigns and his left hand crushed by a shell in the Polish insurrection in 1831. Like Koltsov, he had received no proper education, which did not prevent him from becoming a popular writer about army life and the author of two successful plays: *Kremnev—the Russian Soldier* and *Moscow Scenes*. In his works he extolled the heroism of the Russian soldier in a rather naive, romantic way, his aim being, as he himself expressed it, to inculcate "a pure and ardent loyalty to God and the Emperor, a sincere, child-like attachment to the motherland, a blind, absolute obedience to the authorities and an instantaneous readiness to face death."

Next in seniority at the party was fifty-seven-year-old Alexander Voeykov, a former member of Arzamas (the literary society founded in 1815 by the opponents of the pseudo-classical movement in Russian literature, including the poets Zhukovsky, Dmitry Bludov, Prince Vyazemsky, and later also Pushkin), poet, critic and rather unscrupulous journalist. He was the author of two biting satires on the writers of his day: *The Lunatic Asylum* and *Parnassus Who's Who*. Between 1815 and 1820 he occupied the chair of Russian Literature at the University of Dorpat, in 1821 he founded the journal, *The Son of the Fatherland*, later edited by Nikolai Grech, and in the following year and for the next seventeen years was the editor of the army paper *The Russian War Veteran*, to which he subsequently added various literary supplements. As editor he had earned an unsavoury reputation, chiefly because of his practice of reprinting works of various authors without their knowledge or consent.

Prince Vladimir Odoevsky, who was thirty-four in 1837, had begun his literary career fourteen years earlier in Moscow as editor (together with Wilhelm Kuechelbecker, the poet who was one of the active leaders of the Decembrist insurrection) of the almanac *Mnemosina*, the organ of the Society of Lovers of Wis-

71

dom, the members of which were followers of the German idealist philosophers. In explaining the society's name, Odoevsky wrote in the first number of *Mnemosina:* "Till now a philosopher was imagined to be a French chatterer of the eighteenth century; that is why we call the true philosophers lovers of wisdom." Odoevsky dissolved the society after the Decembrist insurrection and in 1826 settled in Petersburg where he became a close friend of Pushkin and Gogol. He was known chiefly as the author of fantastic tales with a strong didactic and moralist undercurrent, whose aim, according to Belinsky, was "to awaken in the sleeping soul a feeling of disgust towards . . . the vulgar prose of life and a sacred longing for an ideal life consisting . . . in the courageous realisation of human dignity. . . ." His romantic idealism often led him into mysticism, symbolism and philosophic allegorizing, sometimes combined with a satirical attitude towards contemporary society. In "pure art" alone, he maintained, was there an escape from "the vulgarity of life." Such is the theme of his stories *Beethoven's Last Quartet* and *Sebastian Bach*. On the other hand, his two famous stories, *Princess Mimi* and *Princess Zizi,* give quite a realistic representation of "the terrible society" which "has authors, musicians, beautiful women, geniuses and heroes in its power and which is not afraid of anything—laws, truth or conscience."

Of the remaining four minor writers only Grebyonka and Huber deserve brief mention. Yevgeny Grebyonka, who was twenty-five in 1837, became widely known as the author of Ukrainian folktales. A schoolmate of Gogol at the Nezhin grammar school and a member of the circle of Gogol's friends in Petersburg, his stories were greatly influenced by Gogol's Ukrainian tales. Eduard Guber, a young poet of mystical leanings, was only twenty-three when Turgenev met him at Pletnyov's party. His translation of the first part of Goethe's *Faust,* finished two years earlier, had been immediately suppressed, which was quite a good reason for complaining about the vagaries of the censorship.

III

The time, as Turgenev observes, was decidedly "quiet" and the fact that "the government laid its hand upon everything" is perhaps best exemplified by the banning of a number of important periodicals within the preceding five years. One of them, *The European,* was edited by Ivan Kireyevsky, a former member of the Society of Lovers of Wisdom who subsequently became one of the leading lights among the Moscow Slavophils. (His mother, Avdotya Yelagin, was one of Moscow's great hostesses.) *The European* was proscribed in 1832 because of an article by Kireyevsky in which he used the words "enlightenment," "the activity of reason," and "the skilful discovery of a middle way," which Nicholas I interpreted as standing for "freedom," "revolution" and "constitution." Two years later, in 1834, *The Moscow Telegraph,* edited by the critic and novelist Nikolai Polevoy, was suppressed for publishing an unfavourable review of Nestor Kukolnik's flamboyantly patriotic novel, *The Hand of the Almighty Saved the Fatherland.* Polevoy, the son of an Irkutsk merchant, was an ardent admirer of the French romantic movement and, particularly, of Victor Hugo. He is remembered chiefly for his violent attacks on Gogol whom he described as "a sordid writer." Again two years later, in 1836, another important Moscow periodical, *The Telescope,* "a Journal of Modern Enlightenment," with its supplement *Molva* (Rumour), "a Magazine of Fashions and News," founded in 1831, was banned for publishing the first "philosophic" letter by Peter Chaadayev, attacking the "dead stagnation" of Russian society. *The Telescope* was edited by Nikolai Nadezhdin, the son of a humble deacon who became Professor of

73

Fine Arts at Moscow University. Nadezhdin was an enemy of the romantic movement and, as a counterblast to Polevoy's enthusiasm for Victor Hugo, published the first translations of Balzac's novels in his periodical. Belinsky was one of its chief contributors and for a short time during Nadezhdin's journey abroad in 1835 its acting editor.

In 1837 there were only four literary journals in Petersburg and one in Moscow, namely Pushkin's quarterly *The Contemporary*, Voeykov's *Literary Supplement to the Russian War Veteran*, *The Library for Reading* and *The Northern Bee* and, in Moscow, the shortlived *Moscow Observer*, founded by a number of conservative professors of Moscow University, including Mikhail Pogodin and Stepan Shevyryov, both of them close friends of Gogol.

The Library for Reading, the most popular and influential periodical of the first half of the nineteenth century, was founded in 1834 by an enterprising publisher, Alexander Smirdin, and edited by the no less enterprising orientalist and journalist Osip Senkovsky. It took its curious title from its publisher's famous bookshop in Petersburg. Senkovsky, the most flamboyant personality of his time, was born in 1800. The son of a Polish landowner, he studied oriental languages at Vilno University and spent three years travelling in the Near East where he perfected his knowledge of Turkish and Arabic. He seems to have been also proficient in Persian, modern Greek and Italian, and shortly after his return to Russia in 1822 he was offered the chair of Turkish and Arabic at Petersburg University. He used the Russian fairy tale *Frantsyl the Venetian* for his translations from Russian into Turkish with his students, and the hero of the fairy tale being a King Brambeus, he assumed the pen-name of Baron Brambeus when a few years later he embarked on his all too often rather unsavoury journalistic and literary career. His first works to appear under this pen-name were published in Smirdin's almanac

Novoselye (Housewarming), issued on the occasion of the moving of his publishing house into new palatial premises in 1833. They were: *The Big Reception at Satan's,* a satire on the social customs of 1830, inspired by Balzac's *La Comédie du diable,* and *The Fantastic Travels of Baron Brambeus,* more than inspired by Rabelais and Swift. Impressed by Senkovsky's versatility and perhaps even more by his undoubted journalistic flair, Smirdin offered Senkovsky the editorship of *The Library for Reading,* a magazine devoted to "literature, science, the arts, commerce, news and fashions," published—and this was quite an unheard-of innovation in Russian periodical literature—regularly on the first of the month, and—another no less "revolutionary" innovation— paying its contributors without undue procrasination and at rates so high that no other periodical could compete with it. But there was a fly in the ointment: while paying his contributors so lavishly, Senkovsky had so little regard for them or, alternatively, had so high a regard for his own literary genius, that he never hesitated to "revise" the material sent in to him or even, as he admitted himself, "to make up one story out of two or three by different authors." This soon earned him the contempt of every self-respecting writer, including Gogol, who attacked Senkovsky in *The Contemporary* as an utterly unprincipled journalist "who never cares what he says and who never remembers in one article what he has written in another." Senkovsky was therefore forced to gather round him a group of mediocre writers whom he blew up into geniuses, including such minor poets as Alexey Timofeyev, whom he claimed to be "a second Byron," and Alexander Zhukovsky, whose poems he published under the pen-name of Bernet. His politics being reactionary in the extreme, Senkovsky found a natural ally in Faddey Bulgarin, a compatriot of his, who (together with Grech) was editor of the semi-official *Northern Bee* and an agent of the secret political police, the so-called Third Bureau. Bulgarin was one of Pushkin's bitterest enemies. He attacked the poet as a "freethinker," but Pushkin finally succeeded in silencing him by linking his name with that of François Vidocq, the notorious French criminal turned policeman.

Almost everyone, Turgenev remarks in his reminiscences, wrote poetry in those days, but it is no less true to say that fiction was even more popular among writers than poetry. Indeed, it was in the first rather than in the second half of the nineteenth century that the short story and novel became the most widely popular form of artistic expression in Russia. Bulgarin as well as Polevoy, the egregious Kukolnik as well as the philosophic Prince Odoevsky, Vladimir Dahl (Turgenev's chief during his brief civil service career) as well as Mikhail Zagoskin, and scores of others turned out short stories and novels by the dozen, and there can be no doubt that they did so because of an ever growing demand for fiction from the reading public. But the most popular novelist and short story writer was not Gogol, nor Pushkin, nor any of the lesser writers, but Alexander Bestyuzhev, who wrote under the pen-name of Marlinsky. Bestyuzhev, an officer of the Dragoon Guards, was stationed in Peterhof at the Marly Palace (a faithful replica of the fine palace which Louis XIV built at Marly-le-Roi and which was destroyed in the revolution), and he signed the first critical article he wrote in 1821 by the pen-name of Marlinsky, a pen-name that afterwards conveniently concealed the fact that the author of the best selling novels of the thirties had been one of the active participators of the Decembrist insurrection. Indeed, Bestyuzhev appeared at the head of a battalion of the Moscow Regiment in Senate Square, but realizing after the first exchange of shots between the insurgents and the loyalist troops that the game was up, he fled from the square and surrendered to the authorities on the following morning. He was exiled to Siberia (a lenient sentence considering that his closest associate, the poet Kondraty Ryleyev, with whom he had edited the almanac *Pole Star,* had been executed) and four years later, in the autumn of 1829, sent to the Caucasus where he fought as a private against the Circassians. He was killed in action in 1837.

Bestyuzhev began writing his highly coloured romantic tales long before 1825, but he only achieved fame with his novels written in the Caucasus. His heroes were as a rule, "men of lofty ideas and feelings" who could not reconcile themselves to "the world of hypocrisy, falsehood, monstrous egoism and wholesale oppression" in which they were condemned to live. His style is highly artificial and full of the most extravagant metaphors. For example: "The ocean had cherished and preserved his virginal heart like a precious jewel, and it was his heart that he, like Cleopatra, threw into the vinegar of passion for a loving glance. It had to dissolve in it—all, all, without leaving anything behind." How immensely popular Marlinsky was can be seen from the following account which Turgenev gives of it in his short story *Knock! . . . Knock! . . . Knock! . . .* written at the same time as his literary reminiscences: "Marlinsky," the hero of the story declares, "is considered old-fashioned now and nobody reads him, people even make fun of his name, but in the thirties he was regarded as a great literary genius and no one, not even Pushkin, could compare with him, according to the views of the young people of that time. He not only enjoyed the reputation of the foremost Russian writer, but also—what is much harder and much less frequent— he left his mark on his own generation. Heroes *à la* Marlinsky were to be found everywhere, but especially in the provinces and especially among infantry and artillery officers; they conversed and corresponded in his language; they held themselves aloof in society, glaring darkly at everyone—'with a storm in their souls and a fire in their blood.' . . . Female hearts were 'devoured' by them. It was about them that the nickname 'fatal' was invented."

Less a sign of the times but no less popular was the historical novelist Mikhail Zagoskin, who began his literary career as a playwright and later held the post of Director of the Moscow

State Theatres. Zagoskin's historical novel *Yury Miloslavsky or the Russians in 1612* was published in 1829 and immediately became a best-seller. Its cleverly constructed plot, its humour, and its vivid recreation of the customs and the general atmosphere of a past age are its chief attractions; its chief defect is the lifelessness of its heroes. Zagoskin's eight subsequent historical novels never enjoyed the same success.

IV

Turgenev was too much of an artist not to attempt to introduce a fictitious element into his reminiscences and in this way impart greater order and verisimilitude to the events of his life which, viewed across a gulf of thirty years, might appear to be neither so orderly nor so convincing. Thus in his first autobiographical "fragment" he lumped together his meeting of Pushkin with his meeting of the other writers at Pletnyov's, whereas actually he met them not at the beginning of 1837 but shortly before his departure for Berlin on May 27, 1838. Similarly in his second autobiographical "fragment" his first meeting with Belinsky took place several months before and not after the publication of his poem *Parasha*. This is proved by Belinsky's letters to his friends. On February 23, 1843, for instance, Belinsky wrote: "I have recently made the acquaintance of Turgenev. He was so good as to express the wish to meet me *himself*." And a month later, on March 31, Belinsky wrote to Vassily Botkin, the art connoisseur and critic, who was one of his and Turgenev's closest friends: "Turgenev is a good fellow and I find it easy to make friends with him. There is malice in him, gall and humour; he has a profound understanding of Moscow [i.e., of the Moscow Slavophils] and reproduces it so wonderfully that I am transported with pleasure. . . ." And on April 3 he wrote to the same correspondent: "I have grown rather fond of

Turgenev. He is an extraordinarily intelligent man. My talks and arguments with him were a great comfort to me. It is awful to be with people who either agree with you about everything or who keep contradicting you not with facts but with feelings and instinct, and it is nice to meet a man whose original and characteristic ideas produce sparks as they strike against yours. Turgenev has a great deal of humour. He certainly understands Russia. One can detect character and actuality in all his opinions. He is an enemy of everything that is vague."

There was, indeed, a good reason why Turgenev, who was twenty-five at the time, and Belinsky, who was thirty-two, should have taken so quickly to each other. The reason is that both of them had just then shaken off their Hegelian obsessions. These had made Turgenev write a number of highly romantic poems and poetic dramas and drove him into an affair with Bakunin's eldest sister Tatyana, the transcendental nature of which nearly drove both of them out of their minds; as for Belinsky, who had an unhappy love affair with one of Bakunin's younger sisters, his Hegelian ideas had made him write an ultra-patriotic paean to the Tsarist régime (in his article on the anniversary of the battle of Borodino) under the rather comic misconception that since Hegel said that everything real was rational, the Tsarist régime and serfdom, being real enough, must also be rational. Having settled in Petersburg and become a regular contributor to *Home Annals* edited by Andrey Kraevsky ("whose flair for practical affairs," as Turgenev declares in his reminiscences, "was almost equal to his utter lack of aesthetic taste"), Belinsky soon damned Hegel and his followers and never again confused reality with rationality.

Turgenev's enthusiasm for the poems of Vladimir Benediktov, "the singer of mighty passions," as he was hailed by Senkovsky, was also due to his failure to emerge from "the German ocean." When he finally did emerge, he wrote his narrative poem *Parasha*

79

(signed by the initials T.L., i.e., Turgenev-Lutovinov, Lutovinov being his mother's surname), which fully deserves Belinsky's description of it (in a letter to Botkin) as "an excellent poetic work." It dealt with ordinary people and told the story of a very ordinary love affair ending in a most conventional marriage. But, as Belinsky so perceptively observed in his review of the poem in *Home Annals*, "its keen observation of human nature, its profound idea snatched out of the hidden places of Russian life, its exquisite and subtle irony which conceals such a depth of feeling—all this shows that its author not only possesses great creative powers, but that he is also the son of his age who carries all its griefs and problems in his breast." There could indeed be no more wonderful analysis of Turgenev's art as it was to become in his works of fiction and it merely confirms Turgenev's estimate of Belinsky as a great critic whose "aesthetic feelings were almost infallible."

In an article published nine years earlier than his literary reminiscences, Turgenev gives these interesting additional facts of his first meetings with Belinsky in the country near Petersburg in the summer of 1843:

Belinsky occupied one of those boxes made out of barge-planks and covered with crude multicoloured wallpaper which go under the name of summer cottages in Petersburg; to this summer cottage there was attached an unsightly little garden in which the plants could not or would not provide any shade; communication with Petersburg was difficult; the nearest shop had nothing to offer except bad tea and the same kind of sugar—in short, no conveniences whatever! I remember Belinsky, who was a totally unpractical man, bought a nanny-goat on the advice of his doctor so as to be sure of getting fresh milk every day, but the goat was so old that she had no milk to give. But it was a beautiful summer and Belinsky and I used to take long walks together in the pine-woods: their resin-laden air was beneficial to his already weak chest. We used to sit down on the soft dry moss, strewn with thin pine-needles, and it was there that the talks I have mentioned took place. I had only recently returned from Berlin where I had studied the philosophy of Hegel; Belinsky bombarded me with questions, listened, argued, developed his own ideas, and he did it all with a sort of avid eagerness, a sort of insatiable quest for truth. It was sometimes difficult to keep up with him; you obviously needed some rest like any other man, but he knew no rest, and you could not help replying and arguing with him, nor could you blame him for his impatience: for it welled out of the very depths of his agitated soul. Belinsky's preeminently passionate nature revealed itself in every word he uttered, in every gesture, in his very silence; his brain was continually and indefatigably at work; when I recall the talks I had with him, I am most of all struck by his profound common sense, the awareness of his vocation, all the more powerful because he did not seem to be clear about it himself, his sense of vocation that did not allow him to deviate from the only useful activity at that time: his activity as a literary critic in the widest sense of the word. . . . For him literature was one of the fullest manifestations of the vital force of the people; what he demanded of the critic in general and of himself in particular was not so much a thorough study of his people and its history as a love and an understanding of it together with an understanding of art and poetry, and he believed that possessing this the critic had a right to express his opinion. . . .

Turgenev's short digression about Dmitry Pisarev, the only *avant-garde* critic of the time who had written enthusiastically about *Fathers and Sons,* is chiefly interesting for the attempt the forty-nine-year-old novelist seemed to have made to convert the twenty-seven-year-old utilitarian critic to his views on poetry, particularly the poetry of Pushkin. Pisarev, who declared poetry, painting, sculpture and music to be not only useless but also harmful because they diverted society from satisfying its more urgent needs, lashed out at Pushkin in his article *Pushkin and Belinsky* with a fury that dismayed even his followers who saw in the natural sciences a general panacea for all human ills. It would seem from the letter Pisarev wrote to Turgenev on May 30, 1867, that is to say, shortly after their meeting in Petersburg, that Pisarev had been to see Turgenev twice and that, contrary to Turgenev's statement in his reminiscences, the young critic did reply to Turgenev's indignant protest against his cavalier treatment of Russia's greatest poet. "I should be very pleased," Pisarev wrote, "to talk over the reasons of our disagreement with you. Such a talk would be merely a continuation of the conversation I had with you on the first evening of our acquaintance. I spoke very frankly with you then, too. . . ." To try to convince Pisarev of his errors and unfairness was of course a hopeless undertaking. It is interesting, though, to compare what Chekhov thought of Pisarev's attack on Pushkin twenty-five years later. "I have just read again Pisarev's criticism of Pushkin," Chekhov wrote to the publisher Suvorin from his Melikhovo estate near Moscow on March 11, 1892. "Terribly naive. The man is debunking Onegin and Tatyana, but Pushkin remains as safe and sound as ever. Pisarev is the father and grandfather of all our present-day critics. The same pettiness in debunking, the same cold and self-conceited sense of humour and the same rudeness and indelicacy in their treatment of people. It is not so much Pisarev's ideas, which are non-existent, that make one so sick, as his coarseness. His attitude to Tatyana and, particularly, to her sweet letter, which I love so tenderly, seems to me simply disgusting. Such tiresome and capricious criticism reeks of the public prosecutor. However, to blazes with him!"

Such a contemptuous dismissal of Pisarev was impossible for Turgenev, for Pisarev was, or seemed to be, his only ally among the shrieking horde of *avant-garde* critics. Besides, Turgenev was quite pathetically anxious to have Pisarev on his side again after his last novel *Smoke* had met with even greater condemnation than *Fathers and Sons*. But Pisarev's letter held out little hope of such support and, anyway, Pisarev was drowned while bathing in Riga Bay soon afterwards.

Before leaving for France in 1847, Turgenev took part in the preliminary negotiations for the purchase of *The Contemporary* from Pletnyov by Panayev, who supplied most of the cash, and Nekrasov. It was certainly understood at first that Belinsky would be the editor of the new journal, but it was no less evident that he was completely unfit for the job of transforming a moribund quarterly into a financially successful monthly. Turgenev, who had as little business ability as Belinsky, may have thought otherwise, but one can hardly blame Nekrasov, who certainly was an excellent business man (unfortunately, he was also a desperate gambler so that the money he made out of *The Contemporary* he lost at the English Club), for acting rather ruthlessly in this matter.

Turgenev is quite unusually reserved about his last meeting with Belinsky abroad and there is a good reason for it: he had behaved rather shabbily to Belinsky on that occasion, being too busy dancing attendance on Pauline Viardot. Thus, contrary to his statement in the reminiscences, he did not go to meet Belinsky in Stettin, but met him in Berlin on May 22. From Berlin, again drawn irresistibly in the wake of the great primadonna, he dragged Belinsky to Dresden. There he arranged a meeting between Pauline Viardot and Belinsky at the Dresden Museum, where the critic tried to talk to her "in the vilest French used only by horses" and was utterly discomfited. Turgenev and Belinsky arrived in Salzbrunn in June and were joined there by Annenkov a short time after. During the day Belinsky engaged in long arguments with Turgenev, beginning invariably with the phrase, "Take care, boy, I'll stand you in a corner!" The twenty-nine-year-old "boy" however, was not at all put out by his "father and commander," as he called Belinsky, and quite often spoke his mind freely about what he considered the critic's lack of practical sense. Two months later, having received a letter from Pauline Viardot about her proposed concert tour in England, Turgenev left hastily, telling Belinsky that he had to go to

Berlin to take leave of some friends and would return in a few days. He did not return, however, having accompanied Pauline Viardot to England.

It was in Salzbrunn that Belinsky wrote his famous letter to Gogol, which, no doubt, for censorship reasons Turgenev merely mentions in passing. The views expressed in this letter, in which Belinsky furiously attacked Gogol's *Selected Passages from the Correspondence with my Friends,* were of course fully shared by Turgenev, as indeed he makes it clear in his reminiscences of Gogol. On the other hand, Belinsky fully shared Turgenev's views on art, including his objection to Chernyshevsky's thesis about "works of art being inferior to the beautiful in real life" as exemplified in Chernyshevsky's famous statement about a real apple being superior to a painted one. (In *The Devils* Dostoevsky derides Chernyshevsky's aesthetic ideas by quoting the same example of the real and the painted apple.) And that, of course, is what Turgenev meant by saying that Belinsky had died at the right moment, or in other words that had he lived longer, he too would have fallen foul of the utilitarians and been pushed out of *The Contemporary* by Chernyshevsky and Dobrolyubov as Turgenev had been. It is hard to say whether Turgenev was right or not, though what has been happening in Russia in more recent times seems to lend support to his surmise.

V

The reasons for Turgenev's arrest and exile to his country estate were a little more complicated than they appear to be from his reminiscences. His obituary article on Gogol, the ostensible reason for his arrest, was merely the official excuse the authorities gave for it. The thirty-three-year-old Turgenev was known to be a close friend of such an outspoken enemy of the Tsarist government as Herzen, he was at the time closely connected with the left-wing group round *The Contemporary,* he was the author of peasant stories that undermined the very foundation of serfdom, and after Gogol's death he did not exactly endear himself to the authorities by sporting a mourning armband in public and challenging the government to incarcerate him in the Peter and Paul Fortress for it. On top of that he wrote letters to friends in Moscow (opened by the secret police) in which he spoke of Gogol's death as "a historic event that cannot be understood at once" and followed up this hint at the reactionary forces which had combined to drive Gogol to his death by the no less dangerous statement that Gogol had made a mistake in not realizing that "no man, however strong in spirit," could take upon himself "the struggle of a whole people." Furthermore, he singled out the head of the Petersburg Educational District, Count Musin-Pushkin, as chiefly responsible for the government measures to suppress all mention of Gogol in the Russian press. "Count Musin-Pushkin," he wrote, "was astonished at the insolence of people who were sorry for Gogol, but no honest man would waste any honest indignation on that! Up to their neck in filth, these people are quite content to wallow in it—much good may it do them! Honourable men," he concluded, "ought to keep even more closely together now—let Gogol's death have at least this good result." His obit on Gogol was, in fact, just the last straw. . . .

Turgenev's personal acquaintance with Gogol was, as appears from his reminiscences, very slight. He had seen him a few times but had spoken to him only once during his visit with the famous actor Mikhail Shchepkin. Gogol was not an easy man to get on with and Turgenev's political views were diametrically opposed to his own, but he was an artist first and foremost and, recognizing such an artist in Turgenev, he went out of his way to be nice to him. Turgenev was the only man who heard both Gogol and Dickens read in public (he had been present at three public readings by Dickens in Paris at the beginning of 1863) and the comparison he draws between the two is quite unique in literary history.

Turgenev's meeting with Vassily Andreyevich Zhukovsky took place in 1834. The famous romantic poet and translator was forty-nine at the time and his literary career was practically over. He was the illegitimate son of Alexander Bunin, a rich landowner, and a captive Turkish woman, and he got his surname and patronymic from his godfather, a poor nobleman. His father, however, gave him an excellent education and his first literary success came with his translation of Gray's *Elegy written in a Country Church-yard*. He was the tutor of the future Alexander II and that is why Turgenev had to go to the Winter Palace to deliver his mother's birthday present to him.

The meeting with Krylov, the great Russian fable writer, took place in 1839, and Turgenev's magnificent pen portrait of him loses nothing for being so brief. His pen portrait of Lermontov is no less striking, though perhaps a little influenced by the poet's tragic fate. Turgenev saw him in 1840, a year before his death in a duel. Lermontov was twenty-six at the time. A year earlier he had written his little poem to Countess Emilia Musin-Pushkin in which he declared her to be whiter than a lily and her eyes like the skies of Italy, but her heart like the Bastille. No wonder he gazed rather glumly at the beautiful countess as he squatted at her feet! His famous *Meditation* (a favourite title among the poets who were involved in the Decembrist plot) was written in 1838 and in it he condemned his generation whose future he declared to be "obscure and empty" and whom he accused of being "cowards in the face of danger and abject slaves before authority."

Turgenev's last meeting with Zagosin must have taken place in Moscow at the same time as his meeting with Gogol, that is to say, in 1851. Zagosin was sixty-two and he died a year later. At that time, however, the bitter reflection about the transitoriness of literary fame would hardly have occurred to Turgenev who was then at the very beginning of his literary career. Rather does it express Turgenev's views when he was writing his last brilliant pen portrait of the least important of the writers he had met and when his own literary reputation seemed to him to have suffered an eclipse more complete than Zagosin's.

VI

Alexander Ivanov's connection with literature is the indirect one of having been a close friend of Gogol's, but his meeting with Turgenev and Botkin in Rome in the autumn of 1857 certainly resulted in one of Turgenev's most luminous masterpieces of memoir writing.

Turgenev arrived in Rome with his friend Botkin at the end of October and he stayed in Italy for the next five months. He was working at his second novel—*A House of Gentlefolk*—and hoped to finish it by the time he returned to Petersburg in the spring. He and Botkin visited Ivanov's studio on October 30. "I have made the acquaintance here," Turgenev wrote to Annenkov on November 12, "of the painter Ivanov and saw his painting [of the Epiphany]. Judged by the depth of its idea, the force of its expression, and the truth and honesty of its execution it is a first class thing. It is not for nothing that he gave twenty-five years of his life to it. . . . Ivanov . . . is a remarkable man; original, intelligent, truthful, thinking, but I can't help feeling that he is a little touched in the head; twenty-five years of solitude have taken their toll. . . ."

This letter must have been written after the trip to Albano and Frascati, during which Ivanov's paranoiac tendencies came to light, which seems to indicate that the trip actually took place in the first week of November and not in the last days of October. Ivanov was fifty-one at the time and he died in Petersburg of cholera eight months later.

In his brief analysis of Ivanov's art, Turgenev contrasts it with the work of the academician Karl Bryulov, whose famous picture, "The Last Days of Pompeii," was exhibited in Petersburg in 1834 and threw the youthful Gogol into such an ecstasy of delight that he wrote the article that provoked such a crushing criticism from Turgenev in his reminiscences of Belinsky.

VII

Turgenev's apologia for *Fathers and Sons,* written six years after the publication of what later was to be acknowledged even in Russia as his greatest masterpiece, clearly shows that the unscrupulous, shortsighted and downright stupid attacks on him had driven him to despair and to what amounted almost to a conviction that never again would he regain his popularity as a novelist in his own country. But these attacks also provided him with the opportunity of stating his views on the art of the novel and the novelist's attitude to contemporary problems which in itself to some extent makes up for the folly of his adversaries.

Anxious to repudiate the accusation that he had written *Fathers and Sons* with the sole aim of denigrating the younger generation and expressing his contempt for it, Turgenev pointed out that the genesis of his novels was men rather than ideas, or in other words, that it was the human drama that was his chief concern as a novelist rather than the propaganda of any panacea for man's happiness. But in thus challenging (however mildly) the clamorous utilitarian ideologists of his time, Turgenev went rather too far in playing down his ability "to create character" and his "inventiveness." What it comes to is that like any other great creative writer he felt the need for a prototype for his chief characters. This he put much more clearly a few years before his death to Maxim Kovalevsky, the well-known Russian lawyer, historian and sociologist. "I must always have a meeting with a living man," Kovalevsky reports Turgenev as saying, "a direct acquaintance with some vital fact, before I set out to create a type or work out a plot; I am not, of course, just a photographer, I do not make any drawings of my models, but already Belinsky observed that I was quite incapable of getting anything out of my own head. . . ."

In indignantly rejecting the insinuation that in Bazarov, the hero of *Fathers and Sons*, he was trying to caricature Dobrolyubov, whom he was supposed to hate because the young critic had been rude to him and hurt his vanity, Turgenev claimed that the real prototype of Bazarov was an obscure country doctor by the name of Dmitriyev. But his account in the *Literary Reminiscences* omits to state the fact that his meeting with Dmitriyev was much too brief to enable him to make a thorough study of the man. This fact only came out four years after Turgenev's death in the reminiscences published by one of his friends. "Without the district doctor Dmitriyev," Turgenev said, "there would have been no Bazarov. I was travelling from Petersburg to Moscow in a second class compartment. He sat opposite me. We spoke little, mostly about trifles. He was talking at length about some remedy against anthrax. He was too little interested in me to find out who I was and even less interested in literature. I was struck by his Bazarov manner, and I began looking for this newly arisen type everywhere and observing it with care. Soon afterwards I learnt that Dmitriyev had died." Dmitriyev, therefore, was not strictly speaking even the prototype of Bazarov. He merely provided the impulse for the study of a new social phenomenon—"the Bazarov type"—the existence of which no one as yet suspected. Turgenev does not stop to consider the full implications of this conscious creative process in his reminiscences. He does so, however, in the introduction to the collected edition of his novels published in 1880.

I cannot, by the way [Turgenev writes], help expressing my opinion about "the conscious and unconscious creative process," "preconceived and tendentious ideas," "the usefulness of objectivity, spontaneity and naivety," which always seemed to me to be nothing but stock phrases, whoever the authority happened to be who uttered them, nothing but a current rhetorical coin which is not considered false only because too many people accept it as genuine. Every writer *who does not lack talent* (that, of course, is the indispensable condition), every writer, I say, tries his best to give a vivid and true reproduction of the impressions he has obtained from his own life and from the life of others, and every reader has the right to judge how far he has succeeded in this and where he has gone wrong; but who has the right to tell him which impressions are of any use in literature and which aren't? If he is truthful, he is right; if he has no talent, no amount of "objectivity" will be of any help to him. We have now a multiplicity of writers who consider themselves to be "unconscious creative artists" and who choose only "vital" subjects; and yet it is they who are most of all imbued with this disastrous "tendentiousness." Everyone knows the saying: *a poet thinks in images;* this saying is absolutely incontestable and true; but on what ground do you, his critic and judge, permit him to reproduce an imaginative picture of nature, be it something out of the life of the common people or a character who is true to himself (another stock phrase!), and yet as soon as he touches something vague, something that is psychologically complex or even morbid, something that has emerged from the very depth of our social life and is not just some particular case, you shout: Stop! This is no good at all! This is ratiocination, this is a preconceived idea, this is politics, this is journalism! You maintain that the journalist and the poet have different objects in view. . . . No! Their objects can be the same, absolutely the same, except that the journalist looks at them with the eyes of the journalist and the poet with the eyes of the poet. In art the question: how? is more important than the question: what? If all that you repudiate appears as an *image*—note: as an *image*—in the writer's mind, what right have you to suspect his intentions, why do you push him out of the temple where the priests of "unconscious" art sit in state on bedecked altars before which rises the incense all too often kindled by the hands of those selfsame priests? Believe me, no man of real talent ever serves aims other than his own and he finds satisfaction in himself alone; the life that surrounds him provides him with the contents of his works; he is its *concentrated reflection;* but he is as incapable of writing a panegyric as a lampoon. . . . When all is said and done—that is beneath him. Only those who can do no better submit to a given theme or carry out a programme.

This is the most mature reflection on the art of the novelist that Turgenev ever wrote. In his defence of *Fathers and Sons* he gave expression to the same ideas but in a more subjective way. The fact that he thought it necessary to *defend* himself already made his motives suspect and, indeed, Turgenev himself realized that only too well. "It seems," he wrote in a letter to a friend, "that my article about *Fathers and Sons* has not satisfied anyone. . . . And yet every word of it is gospel truth, in my judgment, at any rate. It seems that the author himself does not always know what he is doing. My feelings towards Bazarov—my personal feelings—were rather vague (goodness only knows whether I liked him or hated him!), and yet his character turned out to be so definite that it entered into life at once and went on acting in its own sweet way. After all, what does it matter what an author thinks of his work? His work is one thing and he—another; but, I repeat, my article is as sincere as a confession. . . ."

VIII

The eight "autobiographical fragments" which follow Turgenev's literary reminiscences cover various periods of his life: three of them go back to his early youth, three others deal with various incidents of his life in Paris, one is devoted to his favourite dog and one is merely a piece of critical reportage.

The Man in the Grey Spectacles and *My Mates Sent Me* recount Turgenev's experience in Paris during the 1848 revolution. Turgenev took a keen interest in the political events in France in that year and, while not taking an active part in them, did his best to be on the spot when anything really dramatic happened. He wrote *The Man in the Grey Spectacles* in September 1879 and it was first published in *La Nouvelle Revue* on December 15, 1879, under the heading of *Monsieur François*. A footnote by Turgenev dealt with a rather obvious objection to the story. "This short sketch," Turgenev wrote, "has one serious fault: it contains forecasts made long after the events in question took place. This is a fault which I cannot make good, but I do assert that the man I am talking about did exist and did tell me the things I recorded." But for all that explanation the story of M. François does not carry conviction and the personality of the mysterious Frenchman does not quite come to life. The truth is that Turgenev had precious little to work upon and in the interval of thirty-one years between his meeting with M. François and his description of it the whole sequence of events may have assumed a more mysterious character than they had in reality. Turgenev himself at least does not attempt to explain anything and there can be no doubt that if all the facts were known a fairly good explanation of M. François's forecasts could be found.

Turgenev was much more successful in conveying the atmosphere of the June counter-revolution in Paris in *My Mates Sent Me*. It is one of the finest descriptions of those stormy days. It was first published in the Russian journal *Nedelya* (The Week) in 1874. The German revolutionary poet, Georg Herwegh, who was a close friend of Herzen and Turgenev, had led an unsuccessful campaign against the Duke of Baden-Baden at the begin-

ning of 1848, then fled to France and was living in the same
house as Turgenev during the counter-revolution of June.

The last autobiographical "fragment" dealing with Turgenev's
experiences in Paris—*The Execution of Tropmann*—was first published in 1870 in the June number of the Russian periodical *The
European Herald*. Tropmann, who had been found guilty of the
murder of the proprietor of a small engineering works by the
name of Kink in the village of Pantin as well as of his eldest son
and his wife and their five small children, was executed in Paris
on January 19, 1870. Turgenev must have written his impressions
of Tropmann's execution shortly after he had witnessed it and
that is quite probably why the whole thing is described with such
amazing vividness. It is one of the finest humanitarian documents
left by Turgenev. The article was, of course, a godsend to Dostoevsky who was just then engaged in writing his malicious skit
on Turgenev in *The Devils*. In a letter to the Russian critic Nikolai Strakhov, written in Dresden on June 23, 1870, Dostoevsky
went out of his way to abuse the man he had always hated and
been jealous of, though at times he may have found it politic to
fawn on him and borrow money from him. "I have, by the way,"
Dostoevsky wrote, "just read Turgenev's *The Execution of Tropmann*. You, my dear Strakhov, may be of a different opinion, but
I was revolted by this pompous and squeamish article. Why is he
so coy and why does he keep on saying that he had no right to
be there? Of course, if he had admitted that he had merely gone
to be present at a public show, then one could understand it; but
no man has a right to turn away and ignore what is taking place
on earth and there are higher moral reasons for that. *Homo sum
et nihil humanum*—etc. What is so comic is that at the end he
does turn away and does not see the last stages of the execution:
'Look, ladies and gentlemen, how nicely I have been brought
up! I could not stand it!' However, he gives himself away. As a
result, the chief impression of the article is his terrible concern,

to the point of utter squeamishness, about himself, about his own integrity and peace of mind, and that in the sight of a chopped off head! However, to blazes with them all! I am thoroughly sick of them all. I regard Turgenev as one who of all the Russian writers has most written himself out whatever you, my dear Strakhov, may have to say 'for' Turgenev. I'm sorry. . . ."

And Dostoevsky may well have been sorry. That his personal dislike of Turgenev blinded him to Turgenev's motives for writing the article and to Turgenev's plea for the abolition of capital punishment (a plea that should have appealed to Dostoevsky, for but for the fact that capital punishment for murder had been abolished in the Russia of his day he would not have been able to write *Crime and Punishment* nor *The Brothers Karamazov*), is perhaps understandable, but to interpret Turgenev's inability to look on while a human being, albeit a murderer, was being callously killed as ignoring what was taking place on earth, is surely not only unfair but also quite absurd. The whole purpose of Turgenev's article was, of course, to make people conscious of the beastliness and inhumanity that was taking place before their very eyes and that they ignored and turned away from.

About Nightingales was first published in 1855 as a supplement to *A Huntsman's Reminiscences of Different Kinds of Hunts* by Sergey Aksakov, author of *A Family Chronicle*. Turgenev was very friendly with the Aksakov family, the bulwark of the Slavophil movement, and it would seem from a letter he wrote to a friend in 1869 that he intended to include an article on *The Slavophils and the Aksakov Family* in his literary reminiscences. According to Turgenev, he wrote down the description of the nightingales from the words of Afanasy Ivanov, an old and experienced huntsman, a house-serf of Turgenev's, who used to accompany him on his shoots. Turgenev often mentions Afanasy in his *A Sportsman's Sketches* under the name of Yermolay.

Pégas was first published in Kazan in a separate brochure in

1874 under the heading: "I. Turgenev. Pégas. Pub. P. Vassilyev." Pégas was Turgenev's favourite dog. "A dog like that," he wrote to a correspondent, "is one of the world's wonders. The way he looks for and finds a wounded beast or bird has become quite legendary. . . ."

There is nothing that need be said about the *Pergamos Excavations,* but *The Quail* is interesting not only because it certainly contains some autobiographical elements, but also because it is the only children's story Turgenev wrote. He wrote it at the special request of Countess Sophia Tolstoy as his contribution to her brother's children's magazine. He had first told the story of the dying quail during his visit to Yasnaya Polyana, Tolstoy's country estate, in the spring of 1880. At the beginning of November 1882, Countess Tolstoy asked Turgenev's permission to publish *The Quail,* which he had sent to her, in a volume of children's stories together with Tolstoy's story *What Men Live By.* Turgenev replied on November 22 that he not only agreed to her proposal, but was "genuinely glad of the honour of appearing together with the stories of Leo Nikolayevich, though such proximity is dangerous for my story." Turgenev's delightful story was eventually published with illustrations by the famous Russian artists Vasnetsov and Surikov. On December 15, 1882, Turgenev wrote to Tolstoy: "You do my *Quail* too great an honour in providing it with illustrations by Vasnetsov and Surikov. All it is good for is to serve as material for their talent." On receiving from Tolstoy the volume of children's stories, Turgenev, too weak after his operation to write, dictated on January 8, 1883, a letter thanking Tolstoy for his beautiful present. "The edition," he declared, "is lovely and so are the illustrations. . . . My *Quail* has been greatly honoured." The story shows that, keen sportsman though he was, Turgenev could feel deeply the suffering shooting inflicted on game birds. Indeed, like Thomas Hardy, he was appalled at the indiscriminate slaughter of pheasants during the shooting season in England.

IX

A Fire at Sea was dictated by Turgenev in French to Pauline Viardot three months before his death at Bougival on September 3, 1883. It was then translated into Russian by the woman writer A. Lukanin and the translation, approved by Turgenev, was published posthumously in the edition of his complete works in 1883. It records an incident that had occurred forty-five years earlier, an incident that did not reflect so well on Turgenev's courage in an emergency. It was on May 27, 1838, that the nineteen-year-old Turgenev set out from Petersburg for Berlin by sea via Luebeck. It was his first journey abroad. Not far from the coast of Germany the steamer caught fire and, according to all accounts, Turgenev lost his head in the general panic that ensued among the passengers. Annenkov records that he rushed about appealing to every man to save him as he was the only son of a rich widow. His mother wrote to him about it a few months after the shipwreck. "Why," she asked him, "were only your lamentations noticed on board? Stories about it are reaching me from everywhere and, to my great distress, I have been told about it by many people: *Ce gros Tourguénieff qui se lamentait, qui disait mourir si jeune. . . .* Countess Tolstoy—Princess Galitzine and . . . many others. There were ladies on board, mothers with families: why do they tell this only about you? That you are a *gros monsieur* is not your fault, but!" she concluded bitterly, as usual emphasizing her buts with an exclamation mark, "that you are a coward, which the other passengers could not help noticing in their panic, *that* has left a stain on you, if not of dishonour, then of *ridicule*—you must admit that."

But though everyone must have heard of this incident, it did not seem to worry Turgenev over much. In fact, seventeen years later he himself made fun of it and, to some extent, admitted it when in the spring of 1855 he entertained some of his friends at his country estate. Indeed, on May 26 he himself took part in *The School of Hospitality*, a play composed jointly by them for the occasion, in which he was made to repeat the phrase he was said to have used on the deck of the burning ship: "Save me, save me, I am the only son of my mother!" He was already a famous writer at the time and the fact that as a boy of nineteen he did not behave very creditably did not seem to matter to him or to anybody else. But twelve years later the situation was changed: he was being venomously attacked on all sides and no story, whether genuine or not, was too discreditable for his enemies to make use of. And it was just then that Prince Peter Dolgorukov, a Russian emigré with none too savoury a reputation, published his memoirs in Geneva in which he gave a highly coloured account of the incident on the burning ship, claiming that as a passenger on it he himself heard Turgenev use the phrase: "Save me, save me, I am the only son of my mother!" The story was quoted in a review of the Prince's memoirs in a Russian paper and this time Turgenev could not afford to ignore it. "I knew before," he wrote in a letter to the editor of the paper, "that Prince Dolgorukov had thought fit to dig up the old story of how thirty years ago (in May, 1838) I, who was a passenger on S.S. *Nicholas I*, which caught fire near Travemuende, cried: 'Save me, save me, I'm the only son of my mother!' (the joke being that I called myself an only son while I have a brother). The proximity of death might well have perturbed a boy of nineteen, and I do not wish to claim that I looked upon death with indifference, but the above-mentioned words, made up by a witty prince (not Dolgorukov) on the following day, were never uttered by me."

Turgenev had been urged by his friends in France to publish a description of the incident and in this way confound his enemies once for all. But he would not agree, no doubt, because he felt that it would merely add fuel to the fire which his enemies in Russia (including Dostoevsky who did not shrink from giving a malicious version of it in *The Devils*) were so assiduously stoking up. That his fears were fully justified was proved six years after Turgenev's death by the publication of Mrs. Panayev's memoirs. Mrs. Panayev had always disliked Turgenev, who looked perhaps a little too quizzically on the *ménage à trois* she had established with her husband and Nekrasov, and the unconcealed malice with which she tells her so frequently quoted version of Turgenev's behaviour on the burning ship shows that her chief concern was "to expose" (a favourite occupation of *The Contemporary* group of writers to which she belonged) Turgenev's own version of it. In 1842, Mrs. Panayev records, Turgenev, who was a frequent visitor at her house in Pávlovsk, used to regale her with stories of his exemplary behaviour during the panic on the burning ship, "comforting the weeping women and infusing courage into their husbands who had lost their heads. And indeed," Mrs. Panayev remarks spitefully, "it required a great deal of sangfroid to remember so many small details that took place on the steamer. I had heard before about this disaster," she goes on, "from an acquaintance of mine, who was also travelling on the same steamer with his wife and baby daughter. Among other things, he told me about a very young passenger who had been sternly reprimanded by the captain when, after a lifeboat had been lowered to take the women and children off the burning ship, he pushed his way through them in an attempt to get into the boat first, and then plagued everybody with his complaints about the captain who would not let him get into the boat, crying plaintively: *Mourir si jeune!* At the open air concert [at the Vauxhall Gardens in Pavlovsk] I pointed out to my friend, who lived in the country, the personalities who were remarkable in one way or another, among them Turgenev. . . . 'Good heavens,' my friend exclaimed, 'that's the young man who kept crying *mourir si jeune* on the steamer!' I was sure he was mistaken, but I was surprised when he added: 'He has a very highpitched voice which strikes one immediately in so big and tall a man.' "

There is nothing new in Mrs. Panayev's story except its supposed confirmation by an anonymous witness. But, considering the general lack of veracity, which is such a striking feature of Mrs. Panayev's memoirs, this witness had most probably been invented by herself. The difference between her version and Turgenev's is the difference between the "what" and the "how" that distinguishes a journalist's "story" from a work of art. Quite likely it was not so much the desire to justify himself in the eyes of posterity that impelled Turgenev to record this early incident of his life on his deathbed as the fact that he had seen it *imaginatively* for the first time just at that moment. Indeed, as it stands, *A Fire at Sea* is a truly remarkable reconstruction of a dramatic event that at the time it happened seemed to be too confused for its details to be observed, let alone remembered. That some of these details, such as Turgenev's descent into a lifeboat on an anchor chain with the inert body of a woman hanging round his neck, are no doubt greatly exaggerated, if not entirely fictitious, does not detract from the general effect of the story.

D. M.

INSTEAD OF AN INTRODUCTION

———◆———

About easter 1843 an event took place in Petersburg which was extremely unimportant in itself and which has long since sunk into oblivion, namely, a small poem under the title of *Parasha* was published by a certain T. L. That T. L. was I; with that poem I entered upon my literary career. Since then almost twenty-five years have passed, and now that I am about to publish a new edition of my works, I should like to have a talk with my reader and share with him some of the reminiscences I have accumulated during a quarter of a century. . . . *Grande aevi spatium!*

I cannot promise my reader anything very new, anything "piquant"; I must warn him, too, that a great deal will have to remain unsaid or only partly said. One need not go far in search for the causes of such reservation on my part. We all know that a great deal has changed since 1843 and that a great deal has totally disappeared. . . . But not all the links between our present and our past have been severed; many people are still living and —it is not only the people that remain. . . . But the truth—the whole truth and nothing but the truth—one can only tell about what has finally left the stage. That is why I propose to confine myself to a few fragmentary accounts, a few disconnected chapters, from my reminiscences; I can only hope that their inner unity will be perceived; but I disclaim any outward unity, any strictly consecutive narrative, at once. I think it necessary, however, to acquaint my readers at the outset with a few facts which concern me personally and which reveal the primary cause of my literary activities.

Having graduated from the philological faculty of St. Petersburg university in 1837, I left for Berlin in the spring of 1838 to complete my studies there. I was only nineteen; I have long dreamed of that journey. I was convinced that in Russia one could acquire only a certain amount of elementary knowledge, but that the source of true knowledge was to be found abroad. In those days there was not a single man among the professors and lecturers at the university of Petersburg who could shake that conviction of mine; indeed, they were themselves imbued with it. The Ministry of Education, headed by Count Uvarov, was also of the same opinion, and it sent young men to the German universities at its own expense. I spent about two years in Berlin, having left Germany only once during that period. The Russians who attended the lectures at Berlin university during my first year were: N. Stankevich, Granovsky and Frolov, and during my second year—M. Bakunin, who became such a well known figure afterwards. I studied philosophy, history, Latin and Greek but applied myself with special zeal to a study of Hegel under the guidance of Professor Werder. As an example of the inadequacy of the education we received at the time in our universities I may mention the following fact: in Berlin I read Roman antiquities with Professor Zumpf and the history of Greek literature with Professor Boeck, and at home I had to sweat over Latin and Greek grammar because I knew so little of it. And I was not by any means the worst graduate of Petersburg university.

The aim of our young men—young men of my own age—abroad

reminded me of the search by the Slavs for chieftains from the overseas Varangians. In the same way everyone of us felt that his native land (I am speaking not only of his country, but also of the moral and intellectual attainments of each of us) was great and plentiful, but that there was no order in it. So far as I am concerned, I can truthfully say that personally I realized very well all the disadvantages of being cut off from my native soil and of such a violent interruption of all the links and connexions that bound me to the environment in which I had grown up. . . . But there was nothing to be done about it. That mode of life, that kind of environment and, particularly, the social stratum, if one may put it that way, to which I belonged—the landowning and serf-owning stratum of society—did not represent anything that could hold me back. On the contrary, almost everything I saw around me aroused in me a feeling of embarrassment and indignation and, finally, disgust. There could be no question of any hesitation on my part. I had either to submit and follow meekly the well-trodden track, go along the well-beaten path, or turn away from it without a moment's hesitation and renounce "everyone and everything" even at the risk of losing much that was near and dear to my heart. I chose the latter. . . . I plunged headlong into "the German sea," which was to purify and regenerate me, and when I finally emerged from its waves, I discovered myself to be a "Westerner," and I have remained one ever since.

It has never entered my head to condemn those of my contemporaries who by a different, a less negative, way attained that freedom and that awareness I had striven for. All I want to say is that *I* saw no other way before me. I could not breathe the same air as those who stood for the things I hated so much; I could not remain at their side. I expect I had not the necessary stamina, the necessary strength of character, for that. I had to put a certain distance between myself and my enemy so as to be able to attack him more effectively from the distance that separated us. In my eyes this enemy had a clearly defined form and bore a well-known name: this enemy was—serfdom. Under this name I gathered and concentrated everything against which I had made up my mind to fight to the very end, which I had sworn never to be reconciled to. . . . That was my Hannibal oath; and I was not the only one to take it in those days. The reason I went to Western Europe was to be able to carry it out the better. And I do not think that the fact that I am a Westerner deprived me of any sympathy with Russian life or of any understanding of its idiosyncrasies and needs. *A Sportsman's Sketches,* those studies which were so new at the time and which have been long outstripped since, I wrote abroad; some of them at difficult moments of my life when I was undecided whether to return to my country or not. It might be objected that the bit of the Russian spirit that can be detected in them was preserved not because of my Western ideas, but in spite of those ideas and against my own will. It is difficult to argue about such a thing. All I know is that I should, of course, not have written those studies if I had stayed in Russia. Let me also add that I never admitted the existence of that impregnable line which some solicitous and even zealous, though ignorant, patriots are so anxious to draw between Russia and Western Europe, that Europe to which we are so closely bound by race, language and creed. For does not our Slav race constitute one of the main branches of the Indo-Germanic stock in the eyes of the philologist and ethnologist? And if it is impossible to deny the influence of Greece on Rome, and both on the Germano-Romance world, how can anyone refuse to admit the influence on us of this—whatever you may say—kindred and homogeneous world? Are we really so little original and so weak that we must be afraid of any outside influence and wave it away with childish horror for fear that it may corrupt us? I do not think so; on the contrary, I cannot help thinking that however much you scrub us, you will never be able to deprive us of our

103

Russian nature. Why, what a feeble people we would otherwise have been! I know this from my own experience: my loyalty to the Western principles did not prevent me from guarding zealously and feeling vividly the purity of our Russian tongue. The Russian critics, who imputed such numerous and such diverse faults to me, have never, so far as I can remember, reproached me with any impurity or incorrectness of language or with imitating someone else's style.

However, *basta così*. I have been talking of myself long enough; let me now talk of others. This will be more interesting both for me and for my readers. I should like to point out, however, that the fragments from my reminiscences which I venture to submit to the judgment of the public follow each other in chronological order and that the first of them belongs to the period preceding 1843.

Baden-Baden, 1868.

I

A LITERARY PARTY AT
P. A. PLETNYOV'S

AT THE BEGINNING of 1837, while still a third year student (of the philological faculty) of Petersburg University, I received an invitation from Peter Alexandrovich Pletnyov, Professor of Russian Literature, to a literary party at his house. Shortly before that I had submitted for his criticism one of the first fruits of my Muse (as they used to say in those days), a fantastic drama in iambic pentameters under the title of *Steno*. In one of his subsequent lectures, Pletnyov, with his customary good-humor, analysed, without revealing its authorship, this perfectly preposterous work of mine, in which with childish incompetence I was slavishly imitating Byron's *Manfred*. On leaving the university building and seeing me in the street, he hailed me and rebuked me in a fatherly way, adding, however, that "there was something" in me. Those words gave me the necessary courage to show him a few of my poems; he chose two and published them a year later in *The Contemporary Review*, which he had inherited from Pushkin. I do not remember the title of the second poem, but the first was addressed *To an Oak Tree* and began thus:

An old oak-tree, venerable king of the forests,
  Over the sleepy surface of the water bent his head . . .

This was the first literary work of mine to appear in print, without my name, of course.

On entering the hallway of Pletnyov's apartment, I nearly bumped into a man of medium height who had already put on his hat and coat and who exclaimed in a rich voice as he was taking leave of his host, "Yes, yes, our Ministers are fine fellows! Yes, indeed!" He laughed and went out. I had just time to notice his white teeth and his bright, quick eyes.

You can imagine how sorry I was when I learnt afterwards that that man was Pushkin, whom I had not managed to meet before that evening, and how vexed I was at my slowness! At that time Pushkin was for me as for many other young men of my age something of a demigod. We really did worship him. The worship of authority has recently, as everyone knows, been subjected to mockery, opprobrium and even execration. To confess to it is tantamount to branding oneself for ever as a vulgarian. But I should like, if I may, to point out to our severe young judges that, to begin with, it would not be a bad thing to agree about the meaning of the word "authority." There are authorities and authorities. So far as I can remember, it would never have occurred to any of us (I am speaking of my fellow students) to worship a man only because he was rich or important or a man of high rank; *that* made no impression on us. On the contrary. . . . Even a man of great intellect did not win us over to his side; what we wanted was a *leader,* and our rather liberal and almost republican convictions did in no way conflict with our enthusiastic veneration of those whom we regarded as our leaders and teachers. What's more, I cannot help feeling that enthusiasm of this sort, even in an exaggerated form, is quite natural to a young man of keen sensibilities; for the heart of such a man could scarcely be expected to catch fire from some abstract idea, however beautiful and exalted, if it did not seem to him to be embodied in a living person—in a man he could regard as his teacher. The whole difference between the present-day younger and the older generation is that we were not ashamed of our idol or of our worshipping him, but were, on the contrary, proud of it. The independence of one's own opinions is no doubt a good and estimable thing; until he acquires it no one can call himself a man in the true sense of the word. But the whole point is that one has to *acquire* it, to fight for it, as for everything else that is good on this earth. And to *begin* fighting for it is always much more convenient under the banner of a chosen leader. Still, one must also take into consideration the fact that our young men of today have different conceptions, different views; if when we were young, for instance, anyone belonging to my generation had taken it into his head to demand "respect" for the younger generation, we should most certainly have ridiculed him. Indeed, we should have been offended even. "That's all very well for old men," we would have thought, "but all we want is a wide field for our activities and that, too, we will get by fighting for it." Who is right and who is wrong—those of the older or those of the younger generation—I am afraid I cannot say; it can hardly be denied that the aspirations of youth are always unselfish and honest; and their aims remain the same, it is only the names that are different. Quite possibly, considering that our modern young men possess a more highly developed civic sense and that the difficulties of their tasks are greater, they really do deserve respect.

I saw Pushkin only once more—a few days before his death, at a matinée concert at the Engelhardt Hall. He was standing at the door, leaning against the lintel and, his hands crossed on his broad chest, looking round with a dissatisfied air. I remember his small, dark face, his African lips, the gleam of his large white teeth, his pendent side-whiskers, his dark, jaundiced eyes beneath a high forehead, almost without eyebrows, and his curly hair. . . . He threw a cursory glance at me too; the unceremonious way with which I stared at him probably made an unpleasant impression on him: he shrugged his shoulders as though with vexation—he seemed altogether in a bad mood—and walked away. A few days later I saw him lying in his coffin and could not help repeating to myself—

> *Motionless he lay . . . And strange*
> *Was the languid peace of his countenance . . .*

But to return to my story. . . .

Pletnyov led me into the drawing room and introduced me to his (first) wife, a lady who was no longer young, who looked rather ill and was very taciturn. Besides her, there were about seven or eight people in the room. They are all dead now; of the whole company assembled there that evening I am the only one still living. True, over thirty years have passed since then. . . . But there were young people among the visitors.

The visitors were:

To begin with, the notorious Skobelev, author of *Kremnev* and afterwards commandant of the St. Petersburg Fortress, a memorable figure to all the inhabitants of Petersburg of those days, with some of his fingers missing, with a clever, somewhat crumpled, wrinkled, typically soldier's face and a soldier's far from naive mannerisms—a man who has knocked about the world, in short; then Voeykov, author of *The Lunatic Asylum,* a limping, one might almost say mutilated and half-ruined creature, with the habits of an old-fashioned pettifogging lawyer, a yellow, slightly swollen, face, and an evil look in his tiny black eyes; a certain Vladislavlev, the editor of *Sunrise,* a well-known almanac in those days, an equerry in the uniform of a gendarme, a fair-haired, thick-set man with eyes of different colour (so-called Harlequin eyes), and a cringing, piercing expression of countenance (it was rumoured that the subscription to his almanac was to some extent compulsory); the poet and translator Karlhof, who looked like a State Councillor, a tall, spare man, wearing glasses, with a very small head, restless gestures and a sing-song nasal pronunciation; the translator of *Faust,* Guber, an officer of the Transport Department, with a somewhat sickly, dark face, full, ironic lips and tousled sidewhiskers, which in those days were regarded as a sort of half-hearted acknowledgment of liberal tendencies; Grebyonka, the author of a short novel and humorous stories with a Ukrainian background in which an original, tender vein could just be discerned—a thin, ungainly man with a marked predisposition to consumption, an irresolute smile on his lips and in his eyes, and a narrow but handsome and sympathetic brow—an enemy of Polevoy on whom he had just written a lampoon in the form of a fairy tale in which a field [*polevoy*] grasshopper played a highly improper role; and, last but not least, our most warm-hearted and unforgettable Prince Odoevsky. I need not describe him; everyone remembers his handsome features, his mysterious and affable look, his childishly charming laughter and his good-humoured solemnity. . . . There was one other man in the room. Dressed in a long-skirted, double-breasted frock-coat, a short waistcoat with a watch-chain of blue glass beads and a necktie with a bow, he sat in a corner with his legs modestly tucked in, coughing quietly from time to time and hastily covering his mouth with his hand. This man looked rather shyly at the people in the room, while listening attentively to their conversation. There was a gleam of quite extraordinary intelligence in his eyes, but his face was a most ordinary one, a typical Russian face, the sort of face one often finds among self-educated artisans and house-serfs. The remarkable thing is that these faces, contrary to what one might expect, seldom strike one as energetic; on the contrary, they almost always bear the stamp of timid gentleness and melancholy pensiveness. . . . That was the poet Koltsov.

I cannot remember with any exactitude what the conversation was about that evening; but it was not remarkable for any particular vivacity or for any particular depth or breadth of the questions discussed at that literary gathering. It was concerned with literary topics and with the latest society and service news— and nothing else. Once or twice it assumed a military and patriotic character, probably because of the presence of three men in uniform. The times just then were a little too quiet. The authorities, especially in Petersburg, laid their hands on everything and forced everything to submit to their rule. And yet those years will remain memorable in the history of our spiritual development. . . . Over thirty years have passed since then, but we still live under the influence and in the shadow of the ideas that were just beginning to emerge then; we have not as yet produced anything to equal them. It was in the spring of that year (1836), in fact, that *The Government Inspector* was performed for the first time, and a few months later, in February or March, 1837, came the first performance of *A Life for the Tsar*.[1] Pushkin was still living, at the height of his powers, and he seemed in all probability to have many more years of activity before him. . . . There were all sorts of vague rumours about some excellent works which he carried about in his portfolio. These rumours made lovers of lit-

---

[1] I was present at both performances and, I frankly confess, failed to grasp the significance of what was taking place before my very eyes. During the performance of *The Government Inspector*, at least, I laughed a lot, just as the rest of the audience did. But at the première of *A Life for the Tsar* I was simply bored. It is true, the voice of Vorobyova (Petrova) I had admired so much in *Semiramide* shortly before, was already cracked, while Stepanova (Antonida) screeched unnaturally. But I should have understood Glinka's music.

erature subscribe—in limited numbers, though—to his *Contemporary Review;* but, to tell the truth, it was not on Pushkin that the attention of the public was fixed at that time. Marlinsky was still considered the most popular author, Baron Brambeus still reigned supreme and his *Big Reception at Satan's* was acclaimed as the height of perfection, the achievement of an almost Voltaire-like genius, and the critical section of *The Library for Reading* a model of wit and good taste; Kukolnik was generally looked up to with hope and respect, though it was found that his *The Hand of the Almighty* [*Saved the Fatherland*] could not be compared with his *Torquato Tasso,* while Benediktov was learnt by heart. Incidentally, at the literary party I am writing about, Grebyonka, at the request of our host, read one of Benediktov's last poems. The times, I repeat, were quiet in spirit, but clamorous in outward appearance, and the conversations conformed to the prevalent tone; but there certainly were men of undoubted talent, men of great talent, and they left a deep mark behind them. Now the opposite is taking place before our eyes: the general level has risen considerably, but talents are less frequent and much weaker.

Voeykov was the first to leave; he had barely left the room, when Karlhof began reading an epigram on him in a voice quivering with excitement. "A poet-idealist and for the most part a dreamer," as Karlhof liked to describe himself, could not apparently forget the really cruel quatrain in *The Lunatic Asylum* addressed to him. Skobelev, too, soon took his leave, having exhausted the poor stock of his facetiae. Guber began to complain about the censorship. This subject was often discussed in literary circles in those days. And how could it be otherwise! Everyone knows the anecdotes about "the free spirit," "the false prophet," and so on, but scarcely anyone today can have an idea of the persecution to which printed thought was subjected everywhere and at any moment just then.[1] A writer, whoever he might be, could not help feeling himself a kind of smuggler. The conversation then turned to Gogol who was abroad at the time; but Belinsky had scarcely begun his career as a critic and no one as yet had attempted to explain to the Russian reading public the significance of Gogol in whose works the oracle of *The Library for Reading* saw nothing but "sordid" Ukrainian stories of a cheap humorous genre. I remember that all it came to was that Vladislavlev quoted with approval the phrase from *The Government Inspector:* "You're taking bribes not according to your rank," which he accompanied by a movement of the hand as though catching a fly; I can still see that wave of the hand in its blue cuff and the significant look they all exchanged. Our host said a few words about Zhukovsky, about his translation of *Ondine,* which appeared about that time in an edition de-luxe with illustrations by Count Tolstoy, if I am not mistaken. He also mentioned another Zhukovsky, a very minor poet, who had recently made an appearance in *The Library for Reading* with a great flourish of trumpets under the pen-name of Bernet; a few words were also exchanged about Countess Rostopchin, Mr. Timofeyev, and even Kreshev, for all of them were writing poems, and the writing of poems was still considered an important matter in those days. Pletnyov made an attempt to persuade Koltsov to read his last *Meditation (God's World,* I believe), but Koltsov grew so confused and looked so embarrassed that Pletnyov did not insist. I repeat once more: our whole conversation was characterized by its modesty and restraint. It took place in the days which the late Apollon Grigoryev described as antediluvian. Society still remembered the blow which fell upon its most prominent representa-

---

[1] The censor's excisions reached the height of capriciousness and wantonness; I have for many years kept a galley proof in which the censor K. crossed out the words: "that girl was like a flower," substituting for them the following words (and in red ink, too): "that young lady looked like a gorgeous rose."

tives twelve years earlier,* and nothing as yet so much as stirred of what awakened in it afterwards, especially after 1855, but merely fermented—deeply but indistinctly—in the minds of a few young men. There was no literature in the sense of a living manifestation of one of the social forces that is closely linked with the manifestations of other no less important social forces, as there was no press, no public opinion, no personal freedom. All we had was a pseudo-literature and literary hacks such as we never saw afterwards.

At midnight, almost after everyone else had gone, I went out into the hall with Koltsov. I offered to give him a lift home; I had a sleigh. He accepted my offer and all the way home he kept coughing and wrapping himself in his cheap, thin fur-coat. I asked him why he did not want to read his *Meditation*. "Why on earth should I have read it?" he replied with vexation. "Pushkin had just left, so how could you have expected me to read my stuff! Read it, indeed!" Koltsov venerated Pushkin. My question seemed inappropriate to me too: and how indeed could this diffident man, who looked so meek, start reciting from his corner:

> *"The Father of Light—Eternity,*
> *The Son of Eternity—Power;*
> *The Spirit of Power—Life,*
> *The World is seething with Life!"* etc.

At the corner of the side-street where he lived, Koltsov got out of the sleigh, quickly hooked up the rug over it and, still coughing and wrapping himself in his fur-coat, disappeared in the frosty haze of the Petersburg January night. I never met him again.

Let me say a few words here about Alexander Pletnyov. As a professor of Russian literature he was not distinguished by his

---

* The insurrection of December 14, 1825.—Tr.

scholarship; his academic baggage was very light; on the other hand, he was genuinely fond of his "subject," he possessed a somewhat diffident, though pure and refined, taste, and he spoke simply, clearly and not without warmth. Above all, he knew how to convey to his students his own likes and dislikes, he knew how to arouse their interest. He did not fire his students with any enthusiasm, as, for instance, Granovsky did. Besides, there was no reason for it—*non hic erat locus!* . . . He too was a very quiet person; but he was liked. Moreover, as a man who was in close touch with the famous literary galaxy, as the friend of Pushkin, Zhukovsky, Baratynsky and Gogol, as the person to whom Pushkin dedicated his *Eugène Onegin,* he was regarded by us all with a certain veneration and awe. We all knew by heart the verses: *"With never a thought proud society to amuse,"* and so on.

And, to be sure, Alexander Pletnyov resembled the portrait sketched by the poet: it was not the usual compliment with which dedications are so often embellished. Anyone who knew Pletnyov intimately could not but recognize in him the man whom Pushkin declared to possess "a beautiful soul, full of a sacred dream,[1] of clear and living poetry, of exalted meditations and simplicity."

He also belonged to the epoch which has now gone beyond recall: he was an old-fashioned teacher, a man of letters and not a scholar, but he was wise in his own way. The gentle calmness of his address, his speeches, and his gestures did not prevent him from being clear-sighted and even subtle; but his subtlety never went so far as to become indistinguishable from slyness or cunning; besides, his circumstances were such that he had no need of cunning; everything he wished for he eventually obtained—slowly

---

[1] The meaning of this verse is obscure; it may seem to be a more or less romantic interpolation, what the French call *une cheville;* but in its very obscurity it correctly characterizes that indefinite, but good and honourable "something" which many of the best people of that time carried in their hearts.

but surely; and when he parted from life, he could truly say that
he had enjoyed it to the full; indeed, better than to the full—in
just measure. Such a kind of enjoyment is more reliable than any
other; it is not for nothing that the ancient Greeks used to say
that the last and greatest gift of the gods was a sense of propor-
tion. This side of the spirit of ancient Greece was reflected in
him and he had a special sympathy for it; the *others* were closed
to him. He did not possess any of the so-called "creative" talent;
and he knew it very well himself: the chief quality of his mind—
sober lucidity—could never betray him when it came to analysing
his own personality. "I lack colour," he complained to me one
day. "Everything I do is grey, and that is why I cannot convey
with any accuracy the things I have seen and in the midst of
which I have lived." For a critic—in the educative, in the negative
meaning of the word—he lacked energy, fire, pertinacity; to put
it plainly—courage. He was not born a fighter. The dust and
smoke of battle were as loathsome to his fastidious and clean and
tidy nature as the danger to which he might be exposed in the
ranks of the fighters. Besides, his position in society, his connexions with the court circles made such a role, the role of a
critic who was also a fighter, as alien to him as it was alien to his
nature. Lively contemplation, sincere sympathy, complete loyalty to friends, and joyous adoration of everything poetic—there
you have Pletnyov in a nutshell. He expressed himself completely
in his few works, written in a correct, though rather flat language.

He was an excellent family man and he found everything that
was necessary for his happiness in his second wife and in his children. I happened to meet him twice abroad; ill-health had forced
him to leave Petersburg and give up his editorial duties. The last
time I met him was shortly before his death in Paris. He bore his
painful and distressing illness without a murmur and even with
a dash of gaiety. "I know I must die soon," he said to me, "and yet

115

I feel nothing but gratitude for my fate. I have lived long enough, I have seen and experienced many good things, I have known excellent people—what more do I want? It is time to make my exit!" And as I heard afterwards, his death conveyed the same impression of spiritual calm and acquiescence.

I liked to talk to him. He preserved to his extreme old age his almost child-like freshness of impressions and, as in the days of his youth, was deeply *moved* by beauty: even at that time he never *went into raptures* over it. He never parted with the memories of his life which were dear to him; he cherished them, he was touchingly proud of them. To speak of Pushkin or Zhukovsky was a source of great happiness to him. He never lost his love for Russian literature, the Russian language, or, indeed, for the very sound of Russian speech. His pure Russian origin was clearly manifested in that too: he belonged, of course, to the priestly class. It is to this fact that I ascribe his unctuousness and, perhaps, also his worldly wisdom. He always listened to the works of our new writers with his customary sympathy, and delivered his judgment which, though not always profound, was almost always right and, however mild in form, always in strict conformity with the principles to which, in the case of poetry and art, he was never unfaithful. The student "disturbances" which happened during his absence abroad deeply distressed him, more deeply than I expected, knowing his character; he grieved for his "poor" university and he blamed not only the young men. . . .

Such personalities are rarely met with nowadays; not because there is something extraordinary about them, but because the times have changed. I hope the reader will not mind my having drawn his attention to one of them—to a worthy and good-natured man of letters of the old school.

1868.

II

REMINISCENCES OF BELINSKY

———————◆———————

My PERSONAL ACQUAINTANCE with V. G. Belinsky began in Petersburg in the summer of 1843; but his name had become known to me much earlier. Soon after the appearance of his first critical articles in *Molva* and *The Telescope* (1836–1839), he was beginning to be talked about in Petersburg as an extremely clever and hotheaded fellow, who did not retreat before anything and who attacked "everything"—everything in the literary world, of course. Any other kind of criticism was in those days unthinkable—in print. Many people, even among the young, condemned him, finding that he was too bold and went too far; the old antagonism between Petersburg and Moscow added more trenchancy to the mistrust with which the readers on the banks of the Neva treated the new Moscow luminary. Besides, his plebeian origin (his father was a doctor and his grandfather a deacon) shocked the aristocratic spirit which had become firmly embedded in our literature since the days of Alexander I, the days of *Arzamas*, etc. In those dark, underground days, scandal played a great part in all our judgments, literary and others. . . . Scandal, of course, has not lost its importance even today; it will entirely disappear only in the rays of full publicity and freedom. A whole legend at once arose around the name of Belinsky, too. It was said that he was a State scholarship student who had not completed his course of studies, having been sent down from the university by Golokhvastov, head of the Moscow educational district, for immoral conduct (Belinsky and—immoral conduct!) ; it was claimed that even his personal appearance was quite ghastly, that he was a sort of cynic, a bulldog, taken under his wing by Nadezhdin with the aim of setting him on his enemies; deliberately and as though by way of reproach, his name was mispronounced "Bellunsky." Voices, it is true, were also raised in his favour. I seem to remember that the editor of the only large literary periodical published in Petersburg at the time spoke of him as "a nice little bird" and as "a lively fellow" he would not mind offering a job to, which in fact he did afterwards to the great good fortune of his periodical and to the even greater advantage of—the editor himself. So far as I was concerned, my acquaintance with Belinsky took place in the following way.

Benediktov's poems, published in a small volume in 1836 with the inevitable vignette on the title page—I can see it now, threw the whole of Petersburg society—all the writers and critics as well as the young people—into raptures. I, no less than the rest, was entranced by those poems. Many of them I knew by heart. I was full of admiration for his *Crag,* his *Mountains,* and even his *Mathilda* on her stallion who was so proud of her "seat so broad and beautiful." And just then a fellow student came to see me one morning and told me with indignation that at Béranger's, the pastry-cook's, there was a new number of *The Telescope* with an article by Belinsky in which that "captious fellow" had had the impudence to raise a hand against our idol Benediktov. I went at once to Béranger's, read the whole article from start to finish and, of course, was also boiling over with indignation. But,

strangely enough, while reading the article and afterwards something in me, to my own amazement and even vexation, involuntarily agreed with the "captious" critic and even found his arguments convincing and, indeed, irrefutable. I was ashamed of this
truly unexpected impression, I tried to silence that inner voice
in me, and in the circle of my friends I spoke with even greater vehe-
mence against Belinsky himself and his article, but deep inside me
something kept whispering that *he was right*. . . . A little time
passed and I no longer read Benediktov. Who today does not
know that the opinions Belinsky expressed at that time, opinions
which seemed like blasphemy to us, are now accepted by everyone, are *a truism,* as the English say? Posterity put its signature
under *that* verdict as it did under many other verdicts passed by
the same judge. After that Belinsky's name stuck in my memory,
but our personal acquaintance began later.

When my small poem *Parasha* mentioned earlier was published,
I went on the very day of my departure from Petersburg for the
country to Belinsky's lodgings (I knew where he lived, but had
never called on him and had only met him twice at the houses
of our mutual friends), and without giving my name, left a copy
of my poem with his servant. I spent about two months in the
country and, on receiving the May issue of *Home Annals,* read
Belinsky's long article on my poem in it. He spoke so favourably
of me, praised me so warmly, that I remember being more embarrassed than glad. I simply could not believe it, and when in
Moscow the late Ivan Kireyevsky came up to me with his congratulations, I hastened to deny my own child, maintaining that I
was not the author of *Parasha*. On my return to Petersburg, I, of
course, went to pay a call on Belinsky, and our acquaintanceship
began. He soon left for Moscow to get married and on his return
went to live in a summer cottage at Lesnoye. I, too, rented a
small cottage in Pargolova and till the early autumn visited

119

Belinsky almost daily. I grew deeply and sincerely fond of him; he was very kind to me.

Let me describe what he looked like. The well known lithographic portrait of him (almost the only one in existence) gives quite a wrong impression of him. In drawing him, the artist thought it to be his duty to soar in spirit and improve on nature and for this reason gave the whole head a sort of imperious and inspired expression, a sort of military, almost general-like, turn, an unnatural pose which did not in the least correspond to the real thing and was not at all in accord with Belinsky's character and manner. Belinsky was of medium height, at the first glance rather unhandsome and ungainly, with a hollow chest and a downcast head. One of his shoulder blades stood out conspicuously. Everyone, even those who were not medical men, at once recognized in him all the main symptoms of consumption, the whole of the so-called *habitus* of that terrible disease. Moreover, he coughed almost continuously. He had a small, palely-ruddy face, an irregular, almost flattened nose, a slighty twisted mouth, especially when he opened it, and small, fine teeth; a tuft of his thick, fair hair fell over his white, handsome, though low, brow. I never saw a more exquisite pair of eyes than Belinsky's. Blue, with golden sparks in the depths of the pupils, these eyes, usually half closed by their lids, widened and glittered at moments of animation; when he was gay, they assumed an enchanting expression of cordiality, kindness and untroubled happiness. Belinsky's voice was weak and a little husky, but pleasant; he spoke gutturally and emphasized every syllable in a peculiar way, "dogmatically, excitedly and hurriedly" [Nekrasov]. He laughed happily, like a child. He liked to pace the room, tapping with the fingers of his small, beautiful hands his snuffbox with Russian snuff. No one who saw him only in the street when, in his warm cap, his old threadbare raccoon overcoat and down-at-heel goloshes, he made his way hurriedly and falteringly along the walls, looking round with the timid sternness peculiar to nervous people—no one could form any impression of what he was really like, and to some extent I can quite understand the exclamation of a man from the provinces to whom Belinsky was pointed out: "I used to see such wolves only in the forest and that too only when they were chased by dogs!" Among strangers, in the street, Belinsky was easily abashed and embarrassed. At home he usually wore a padded grey frockcoat and was generally very neat and tidy. His accent, manners and gestures reminded one vividly of his origin; his whole demeanor was a typically Russian one; one could at once recognize a native of Moscow in him; it was not for nothing that the blood that flowed in his veins was pure and unadulterated—belonging as it did to the Great-Russian priesthood which for so many centuries was impervious to the influence of any foreign race.

Belinsky—which is so rare with us—was a truly passionate and truly sincere man, capable of selfless enthusiasm, but devoted entirely to truth, irritable but not egoistic, who knew how to love and to hate disinterestedly. People, passing judgment on him unthinkingly, were indignant at his "impudence," took offense at his "rudeness," wrote denunciations against him, spread scandalous stories about him—these people would probably have been surprised if they knew that the soul of this cynic was chaste to the point of bashfulness, soft to the point of tenderness, and honest to the point of chivalry; that he lived almost a monastic life and that wine never passed his lips. In this last respect he did not resemble the Muscovites of those days. It is impossible to imagine to what an extent Belinsky was truthful with others and with himself; he felt, acted and lived only in accordance with what he recognized as truth, in accordance with his principles. I will give one example. Soon after we had become acquainted he began once more to be troubled by those questions which, remaining unsolved or being solved only one-sidedly, do not let a person rest, especially in his youth: philosophic questions about the meaning of life, about the relations of people to one another and to God, about the origin of the world, about the immortality of the soul, etc. Not knowing foreign languages (he read even French with difficulty) and finding nothing in Russian books to satisfy his inquisitiveness, Belinsky had willy-nilly to have recourse to talks with his friends, to lengthy discussions, expressions of opinions and questionings; and he gave himself up to them with all the feverish ardour of his truth-yearning soul. It was in this way that, while still in Moscow, he incidentally mastered the chief conclusions and even the terminology of the Hegelian philosophy, which held absolute sway over the minds of the young people in those days. There were, of course, inevitably all sorts of misunderstandings, sometimes highly comic ones; Belinsky's friends, who acted as his instructors and who conveyed to him the entire pith and essence of Western science, often understood it badly and superficially themselves; [1] but Goethe has said:

> *Ein guter Mann in seinem dunklen Drange*
> *Ist sich des rechten Weges wohl bewusst*

["A good man, in his blind yearning, is well aware
of the right path."]—

---

[1] A great deal of trouble was caused in Moscow at that time by the familiar saying of Hegel: "What is rational is real and what is real is rational." Everyone agreed with the first part of the saying, but how was one to understand the second? Was one to acknowledge everything that existed in Russia then as rational? After a great deal of discussion it was decided *not to admit* the second half of the saying. If someone had at the time whispered to the young philosophers that Hegel *did not acknowledge everything that existed as real,* a lot of mental work and brainwracking discussions would have been avoided; they would have realized that the famous formula, like so many others, was a mere tautology and virtually meant that *opium facit dormire, quare est in eo virtus dormitiva,* that is to say, opium puts people to sleep because it possesses soporific powers (Molière).

and Belinsky was essentially *ein guter Mann*—he was a truthful and honest man. Moreover, in such cases he was always saved by the remarkable instinct with which he was endowed; but of that later.

And so when I got to know Belinsky, he was tormented by doubts. I often heard that phrase and used it myself more than once; but in reality it was fully applicable to Belinsky alone. His doubts actually did torment him, deprived him of his appetite and sleep, worried and gnawed at him incessantly; he did not allow himself a moment's peace and did not know the meaning of fatigue; day and night he kept worrying over the solution of the questions which he put to himself. It often happened that as soon as I came to see him, he would at once get up from the sofa, looking haggard and ill (he had just got over an attack of pneumonia which nearly carried him off to his grave), and in a scarcely audible voice, coughing continuously and with a pulse of one hundred a minute and a hectic flush on his cheeks, he would begin the conversation at the point where we had left off the day before. His sincerity infected me, his fire communicated itself to me too, and I was carried away by the importance of the subject under discussion; but after talking for two or three hours I weakened, the frivolity of youth asserted itself, I wanted to have a rest, I was thinking of going for a walk, of having dinner, Belinsky's wife herself begged her husband and me to break off our discussion for a little while and take a rest, reminded him of the doctor's orders, but—it was not easy to cope with a man like Belinsky. "We haven't yet decided the question of the existence of God," he said to me once with bitter reproach, "and you want to eat!" I confess that, having written these words, I nearly crossed them out at the thought that they might raise a smile on the faces of some of my readers. . . . But anyone hearing Belinsky utter them would not have dreamed of smiling; and if at the recollection of that absence of fear of the ridiculous, a smile might rise to one's lips, it would only be a smile of surprise and tender affection. . . .

Only after having obtained the result that seemed satisfactory to him at the time, did Belinsky compose himself and, laying aside the consideration of those fundamental problems, returned to his daily work and occupations. He was especially eager to speak to me because I had shortly before returned from Berlin, where I had studied Hegelian philosophy during two semesters and was thus able to pass on to him the newest and latest conclusions. At that time we still believed in the reality and the importance of philosophic and metaphysical conclusions, though neither he nor I were philosophers and did not possess the ability of pure and abstract reasoning in the German manner. . . . Still, in those days we looked to philosophy for everything in the world except pure reasoning. . . .

Belinsky's knowledge was not vast; he knew little and there is nothing surprising about that. Even his enemies did not accuse him of any lack of industry or of laziness; but the poverty that had surrounded him ever since he was a child, his bad upbringing, his unfortunate circumstances, his early illnesses, and afterwards the necessity of earning a living by work done in a hurry—all this taken together prevented Belinsky from acquiring a sound knowledge of all sorts of subjects, though he did make a thorough study, for instance, of Russian literature and its history. But I will go further and say that it was just this insufficient knowledge that was so characteristic of him and, in his case, almost a necessity. Belinsky was what I might call a *basic nature;* he was with every fibre of his being close to the heartbeat of his people, he was the fullest possible embodiment of it, both of its good and bad sides. A learned man, I do not say an "educated man"—that is another story—but a learned man could, just because of his learning, never become such a basic Russian nature in the 'forties;

he would not entirely fit into the environment on which he would have to exert his influence; he and it would have had different interests; there would have been no harmony and, I suppose no mutual understanding, either. The leaders of their contemporaries in the field of social and aesthetic criticism, in the field of critical self-knowledge (I cannot help thinking that my remark is of general application, but this time I shall confine myself to this *one* aspect only), the leaders of their contemporaries, I say, must of course tower above them, must possess a more balanced mind, a clearer outlook, a greater strength of character; but between those leaders and their followers there must be no impassable gulf. The word "follower" by itself implies the possibility of marching in one and the same direction, the possibility of a close connexion. A leader may arouse indignation and disappointment in those whom he disturbs, forces to rise from their places, moves forward; they may curse him, but they must always understand him. He must tower above them, yes, but he must also be close to them; he must possess not only some of their qualities and idiosyncrasies, but also some of their faults: by possessing these faults, he feels them more profoundly and more painfully. Senkovsky was infinitely more learned not only than Belinsky but than the greater part of his Russian contemporaries; but what trace did he leave behind him? I will be told that his activity was futile and harmful not because he was a scholar, but because he had no convictions, because he was alien to us, because he did not understand us, because he did not sympathize with us; I will not argue against that, but I can't help feeling that his scepticism, his pretentiousness and fastidiousness, his contemptuous scoffing, his pedantry and coldness—all his peculiarities, in fine, were partly due to the fact that as a scholar and specialist his aims and sympathies were different from those of the majority of the people. Senkovsky was not only learned, he was clever, amusing, brilliant; the young civil servants and army officers were full of admiration for him, especially in the provinces; but it was not that that the great mass of readers needed; what they needed was a critical and social flair, good taste, an understanding of the crying needs of the times and, above all, warm affection for their unfortunate and ignorant brethren—and he possessed none of it. He amused his readers, while despising them in his heart as ignoramuses; they were diverted by him and—did not believe a word he said. I hope that I shall not be accused of defending and advocating ignorance: I am merely pointing out a physiological fact in the development of our consciousness. It is obvious that to become the leader of *his* generation and the representative of the spirit of *his* people, a Lessing would have to be a man of almost universal learning; for in him was reflected Germany, in him Germany found her voice and her thought—he was *the German basic nature.* But Belinsky, who to a certain extent deserves to be described as the Russian Lessing, Belinsky, whose significance really recalls by its meaning and influence the significance of the great German critic, could become what he was without a great store of learning. He used to confuse the elder Pitt (Lord Chatham) with his son William Pitt—what does it matter? "We all picked up a little knowledge here and there." For what he had to do, he knew enough. Where would he have got that heat and that passion with which he fought everywhere so continuously for education, if he had not in fact experienced the whole bitterness of ignorance? A German tries to remedy the faults of his people after having convinced himself of their harmfulness by reasoning; a Russian will for a long time to come suffer from them himself.

Belinsky undoubtedly possessed the chief qualities of a great critic, and if in the sphere of knowledge and learning he had to fall back on the assistance of his friends and take their words on trust, he had not to seek anyone's advice in the sphere of criticism; on the contrary, others sought his advice; the initiative always remained with him. His aesthetic sense was almost infallible; his judgment was unusually profound and it never became obscure. Belinsky was not deceived by appearances or surroundings, he never submitted to any influences or ideas; he instantly recognized the beautiful and the hideous, the true and the false, and pronounced his verdict with fearless courage, pronounced it outspokenly, without any reservations, warmly and powerfully, with all the impetuosity and assurance of conviction. Anyone who witnessed the mistakes in criticisms made even by men of outstanding intellectual abilities (one has only to remember Pushkin who saw "something Shakespearean" in Mr. Pogodin's *Marfa the Mayoress!*), could not help feeling respect for Belinsky's precise judgment, correct taste and *instinct,* for his ability to "read between the lines." I need hardly mention the articles in which he allotted their proper places to the writers belonging to the past epochs of our literature, nor need I mention those articles in which the importance of still living writers is carefully defined, their activities summed up, and his summing up accepted and confirmed, as I pointed out already, by posterity; but at the appearance of a new talent, a new novel, poem or short story, no one, either before Belinsky or better than he, ever gave a more correct appraisal or said a truer, or more decisive word. Lermontov, Gogol, Goncharov—was he not the first to point them out and explain their significance? And how many others! It is quite impossible, incidentally, to read without a feeling of amazement at Belinsky's critical diagnosis the short notice he wrote in one of his early annual surveys predicting a brilliant literary future for the author of *The Song about the Merchant Kalashinikov,* published anonymously in *The Literary Gazette.* One comes across such things continuously in Belinsky's writings. Let me give one example. In 1846 there was published in *Home Annals* a short novel by Mr. Grigorovich under the title of *The Village*, the *first* attempt ever made to bring our literature in contact with the life of our peasants, the first of our "village stories"—*Dorfgeschichten*. It was written in a somewhat refined style, not without sentimentality; but there could be no doubt of the author's desire for a realistic reproduction of peasant life. The late Ivan Panayev, a good-natured, though rather thoughtless man, who was able to grasp the significance of only the highest literary peaks, seized on some absurd expressions in *The Village* and, glad of the opportunity of making fun of the author, began ridiculing the whole novel, even reading aloud some pages which he thought were very funny indeed in the houses of his friends. Imagine his astonishment as well as the bewilderment of his laughing friends, when Belinsky, after reading Mr. Grigorovich's novel, not only found it to be very remarkable, but instantly defined its significance and predicted the new movement in our literature, the new turn which it was soon to take. All that was left for Panayev to do was to continue his readings of extracts from *The Village*, but this time expressing his admiration for them—which he did.

I cannot help mentioning in this connexion the case of the editor of a literary periodical whose flair for practical affairs was equal to his complete lack of aesthetic taste and whose leg was mercilessly pulled on several occasions. Someone belonging to Belinsky's circle, for instance, would bring him a new poem and begin reading it without telling his victim beforehand what the poem was about or why it was thought worthy of being read aloud. The reader would begin in an ironical tone, while the editor, concluding from the tone that he was going to be presented with a model of tastelessness and absurdity, began smiling and shrugging his shoulders; then the reader would gradually change his tone from ironic to serious, grave and rapturous; the editor, thinking that he had made a mistake, would begin grunting appreciatively, shaking his head, and sometimes even exclaiming, "Not bad! Very good!" Then the reader reverted to his ironic tone and once more carried his listener along with him, then returned to his rapturous mood, the editor again expressing his admiration. If the poem happened to be long, such variations, reminding one of the game with a little rubber head which changes expression under the pressure of a man's fingers, could be repeated several times. It all ended with the unhappy editor getting completely muddled, and no longer expressing either sympathetic approval or sympathetic disapproval on his highly expressive face. Belinsky's nerves were not too strong and he never engaged in such pastimes; besides, he was much too truthful a person and he could not have done it even for the sake of a joke, but he was doubled up with laughter every time he was told the details of such a prank.

Another remarkable quality of Belinsky as a critic was his grasp of what was of major importance at a given juncture, of what demanded an immediate solution, of what was going to be "the talk of the town." A Russian proverb says that an uninvited guest is worse than a Tartar, and in the same way a truth announced at the wrong time is worse than a falsehood, and a problem raised at the wrong moment merely leads to confusion and distraction. Belinsky would never have made the mistake into which the gifted Dobrolyubov had fallen; he would not, for instance have violently attacked Cavour,[1] Palmerston and parliamentary government in general, as an imperfect and therefore wrong form of government. Even admitting the justice of the reproaches earned by Cavour, he would have realized the inopportuneness (in 1862 in Russia) of such attacks; he would have

---

[1] The writer of these lines heard with his own ears an admirer of Dobrolyubov at a card table, wishing to chide his partner for a bad move, exclaim, "Well, sir, you're a perfect Cavour!" I confess I felt sad; not for Cavour, of course!

understood what party they would render a service to, who would have been pleased with them! Belinsky realized perfectly well that in the conditions under which he had to work he must never go out of the range of purely literary criticism. To begin with, the political and general situation was such that to act otherwise was too far difficult; nor did the censorship make things any easier. As it was, he could scarcely hold out against the storm of threats and denunciations which his refusal to accept our pseudo-classical authorities had aroused; furthermore, he saw and understood very clearly that in the development of every people a new literary epoch comes before any other, that without experiencing and going beyond it, it is impossible to move forward, that criticism in the sense of challenging lies and falsehoods must first subject to analysis literary events and—it was precisely *that* that his duty as a writer demanded of him. His political and social views were very strong and decidely trenchant; but they remained in the sphere of instinctive sympathies and antipathies. I repeat: Belinsky knew that there could be no question of applying them, of putting them into practice; and even if it were possible, he had neither the necessary training nor the necessary temperament for it; he knew that, too, and with the practical understanding of the rôle he had to play, that was so characteristic of him, he restricted the sphere of his activities himself, confining it within certain set limits. (See the second appendix at the end of this fragment.) On the other hand, as a *right man in the right place,* which cannot be said of his succes-*literary* critic he was exactly what the English describe as *the* sors. It is true, though, that their task was much more difficult and more complicated. Shortly before his death, Belinsky began to feel that the time had come for him to take a new step and to get out of the confined sphere of his activities. Political and economic questions had to take the place of aesthetic and literary ones, but he himself stood aside and pointed to another person whom he regarded as his successor, to V. N. Maykov, the brother of the poet. Unfortunately, that talented young man died at the very beginning of his career, just as D. I. Pisarev, another young man of great promise, died recently.

Pisarev's name reminds me of the following incident: in the spring of 1867 I happened to pass through Petersburg and he was so good as to call on me. I had not met him before, but I had read his articles with interest, though I could not agree with many of the statements in them and, generally, with their tendency. I was particularly indignant with his articles on Pushkin. During our conversation I told him frankly what I thought of them. At first sight Pisarev gave the impression of an intelligent and honest man with whom one not only could but should speak the truth. "You," I began, "bespattered one of Pushkin's most moving poems (his address to his last fellow-student at the lycée who had been amnestied [for his part in the Decembrist insurrection]: 'Unhappy friend,' etc.). You claim that the poet simply advises his friend to drown his grief in drink. You have a highly developed aesthetic sense: you could not have meant it seriously, you said it *on purpose,* with a definite aim. Let us see if your aim justifies you. I understand exaggeration, I have nothing against caricature, but exaggeration of truth, caricature in the right sense, in the right direction. If our young men today did nothing but write poetry, as in the blessed period of the almanacs, I should have understood it and I might even have justified your spiteful reproach, your jibe; I should have said to myself: it is unfair, but it's useful. But as it is, good Lord, who are you firing at? At sparrows from a field-gun! We have only three or four men left, elderly men of fifty or more, who are still practising the art of poetry. Is it worth while getting furious with them? Are there not thousands of other questions of the utmost importance to us today which you, as a journalist, who is *in duty bound* to apprehend before everyone else what is important, necessary and momentous, *ought* to bring to the attention of the public? A campaign against poets in 1866! Why, it's an out-of-date frolic, an archaism! Belinsky would never have been guilty of such a *faux pas!"* I do not know what Pisarev thought of it, but he made no reply. I don't suppose he agreed with me.

It goes without saying that Belinsky's understanding of his time and his vocation did not interfere with the expression of his deepest convictions that could be apprehended in every word of his articles, particularly as his negative activity in the field of criticism was entirely in tune with the rôle he would most certainly have chosen in a politically developed society. He alone and a few of his friends knew what his feelings and thoughts were, but what he did and what he published was kept rigorously and strictly within the limits of literary values and was devoted to them exclusively. Only in one famous letter did this passion which he—

> *. . . in the dark of the night*
> *With tears and grief had nourished,*

break through, like the fire of which Lermontov speaks [in his poem *Mtsyri*].

I should like to ask my reader's permission to quote in this place an extract from a lecture on Pushkin which I delivered in 1859 before a small audience. To describe the character of the 'thirties and 'forties, I had to refer to Gogol's satire, to Lermontov's protest and then to the significance of Belinsky's criticism. The very mention of Belinsky's name aroused the indignation of the major part of my audience. Here is this extract. (I shall have to start a little ahead of the passage in question, but that, I am afraid, cannot be helped.)

"And while our great artist [Pushkin], turning away from the crowd of mediocrities and getting as near as he possibly could to the common people, was pondering his long cherished works, while his soul was immersed in those images, the study of which involuntarily arouses in us the thought that he might have given us a people's drama and a people's epic—important, if not great, events were taking place in our literature. Under the influence of certain fortuitous circumstances in the life of Europe of that time (from 1830 to 1840), we gradually arrived at the somewhat premature, though no doubt justified, conviction that we are not only a great people, but also a great state, which is in full control of itself and indestructibly stable, and that our art and poetry was consequently called upon to be the worthy heralds of our might and our grandeur. Simultaneously with the spread of that conviction and, perhaps, stimulated by it, there appeared a whole phalanx of men who were undoubtedly gifted but whose gifts bore the stamp of rhetoric, of externality, corresponding to that great but purely external power of which it was an echo. These men appeared in poetry as well as in painting and in journalism and even on the stage. Need I name them? Everyone of us remembers them—all we have to do is merely to recall whom we acclaimed and applauded at a time when the name of Pushkin, who had fallen silent, was hardly ever mentioned.[1] This intrusion into public life of what we have decided to call the *pseudo-sublime* school did not last long, though its influence in the spheres which are less subject to critical analysis than literature and art persists to this day. It did not last long, but what a terrific din it raised while it lasted! How far flung was the influence of that school in those days! Some of its adherents good-naturedly regarded themselves as geniuses. But for all that there was something false, something lifeless about it even at the moments

---

[1] These names, which I was loath to mention at the time, will probably occur to every reader—the names of Marlinsky, Kukolnik, Zagosin, Benediktov, Bryulov, Karatygin, etc.

of its apparent triumph, and it never succeeded in gaining a permanent ascendancy over any live, original mind. The works of this school, so full of self-confidence that it often assumed the form of bombast, were devoted to the glorification of Russia at all costs, though at bottom there was nothing Russian about them: they were like vast pieces of scenery, busily and carelessly erected by patriots who did not know their country. All this thundered, swaggered and blustered, all this considered itself to be a worthy ornament of a great country and a great people, but— the hour of its downfall was near. It was not, however, Pushkin's last highly artistic works that were the cause of this downfall. Even if they had appeared during his lifetime, I doubt whether the deafened and confused public would have appreciated them at the time. They could not become subjects of polemical discussions; they could only win the day, as indeed they did, by their own beauty, and by the mere juxtaposition of their strength and beauty and the weakness and hideousness of that pseudo-sublime phantom. But at first other weapons were needed in order to expose this phantom in all its emptiness, other more deadly forces—the forces of Byronic lyricism which had made its appearances in our country once already, but only superficially and not seriously, and the forces of criticism and humor. And they were not slow in appearing. In the sphere of art Gogol spoke up and after him Lermontov; in the sphere of criticism and ideas—Belinsky.

". . . In my last talk to you I spoke of the importance which a future historian of our literature would ascribe to the appearance of Pushkin; but I have no doubt that the attention of our Macaulays (if we shall ever have any Macaulays) will also be drawn to that moment when the inflated and blown up and, as it were, official giant was confronted on the one hand by a hussar officer, a lionized society dandy, from whose mouth high society for the first time heard such a merciless rebuke,[1] and an obscure Ukrainian teacher with his terrifying comedy, headed by the epigraph: 'Don't blame the mirror if your face is ugly'; and on the other, by a similarly obscure student, who had not finished his course at the university, but who had the audacity to declare that we had not yet had a literature, that Lomonosov was not a poet, that not only Kheraskov, but also Derzhavin and Dmitriyev could not serve as our models, and that even our most recent great men had done nothing. By the combined efforts of these three men, who scarcely knew one another, not only the literary school we had called pseudo-sublime had collapsed, but a great many other things that were old-fashioned and unworthy had been turned into ruins. Victory was soon achieved. At the same time the influence of Pushkin, too, diminished and faded, the same Pushkin whose name was so dear to the reformers themselves and which they had surrounded with such love. The ideal they served—consciously or unconsciously (Gogol, as is known, denied and held aloof from it to the very end)—this ideal could not exist side by side with Pushkin's ideal, much as they might regret it themselves. The force of circumstances is stronger than any individual, personal force just as the general tendencies in us are stronger than our personal inclinations. The time of pure poetry has passed just as the time of the pseudo-sublime phrase; the time of criticism, politics and satire has arrived. Instead of the words: 'has arrived,' we could, remembering Fonvisin and Novikov, use the words 'has returned.' Such 'recurrent' turns of the ever turning historic wheel are familiar to all observers of the lives of nations. Society, struck by the sudden realization of its own shortcomings and foreseeing other, more bitter,

---

[1] I should like to quote the remark made by a lady of high society who met me with the following exclamation: *"Avez-vous lu la 'Douma'? Qui pouvait s'attendre à cela de la part de Lermontoff? Lui qui venait de dire:* I, Mother of God, *now* with a prayer! *C'est affreux!"*

disappointments in the future—which came to pass, too [1]—listened eagerly to the new voices and accepted only what answered their new needs. Kukolnik's *Torquato Tasso* and *The Hand of the Almighty* [*Saved the Fatherland*] vanished like soap bubbles; but—one could not admire [Pushkin's] *Bronze Horseman* at the same time as [Gogol's] *Overcoat,* either."

Here followed a rather detailed characterisation of Gogol and Lermontov, ending as follows:

"The force of an independent, critical, protesting personality had risen up against falsehood, against vulgarity—and at what level of society did not vulgarity reign in those days?—and against those false generalisations, those wrongly accepted principles that lacked any rational rights to demand that the human personality should be subjected to them. . . ." And I went on as follows: "Now I should like to ask for your permission to dwell on another personality whose name, I know, is not altogether agreeable to you. I am speaking of Belinsky. His name conjures up memories of some indiscretions but also, I am glad to say, of some great merits. His writings live to this day and we cannot possibly assume that the Russia which is so eagerly reading him at this very moment [it was just then that the first volumes of his complete works were published], should be wrong in her love for him. I have mentioned him not because I was attached to him by personal ties of friendship; I want to draw your attention to the guiding principle of his activities. This principle is idealism. Belinsky was an idealist in the best sense of the word. In him lived the traditions of the Moscow circle which existed at the beginning of the 'thirties and whose traces can be discerned to this day. This circle, which was under the strong influence of German philosophic ideas (this constant connexion between Moscow and those ideas is, surely, remarkable), deserves a special historian. It is from there that Belin-

---

[1] Three years have barely passed since the Peace of Paris of 1856 when I read those lectures.

sky acquired those convictions to which he remained faithful to his dying day, the ideal which he served. In the name of that ideal Belinsky proclaimed the artistic significance of Pushkin and pointed out his lack of civic principles; in the name of that ideal he also hailed Lermontov's protest and Gogol's satire; in the name of that ideal he kept demolishing the old authorities, our so-called glories on which he was unable and unwilling to look from the historic point of view. . . ."

Some of my readers will perhaps be surprised at the word "idealist" with which I thought it necessary to characterize Belinsky. I can only observe that, in the first place, it was impossible in 1859 to call many things by their right names and, secondly, that, I confess I was rather pleased to declare that Belinsky was an "idealist" before an assembly of people who imagined his name to be indissolubly bound up with the conception of a cynic, a coarse materialist, etc. Besides, such a description suited him admirably. Belinsky was as much an idealist as a negationist; he negated in the name of his ideal. That ideal had quite a definite and homogeneous quality, though it was called and still is called by different names: science, progress, humanity, civilization—the West, in fine. Well-meaning though ill-disposed people even use the word—revolution. What matters is not the name, but the substance, which is so clear and indubitable that it is not worth while dwelling upon it: there can be no misunderstandings here. Belinsky devoted himself wholly to the service of this ideal; he belonged to the camp of the "Westerners," as their opponents called them, with all his sympathies and with the whole of his activity. He was a Westerner not only because he acknowledged the superiority of Western science, Western art and the Western social order, but also because he was deeply convinced of the need for Russia to absorb everything the West had produced for the development of her own powers and her own importance. He believed that there was no salvation for us other than to follow the path Peter the Great pointed out to us and upon which the Slavophils hurled their choicest execrations at that time.[1] To accept the results of Western life, to adapt them to ours, taking into account the peculiarities of our history and climate and, treating them, too, of course, freely and critically—it was in this way that he thought we could at last achieve originality, a quality he prized much more than is generally believed. Belinsky was an out-and-out Russian, indeed, a Russian patriot, though not, of course, à la M. N. Zagoskin; the good of his country, her greatness and her glory aroused a deep and powerful response in his heart. Yes, Belinsky loved Russia; but he loved freedom and enlightenment as ardently: to unite into one those, to him, highest interests—therein lay the whole meaning of his work, that was what he aspired to. To argue that he worshipped the West from the slavish and unintelligent humility of a half-educated person means that one did not know him at all; besides, it is not by their humility that half-educated persons are known. Another reason why Belinsky had so high an opinion of Peter the Great and, without a moment's hesitation, declared him to be the man who saved Russia, was that already in the reign of Peter the Great's father, Alexey Mikhailovich, he found undoubted signs of decay in our old social and civil order and, therefore, could not believe in the correct and normal development of our state organism as it can be observed in the West. Peter the Great's reforms were, to be sure, based on coercion; it was what we would call today a *coup d'état*, but it was only thanks to a whole series of these coercive measures imposed from above that we were pushed into the family of European nations. Such reforms are still necessary today. I could bring most recent examples in confirmation of that view. What place we

---

[1] Belinsky often read to his friends the poem *Peter the Great* by Leo Pushkin, the poet's brother, and declaimed with special feeling the verses in which the reformer was represented as dragging along "rows of amazed generations with his mighty hand."

already occupy in that family, history will show; but it is undeniable that we have been following and that we *had* to follow (the Slavophils will not of course agree), *had* to follow a course other than that of the more or less organically developed nations of Western Europe.

And every article he wrote proved that Belinsky's Western convictions had not weakened by a hair's breadth his understanding of, and his flair for, everything Russian and had not stemmed the Russian torrent that flowed through his entire being. Yes, he felt the intrinsic nature of Russia as no one else did. Refusing to accept our would-be classical and would-be national authorities and doing his best to confute them, he at the same time knew how to appreciate more subtly and more correctly what was truly original in our literary works and to make others see it. No one had a more sensitive ear, no one felt more vividly the beauty and harmony of our language; a poetic epithet, an exquisite turn of phrase immediately attracted his attention, and to listen to his simple, somewhat monotonous, but exciting and truthful reading of some Pushkin poem or Lermontov's *Mtsyri* was a real delight. Prose, especially that of his favourite Gogol, he did not read so well; his voice, too, used to grow weak after a short time.

Another remarkable quality of Belinsky as a critic was that, as the English say, he was always "in earnest." He never jested with the object of his researches, nor with his reader, nor with himself, and he would have repudiated the latest all too prevalent fashion of indulging in jeering as unworthy thoughtlessness or cowardice. It is a well known fact that a man given to jeering quite often has no clear idea what he is jeering at or speaking so ironically about; he can, at any rate, make use of that screen to conceal the weakness and obscurity of his own arguments. A man whistles, laughs. ... Try to make any sense of what he is talking about or what he is driving at. Maybe he is laughing at something that is indeed worth laughing at and maybe he is simply sneering at his own laughter. I will be told that there are times when one can only hint at the truth and that it may be easier to express it with a laugh. . . . But did Belinsky live at a time when it was possible to express everything without concealment? And yet he did not resort to jeering or to the "fashionable" whistling and sneering. The acquiescent laughter aroused in a certain section of the public by this "whistling" is not far removed from the laughter with which Senkovsky's unprincipled sallies were met. . . . Here and there the propensity towards coarse amusement and buffoonery could be clearly perceived; it is a propensity that is unhappily peculiar to the Russian and which ought not to be encouraged. The coarse laughter of ignorance is almost as disgusting—and as harmful—as its spitefulness. But then Belinsky himself used to say that he was not very good at jesting. His irony was very heavy and clumsy; it turned at once into sarcasm and was all too prone to hit the nail on the head. He did not sparkle with wit either in his conversation or with his pen; he did not possess what the French call *ésprit;* he did not dazzle by a skilful exhibition of dialectical powers; but he possessed that irresistible force which is the result of honest and unflinching thought, and it expressed itself in an original and, after all, an absorbing fashion. Although completely lacking what is usually described as eloquence and although quite frankly unable and unwilling "to paint the lily" or indulge in fine phrases, Belinsky was one of the most eloquent of men, if "eloquence" is to be understood in the sense of a force of conviction, the force which the Athenians, for instance, acknowledged in Pericles when they said that his every speech left a sting in the soul of every listener.

Belinsky, needless to say, was not an admirer of the principle of "art for art's sake"; and it could hardly have been otherwise when the whole trend of his thoughts is taken into consideration. I remember with what a comic fury he attacked Pushkin (who was not there, of course) in my presence for the two lines in his poem *The Poet and the Mob*—

A pot on the stove to you is dearer:
Your dinner in it you cook!

"Why, of course," Belinsky declared with flashing eyes, running from one corner of the room to the other, "it is dearer. I do not cook my dinner in it for myself alone but for my family, for another poor wretch like me, and rather than admire the beauty of some statue—be it a thousand times an Apollo by Phidias—it is my right, my duty to feed my own wife and children and myself too, whatever all sorts of indignant gentlemen and versifiers may say!"

But Belinsky was much too intelligent, he had much too much common sense to deny art, to fail to understand not only its great significance, but also its very naturalness, its physiological necessity. Belinsky recognized in art one of the fundamental manifestations of the human personality, one of the laws of our nature, a law whose validity was proved by our daily experience. He did not admit of art only for art's sake in the same way as he would not admit of life only for life's sake; it was not for nothing that he was an idealist. Everything had to serve one principle, art as well as science, but in its own special way. The truly childish and, besides, not new, "warmed-up" explanation of art as an imitation of nature he would have deemed worthy neither of a reply nor of his attention; and the argument of the superiority of a real apple over a painted one would not have made any impression on him because this famous argument loses any validity the moment we apply it to a well-fed man. Art, I repeat, was for Belinsky as much a legitimate sphere of human activity as science, as society, as the State. . . . But from art as from any other human activity he demanded truth, vital, living truth. (See the First Appendix at the end of this essay.) In the domain of art, however, he felt at home only in poetry and literature. He did not understand painting and was

141

only little interested in music. He realized his shortcomings very well himself and did not try to butt in where entrance was barred to him. Gogol's articles on Bryulov and Ivanov can serve as a warning of the depths of imbecility and pretentious bathos a man may reach who encroaches on territory that is not his own. The only melody Belinsky knew by heart was the Devils' Chorus from *Robert le Diable:* whenever he was in a good mood he would hum this devilish refrain in his bass voice. He was deeply moved by Rubini's singing; but it was not his musical perfection that he appreciated, but his exciting, violent energy and the dramatic force of his expression. Everything theatrical and dramatic stirred Belinsky to the depth of his soul and seemed to set it ablaze. His articles on Mochalov, Shchepkin, and the theatre in general, are imbued with passion; one had only to see the impression made on him by the mere recollection of Mochalov as Hamlet in the scene of the play within a play when he declared, breathless with exaltation and hatred—

Why, let the strucken deer go weep . . . . .

There was one reason that sometimes made Belinsky avoid talking about the theatre and about dramatic literature, especially with people he did not know well: he was afraid of being reminded of his comedy *The Fifty-Year-Old Uncle,* which he had written in Moscow and which was published in *The Moscow Observer.* This comedy is, in fact, a very poor work; it belongs to the worst possible genre—the lacrymose-sentimental and the sentimental-virtuous one; its chief character is a generous-hearted uncle who is in love with his niece and who sacrifices his love in favour of a young rival. All this is set forth in a longwinded, stilted, dull style. . . . Belinsky did not possess any "creative" talent. This comedy as well as an article of his on Menzel were Belinsky's Achilles' heel and to mention them in his presence was to grieve and insult him. It was his

article on [Wolfgang] Menzel in particular that he could not forgive himself: he admitted that his comedy was an aesthetic and
literary mistake, but that article he considered a mistake of a much
worse kind. He wrote it in a moment of impatience and under the
influence of a wistful desire to pass from the sphere of unattainable ideals to something positive and real, as though the things
that existed then could have had any real meaning or could have
satisfied a conscientious man! Poor Belinsky, of course, had no idea
of the sort of person Menzel was and wrote about him from a purely
abstract, *a priori* point of view. In this particular case, an insufficient knowledge of the facts played a bad joke on him. . . . There
was also his article on the anniversary of the battle of Borodino.
I tried to speak to him about it one day, but he stopped his ears
with both his hands and, bending low and swaying from side to
side, began pacing the room. However, he was infected with jingo-
ism for a very short time. Generally speaking, Belinsky's best articles were written at the beginning and towards the end of his literary career; in the middle of it he went through a period lasting
two years in the course of which he stuffed himself with Hegelian
philosophy and, failing to digest it, kept scattering its axioms, its
familiar theses and technical terms, its so-called *Schlagwoerter*
everywhere with feverish zeal. One was simply dazzled by the multitude of favourite phrases and expressions that were in fashion in
those days! Well, Belinsky, too, had to pay tribute to his times! But
that flood soon subsided, leaving only good seeds behind and Belinsky's splendid, clear and sensible Russian language reappeared
once more in all its courageous and artless simplicity. Belinsky,
one might say, improvised his articles; he wrote them during the
last few days of the month, standing before his bureau, on loose
quarto pages, without corrections, in a large, round hand. He had
no time to polish his style, to weigh and think over every expression, and that was why he willy-nilly became somewhat prolix; but
he was far from becoming long-winded, a manner of writing which,

I am afraid, has, thanks to Pisarev, become the rule in the critical sections of our periodicals. Belinsky's articles, for all their short-comings, remained literary works and did not become transformed into flaccid conversation pieces, into puffed up variations on hack-neyed themes, variations which, in spite of all their fervour, reek of the schoolboy's exercise book.

Everyone knows what a heavy burden was heaped upon Belinsky by the hard-headed editor of the periodical to which he contrib-uted. The sort of books he had to review: cookery books, interpre-tations of dreams, books on mathematics, which he could not make head or tail of! But when after the punctual publication of the periodical on the first of the month, he had a few days of complete rest, he enjoyed them to the full, he abandoned himself to the pleasures of idleness, to talks with friends and occasionally to a game of cards for penny stakes. He played badly, but with the same genuine sincerity, with the same passion, which were charac-teristic of him whatever he happened to be doing. I remember we were playing with him one day not for money but just for pleas-ure; he was winning and looked triumphant, but suddenly he lost a trick and was left without a four. Poor Belinsky's face grew darker than an autumn night, he hung his head, looking like a man sentenced to death. His expression of suffering and despair was so genuine that at last, unable to restrain myself, I exclaimed that that was really going a bit too far and that he had better stop play-ing cards altogether. "No," he replied hollowly, giving me a sullen look, "this is the end: I staked my life on the diamonds!" And I am sure that at that moment he really meant what he said.

I often went to see him in the afternoon to pour out all my troubles to him. He had rented an apartment on the ground floor on the Fontanka Embankment, not far from Anichkin Bridge, con-sisting of several sombre and rather damp rooms. I can't help say-ing it again: we had been going through very difficult times just then. Our young men today have never had to experience anything like it. Let the reader judge for himself: in the morning you may have got back your proofs from the censor, all mangled and mutilated and stained with red ink as though with blood; you may even have had to pay a personal call on the censor and after offering all sorts of useless and humiliating explanations and justifications, listen to him delivering his all too often sneering sentence from which there was no appeal. . . .[1] In the street you probably ran across Mr. Bulgarin or his friend Mr. Grech; or some general, any general, not even your civil service chief, who snubbed or, what is worse, praised you. . . . You looked round: bribery was rampant, serfdom remained as firm as a rock, the barracks were in the forefront of everything, no courts of justice, rumours about the impending closure of the universities, the number of admissions to which were soon to be reduced to three hundred, journeys abroad were becoming impossible, no decent book could be ordered from abroad, a sort of dark cloud was constantly hanging over the whole of the so-called department of learning and literature and, to cap it all, denunciations whispered and spread on all sides; no common bond among the younger generation, no common interests, everyone afraid and grovelling—you might as well give it up! Well, you went to see Belinsky, somebody else came along, too, you started talking and—you felt better. The subjects of our talks were mostly of such a nature that no censor would in those days have passed them in print, but actually we never discussed politics: the utter uselessness of such discussions was clear to anyone. The general complexion of our talks was philosophic-literary, critical-aesthetic

---

[1] The censor F. was particularly distinguished for his humour at such interviews. "Good Lord," he used to say, "I don't want to cross out a single letter of your article. All I want is to destroy its spirit." He said to me one day, looking with feeling into my eyes: "You don't want me to cross anything out. But just think: if I don't cross anything out, I may lose 3,000 roubles a year, and if I do—who cares? There were a few words before and now there aren't any more—what does it matter? How then can you expect me not to cross out? Really, young man!"

and, I suppose, social, but rarely historical. Sometimes our discussion happened to be interesting and even powerful, sometimes it was a little superficial and rather light. For all the seriousness and genuine sublimity of his nature, Belinsky sometimes acted like a child: on hearing something that appealed to him very much, some passage from Georges Sand or Pierre Leroux (who was getting very fashionable in those days, people corresponding about him mysteriously(!) under the name of Red-haired Peter), on hearing it, he would at once ask for the passage to be written down for him and he kept gloating over it. But all this became him; in this, too, you could see that you were dealing with a Russian whose mind was always alive. Sometimes some trifle stung him to the quick. Once he carried Goethe's *Westoestlicher Divan* about in his pocket for six weeks and for this reason: one day I happened to quote from it the verse—*Lebt man denn, wenn andre leben?* (Is it possible to live when others are living?) He repeated it to A.N.S [trugovshchikov], a well-known translator of Goethe, as a criticism of the German poet. S[trugovshchikov] doubted the authenticity of the quotation and almost made fun of Belinsky's gullibility. So he begged me to lend him a copy of the *Divan* and carried it constantly about so as to be able to discomfit S[trugovshchikov] the moment he met him, but to Belinsky's great annoyance this meeting never took place. During the last two years of his life, as a result of the rapid advances made by his illness, he became very irritable and he was often depressed.

I saw Belinsky regularly during four winters, from 1843 to 1846, and particularly often before January 1847, when I left for a long stay abroad and when the *Contemporary* was founded, that is to say, bought from the late Pletnyov. The history of the *foundation* of this journal is highly edifying. . . . But to describe it in detail is rather difficult at present: I should have to revive old squabbles. Suffice it to say that Belinsky was gradually and very skilfully removed from the journal, which had been really created for him, which had acquired many contributors because his name was associated with it, and which for a whole year was filled with excellent articles Belinsky had acquired for a large almanac he had planned to publish. Belinsky broke off his relations with *Home Annals* for the sake of *The Contemporary,* and it turned out that instead of running the journal as its editor, to which he was fully entitled, he occupied the same position of an outside contributor, a hired man, as he had held in the old one. I possess a number of interesting letters written by Belinsky at that time: the reader will find short extracts from them below. As regards myself, I must say that having at first welcomed my literary work, he very soon grew indifferent to it, and quite rightly, too, for he could hardly have encouraged me in writing those poems which were my sole literary occupation in those days. Still, I quite soon realized myself that there was no need for me to carry on with such like exercises and—made up my mind to give up literature altogether. It was only because of the repeated requests by I. I. Panayev, who had nothing with which to fill the miscellaneous section of the first number of *The Contemporary,* that I left him a sketch entitled *Khor and Kalinych* (The words: "From the Sketches of a Sportsman" were invented and added by the same Panayev with the intention of winning the reader's favour). The success of this sketch made me write the others; and I returned to literature. But the reader will see from the same Belinsky letters that although he was more satisfied with my prose works, he did not repose any great hopes in me. Belinsky encouraged young writers with good-natured indulgence and sympathetic warmth and, provided he recognized their talent, he lent his support to their first steps; but he treated their further efforts with the utmost severity, pointing out their faults mercilessly and criticising and praising them with equal impartiality. But occasionally he would treat beginners with great tenderness, being carried away most charmingly, almost touchingly, almost amusingly. When he got hold of Mr. Dostoevsky's *Poor People* he was positively delighted. "Yes," he used to say proudly, as though he had himself been responsible for some terrific achievement, "yes, my dear fellow, let me tell you it may be a tiny bird," and he would put his hand about a foot from the floor to show how tiny it was, "but it's got sharp claws!" Imagine my surprise when I met Mr. Dostoevsky a little later and saw before me a man of more than medium height, taller than Belinsky himself at any rate. But in his access of paternal tenderness to a newly discovered talent, Belinsky treated him like a son, just as if he were his own "little boy." In the same way, when I first met him in 1843, he made much of Nekrasov, introducing him to everybody and putting him on his feet. . . .

As with all ardent-hearted persons, with all enthusiasts, there was a large dose of intolerance in Belinsky. He did not admit, especially in the heat of an argument, a single grain of truth in the opinions of his opponents and turned away from them with the same kind of indignation with which he gave up his own opinions when he found them to be mistaken. But he could be easily moved to tears, as I told him once, which made him laugh a lot. Truth was too precious to him: he could not remain obstinate for ever. Only the Moscow party, the Slavophils, he treated all his life with hostility: they opposed too violently all that he loved and all he believed in. In general, Belinsky knew how to hate—*he was a good hater*—and despised with all his heart whatever he deemed worthy of contempt. Leibnitz says somewhere that he despised almost nothing (*je ne méprise presque rien*). This is understandable and praiseworthy in a philosopher who spent all his life on the heights of spiritual contemplation; but an ordinary man walking the earth is not able to raise himself to such cold indifference, to such sublime calm; the feeling of contempt which men like Bulgarin inspire in us, confirms and strengthens our moral sense, our conscience. Belinsky admitted his own mistakes without hesitation: there was no trace of petty vanity in him. "Good Lord," he used to say with a smile, "I did talk a lot of nonsense, didn't I?"—and what a fine trait of his character that was! Belinsky was not of a very high opinion of himself or of his abilities. His modesty was genuine and absolutely sincere. But the word "modesty" is not perhaps quite right: he was not at all pleased with being, according to his own idea, such an unimportant person; but, as he used to say, "You can't jump out of your skin!" There was, on the other hand, nothing more important or higher to him than the cause for which he stood, than the ideas which he defended and tried to put in practice: for them he was ready to work himself up into a rage, and woe to him who happened to cross his path; for them he showed true bravery, desperate courage, in spite of his poor physique and weak nerves; for them he was ready to sacrifice everything! Such great irritability and so little personal sensitiveness! No, I never met a man like him, neither before nor after.

In the summer of 1847 Belinsky went abroad for the first and the last time. I spent several weeks with him in Salzbrunn, a small Silesian town, famous for its waters, which were supposed to cure consumption. They were of little use to him. It was in Salzbrunn that, his indignation aroused by Gogol's notorious *Selected Passages from the Correspondence with My Friends,* he wrote him a letter. . . . I met him again in Paris where he entered the clinic of a certain Dr. Tirà de Malmory, a t.b. specialist. Many people regarded him as a charlatan, but he certainly seemed to have set Belinsky on his feet. He stopped coughing and his face was no longer green. His premature departure for Petersburg undid it all.[1]

---

[1] Here is another example of Belinsky's humorous attitude towards himself. On leaving Paris, he was provided with an escort who had to travel to Berlin with him. But at the last moment some misunderstanding arose and Belinsky left alone. "Imagine my position," he wrote to a friend in Paris. "On the Bel-

A funny thing! He was bored to tears abroad; he was longing to be back in Russia. He was too much of a Russian and out of Russia he felt like a fish out of water. I remember that when he saw the Place de la Concorde for the first time, he said to me at once: "It is one of the most beautiful squares in the world, isn't it?" And on my replying in the affirmative, he exclaimed: "Well, that's fine, come along!" And he began talking about Gogol. I told him that during the French Revolution the guillotine had stood in that very square and that Louis XVI had his head cut off there. He looked round, said: "Ah!" and recalled the scene of Ostap's execution in *Taras Bulba*. Belinsky's knowledge of history was very weak: he could not possibly be interested in places where great events of European history had taken place; he knew no foreign languages and therefore could not study the people in foreign countries, while idle curiosity, staring at things, *badauderie*, was not in his nature. Music and painting, as already mentioned, made scarcely any impression on him; and the things that do make a great impression on our fellow-countrymen in Paris revolted his pure, almost ascetic, moral feelings. And he had only a few more months left to live. . . . He was tired and had lost interest. . . .

I do not know whether I ought to say anything about Belinsky's relations with women. He hardly ever touched on this delicate subject himself. He was not, as a rule, very fond of talking at length about himself, his past, etc. I had tried many times to make him talk about it, but he always declined. He seemed to be ashamed of it, he did not seem to understand why he should be wasting his time talking about all sorts of disagreeable personal affairs when there were so many much more useful and more important things to talk about! If he did refer to his past, it was almost always in a

---

gian frontier I was asked something, but I couldn't understand a word and just stared stupidly at the customs official. Luckily, he realized that I was *a damned fool* and—let me pass."

humorous vein: so, for instance, he told me that when he had been *sent down* from the university, he had literally nothing to live on and he undertook to translate a novel by Paul de Kock for twenty-five roubles and, he added, "what awful howlers I made!" He had evidently experienced terrible poverty, but he never took any pleasure in describing it at length in the circle of his friends, as many people who have been through such a painful experience all too often do. Belinsky had too great a store of simple dignity to indulge in such effusions, and perhaps too much pride, too. . . . Pride and vanity are two quite different things.

In Belinsky's view, his personal appearance was such that it could not possibly appear attractive to women; he was absolutely convinced of that and that conviction, of course, increased his shyness and timidity in his relations with women. I have every reason to believe that with his warm and impressionable heart, with his affectionateness and his passionateness, Belinsky, who was after all one of the most eminent men of his time, had never been loved by a woman. He did not marry for love. As a young man he was in love with a young girl, the daughter of the Tver landowner B[akunin]; she was a highly romantic creature, but she loved another and, besides, she died shortly afterwards. There was also in Belinsky's life a rather strange and sad incident with a peasant girl; I remember his fragmentary and sombre story about her. . . . It made a profound impression on me, but here, too, nothing came of it. He could have exclaimed in the words of the poet:

> *O heaven, if only once the fire*
> *In my heart had blazed up entire,*
> *And died away without suffering or pain,*
> *My life would not have been in vain!*

But men's dreams never come true, and their regrets are futile. He who has not drawn a winning number may as well be satisfied with a losing one and not breathe a word about it to anyone.

I cannot help mentioning in passing, however, Belinsky's gener-
ous and honourable views about women in general and Russian
women in particular, about their position, their future, their
inalienable rights, their lack of education, in short, what is now
termed the woman question. His respect for women, his recognition of their right to freedom, of their social as well as their family importance becomes apparent in everything he wrote on the
subject, though not, it is true, with that challenging, vociferous
glibness which is so much in fashion now.

One often hears people say: so-and-so has died at the right moment, just when he should. . . . This is certainly true of Belinsky
as of no one else. Yes, he died when he should, at the right moment! Before his death (Belinsky died in May, 1848), he was in
time to witness the triumph of his dearest hopes and he did not
live to see their final ruin. . . . And the troubles that awaited him if
he had remained alive! It is a well known fact that the police were
daily making inquiries about the state of his health, about the
progress of his agony. . . . Death delivered him of hard trials. Besides, his physical strength was gradually ebbing away. . . . What
was the sense of carrying on, procrastinating?

A struggle more—and I am free! [Byron]

It is all very well, but while you are alive you are alive and you
cannot suppress the feeling of regret for one of us whom death
carries off to "the undiscovered country from whose bourn no traveller returns." I can't help asking myself sometimes, I can't help
trying to imagine what Belinsky would have said and felt had he
been alive to see the great reforms of the present reign—the libera-
tion of the serfs, the introduction of public trials, etc.? With what
enthusiasm would he have greeted these promising beginnings!

But he did not live to see them. . . . He did not live even to see something else that also would have filled his heart with great delight: he did not live to see the many great things that happened in our literature after his death. How delighted he would have been at the poetic gifts of L. N. Tolstoy, the force of Ostrovsky, the humour of Pissemsky, the satire of Saltykov, the sober truth of Reshotnikov! Who but he should have witnessed the sprouting of the seeds many of which had been sown by his hand? But it seems it was not to be. . . .

Let me finish my reminiscences of Belinsky by a quotation from a letter from a close woman friend of his, whom I asked to tell me the details of his death (I was abroad, in Paris, at the time), as well as by a few extracts from his letters to me.

Here is the letter from his woman friend (dated June 3, 1848):

"You want to know something about Belinsky. . . . But I am afraid I am not very good at describing things and, indeed, there is hardly anything I can tell you about a man who for the last few weeks was completely worn out by his physical sufferings. I can't tell you how terribly painful it was to watch the slow dissolution of this poor sufferer. He had returned from Paris in such excellent health and spirits that all of us, not excepting the doctor, had great hopes of his recovery. He spent several mornings and evenings with us talking vigorously and animatedly all the time and everyone was glad to find the old Belinsky in him, the Belinsky who was still in comparatively good health. But, strangely enough, his character seemed to have greatly changed since his return from abroad: he became more gentle, more sweet-tempered, much more tolerant than before; even at home it was difficult to recognize him, so calmly and apparently without any struggle did he put up with everything that used to upset him so greatly before. He did not enjoy his good health long, however; he soon caught a cold in Petersburg and his condition grew worse with every day that passed. Every time we went to see him we found him terribly changed. It seemed to us that he could not possibly grow thinner, and yet when we met him again we found him looking more terrible than ever. I went to see him for the last time a week before his death. We found him half reclining in an armchair; his face looked dead already, but his eyes were huge and glittering; every breath he drew was a moan, and he greeted us with the words: 'I am dying, I am dying!' But he uttered those words hesitantly, without conviction, but rather as though wishing that we should contradict him. I need not tell you how awful the two hours were that we spent in his rooms. He could not, of course, talk, but he no longer showed any interest in those *subjects* that were of so vital an importance to him throughout his life. They stirred him no longer. He took to his bed three days before he died and apparently never gave up hope while still conscious; a day before his death he began to ramble, but he did recognize Granovsky who had arrived from Moscow on that day. Before his death he talked for two hours without stopping, as though addressing the Russian people, and he frequently turned to his wife and asked her to remember his words and pass them on correctly to those they were meant for; but it was hardly possible to make any sense of his long speech; then he suddenly fell silent and after half an hour of great agony he died. His poor wife . . . never left him for a moment, looking after him herself all the time, raising him and turning him over in his bed. That woman . . . I am sure deserves universal respect; she looked after her sick husband with such unmurmuring devotion and patience all winter. . . ."

Here are some extracts from Belinsky's letters to me:

Petersburg,
19th February (3rd March) 1847
". . . When you were preparing to go aboard, I knew beforehand that I should miss you, but when you were gone, I realized

154

that I missed you more than I thought. . . . After you had gone I resigned myself to boredom with a sort of apathetic renunciation and I was bored as I have never been bored in my life before. I go to bed at eleven, even at ten, sleep till twelve, get up at seven, eight or nine, and doze all day, especially all evening (after dinner)—that's what my life is like!

". . . Received an abusive letter from K[etcher], but did not show it to [Nekrasov]. The latter knows nothing, but I suppose he guesses, and goes on doing exactly what he likes. During our interview he was not at his ease: he coughed, stuttered, said that for my own good, it seems, he could not agree to do what I wanted, for reasons which he would explain to me in a moment but which he could not possibly tell me. I told him I did not want to know any reasons and mentioned my conditions. He cheered up and every time he meets me now he holds out both his hands—one can see that he is completely satisfied with me! You can see clearly from the tone of my letter that I am neither furious nor *exaggerating*. I was fond of him, so fond that now I am sometimes sorry for him and sometimes annoyed with him—with him and not with myself. It *hurts* me very much to have to give up an old friendship—but afterwards I don't mind. Nature has not given me the ability to hate a man for a personal injustice he has done to me; I am more likely to hate a man for a difference of opinion or for his faults and vices which do not affect me in the least. I think a great deal of [Nekrasov] even now; and yet I look upon him as a man who is going to amass a great fortune, who is going to be rich, and I know how that is done. He had already begun with me. But enough of this.

"Let me give you a piece of news: I shall probably be in Silesia. B[otkin] is raising 2,500 roubles for me. At first I would not hear of it, for what would I be leaving my family with, and I did not want to ask to be paid my salary while I was away. But after my interview with [Nekrasov] I decided that it would be stupid to stand on ceremony. . . . He was very pleased, he was willing to do anything provided I . . . I wrote to B[otkin] and his reply will decide the matter.

"Your *Karatayev* is good, though far below *Khor and Kalinych*. . . .

". . . It seems to me that you either have not got a purely creative talent at all or have very little of it and that your talent is rather like Dahl's. That is your real *genre*. Take, for example, your *Yermolay and the Miller's Wife*. It's nothing much, but it is good because it is intelligent and sensible, with an idea behind it. But in your *Bully*, I am sure, you showed real creative talent. To find one's right path, to get to know one's real place means everything to a man; it means to find oneself. If I am not mistaken your true vocation is to observe actual facts and describe them after letting them filter through your imagination, but not depending entirely on your imagination. . . . Only for Allah's sake don't publish anything that is not so much bad as not very good. This does great harm to the totality of one's reputation (I'm sorry for the stilted expression, I can't think of anything better). But *Khor* shows promise of a remarkable writer—in the future.

". . . Gogol has been thoroughly trounced by public opinion and violently attacked in all journals; even his friends, the Moscow Slavophils, have turned away, if not from him, then from his odious book. . . ."

"My wife and my entire household, including your godson [I stood godfather to his son] send you their best regards. . . ."

Petersburg, 1 (13) March 1847

". . . I must tell you I have now almost changed my mind about the origin of certain actions of [Nekrasov]. It now seems to me that he acted conscientiously, basing himself upon objective rights, for he has not yet grown up to the conception of others, higher ones, and he could not acquire it because he grew up in a dirty matter-of-fact world and was never an idealist or a romantic like one of us. I can see—from his example—how this idealism and romanticism can be useful to some people who are thrown back upon their own devices. This idealism and romanticism may be horrible, but what does it matter to a man if a badly tasting medicine has helped him even though, having cured him of a mortal illness, it has infected his organism with other, though no longer mortal, illnesses; the point here is not that it is horrible, but that it has been of some help . . .

"My journey to Silesia is now settled. I owe this to Botkin. He found the means and forced me to make up my mind. I shall never do nor have I ever done so much for myself as he did for me. How many letters he wrote about it to me as well as to A[nnenkov], H[erzen] and to his brother, and how many talks and discussions he had with all sorts of people about it! The other day he received an answer from A[nnenkov] and forwarded it to me. A[nnenkov] has given me four hundred francs. You know that he is a man of independent means but certainly not rich, and you know from your own experience that four hundred francs abroad are not to be sneezed at. But that is nothing, I always expected it of A[nnenkov]. What really did touch me deeply was that the man had changed his plans *for me* and instead of going to Greece and Constantinople is going to Silesia! That sort of thing, let me tell you, makes one feel really embarrassed and if I had not known, if I had not felt deeply how very fond I am of A[nnenkov], I should have been greatly annoyed by such a thing. I hope to leave by the first boat. . . ."

Petersburg, 12 (24) April 1847

"Just a few lines, my dear T. Shortly after receiving your second letter, in which you say how glad you are to hear of my son's good health, he died. That was a great blow to me. I am not living, but dying a slow death. But to business. I have got my ticket for the Stettin boat; she is leaving on 4 (16) May. . ."

On May 9 (21) I met Belinsky in Stettin where I had gone to meet him. I received news from Petersburg that the death of his three-months-old son was a terrible shock to him. Within one year he, too, followed him into the grave.

And now over twenty years have passed since then—and I have called up his dear shade. . . I don't know whether or not I have succeeded in describing the main traits of his character to my readers, but I am, at any rate, glad that he has been with me—in my memory. . .

"This was a man!"

1868.

157

First Appendix

I received a letter from A. D. Galakhov in connexion with my article on Belinsky, published some time ago in *The Russian Herald* [April 9, 1869]. I am reproducing here an extract from that letter. In it the esteemed author, who in the field of literary history and criticism carries great weight and enjoys well-deserved respect, to some extent complements my views:

"As regards any errors of literary judgment or facts, I have discovered none. I can only point out what I consider to be a single inaccuracy. You say that prizing art as a special, entirely natural and legitimate sphere of man's spiritual activity, Belinsky was not an adherent of the theory of art for art's sake, and to prove your statement you quote his remark about Pushkin's *The Mob*. I don't think this is so, at least, not chronologically. His remark was made at the time of your acquaintance with Belinsky. Before that time (before 1843) he had been working in *Molva* and *The Telescope*, in *The Observer* and in *Home Annals*. It can be seen from some of his articles published there (especially in *The Observer*) that he recognized the justice of the famous formula: the aim of art is art itself. That, surely, is why he attacked Menzel so violently (in *Home Annals*), for in his *History of German Literature* Menzel subordinates the aim of art to all sorts of aims outside the sphere of literature and demands that it should serve civic, political and other interests, attacking Goethe and praising Schiller because of it. I remember that on one occasion when I paid him a visit, he showed me with genuine emotion the portraits of Hegel and Goethe as the highest representatives of pure thought and pure art."

It seems to me that I ought to explain that when I first met Belinsky his views were exactly as I described them; he had changed them shortly before that. He became once more much more politically minded.

Second Appendix

In his well-known biography of Belinsky, A. N. Pypin disputes my views about what I described as the non-political elements in Belinsky's temperament. He regards Belinsky's "restraint" as the inevitable concession made to the special conditions of his time. I am quite ready to agree with the esteemed scholar: quite likely Mr. Pypin's evaluation of *that* side of our great critic's character is more correct than mine, and I think I ought to make that clear to my readers. The "fire" which I mentioned was never quenched in him, though it could not always be seen.

Paris, September, 1879.

III

GOGOL,
ZHUKOVSKY, KRYLOV, LERMONTOV,
ZAGOSKIN

I WAS TAKEN TO MEET GOGOL by the late Mikhail Semyonovich Shchepkin. I remember the day of our visit: 20th of October, 1851. Gogol lived in Moscow at the time, in Nikitsky Street, Talyzin's house, with Count [Alexander] Tolstoy. We arrived at one o'clock in the afternoon: he received us at once. His room was on the right of the entrance hall. We entered and—there was Gogol standing before a tall bureau with a pen in his hand. He was wearing a dark coat, a green velvet waistcoat and brown trousers. A week before I had seen him in the theatre at a performance of *The Government Inspector;* he was in a box in the stalls, near the very door and, craning his neck, looked with nervous anxiety at the stage over the shoulders of two stout ladies, whom he used as a screen from the curiosity of the public. F[eokstitov], who was sitting next to me, pointed him out to me. I turned round quickly to have a look at him; he must have noticed my movement, for he shrank back a little into the corner of the box. I was struck by the change that had taken place in his appearance since 1841. I had met him twice then at Avdotya Petrovna Ye[lagin]'s. At that time he was a stout, thick-set Ukrainian; now he looked a very thin, haggard man who had been through a great deal of trouble in life. A sort of hidden anxiety and pain, a sort of melancholy restlessness hung over the usually shrewd and intelligent expression on his face.

Seeing Shchepkin and myself, he went up to us gaily and, shaking hands with me, said: "We should have become acquainted long ago." We sat down—Shchepkin in an armchair beside him and I next to him on the sofa. I looked at him more closely. His fair hair, which fell straight from the temples, as is usual with Cossacks, still preserved its youthful tint, but had thinned noticeably; his smooth, retreating white forehead conveyed, as before, the impression of great intelligence. His small brown eyes sparkled with gaiety at times—yes, gaiety and not sarcasm; but mostly they looked tired. Gogol's long, pointed nose gave his face a sort of cunning, fox-like expression; his puffy, soft lips under the clipped moustache also produced an unfavourable impression; in their indefinite contours—so at least it seemed to me—the dark sides of his character found expression. When he spoke, they opened unpleasantly, showing a row of bad teeth. His small chin disappeared in his wide, black velvet cravat. In Gogol's bearing, in his gestures, there was something not so much professorial as schoolmasterly—something reminiscent of teachers in provincial institutes and secondary schools. "What an intelligent, queer and sick creature you are!" I could not help thinking as I looked at him. I remember that Shchepkin and I had gone to him as to an extraordinary man, a man of genius, who was a little touched in the head . . . all Moscow was of that opinion of him. Shchepkin had warned me not to talk to him about the continuation of *Dead Souls*, about the second part of his novel, at which he had been working so long and so assiduously and which he burnt before his death. He did **not** like to talk about it, Shchepkin said. I should not have mentioned his *Selected Passages from the Correspondence with my Friends* myself, for I could not have said anything good about it. As a matter of fact, I was not particularly anxious to discuss anything with him; all I wanted was to see the man whose works I knew almost by heart. It is difficult to explain to our young people of today the fascination his name exerted on us in those days; there is, in fact, no one living today who could become the focus of general attention.

Shchepkin had warned me beforehand that Gogol was anything but talkative; but actually it turned out quite otherwise. Gogol talked a lot and with great animation, enunciating every word clearly and emphasizing it, which not only did not seem unnatural but, on the contrary, lent his speech a sort of agreeable weight and impressiveness. I could not detect any particular Ukrainian accent in his speech, except that he pronounced the letter O without slurring over it. Everything he said was absolutely right and to the point. The impression of fatigue and morbid nervous restlessness, which had struck me at first, disappeared. He spoke of the importance of literature, the vocation of the writer, and what one's attitude to one's own works should be; he made a few subtle and true observations about the process of literary work itself, the physiology, if one may put it that way, of authorship; and all that in an imaginative and original language and, as far as I could see, without any preliminary preparation, as is all too often the case with "famous men." It was only when he began speaking of the censorship, almost glorifying it, almost approving of it as a means of developing the writers' acumen and skill in protecting his beloved child as well as his patience and a multitude of other Christian and worldly virtues, it was only then that I could not help feeling that he was drawing it all out of a ready-made arsenal. Besides, to prove the need for censorship in this way—is it not tantamount to recommending and almost praising the cunning and craftiness of slavery? I could, I suppose, to some extent accept the verse of the Italian poet: *Si, servi, siam; ma servi ognor frementi* [Yes, we are slaves; but slaves who are always mad with rage]; but self-satisfied submission and double-faced hypocrisy of slavery—no; I'd rather not speak of it. In such excogitations and rationalisations of Gogol one could clearly detect the influence of those high-placed personages to whom he had dedicated the greater part of his *Selected Passages;* it was from there that that stale and musty odour came. In fact, I soon felt that there was an impassable gulf between Gogol's outlook on life and mine. It was not the same things that we hated and not the same things that we loved; but at that moment that did not matter to me. A great poet, a great artist was before me, and I looked at him and listened to him with veneration even when I did not agree with him.

Gogol, I expect, must have known of my relations with Belinsky and Iskander [Herzen]; he never mentioned the first nor Belinsky's letter to him; that name would have scorched his lips. But just at that time there appeared an article by Iskander, an article, published abroad, in which he reproached Gogol with going back on his former opinions in connexion with the notorious *Selected Passages.* Gogol began talking of that article himself. From his letters, published after his death (oh, what a great service their editor would have done if he had thrown out two-thirds of them or at least those written to society women—there is a no more hideous mixture of arrogance, servility, sanctimoniousness and vanity, prophetic and cringing tone in all literature!)—from Gogol's letters we know what a festering wound the fiasco of his *Selected Passages* had inflicted on his heart, a fiasco which one cannot help hailing as one of the few salutary manifestations of public opinion in those days. On the day of our visit Shchepkin and I could see how terribly painful that wound was. Gogol began to assure us in a suddenly changed and flurried voice that he

could not understand why some people found some sort of contradiction to his former works, something that he had betrayed
afterwards; that he had always adhered to the same religious and
conservative principles, and to prove it he was ready to show us
certain passages in a book of his he had published ages before.
Having said this, Gogol jumped up from the sofa with almost
youthful agility and rushed into the next room. Shchepkin just
raised his eyebrows and—his forefinger. . . . "I've never seen him
like that," he whispered to me.

Gogol returned with the volume *Arabesques* and began reading extracts from one of those childishly bombastic and tiresomely
insipid articles with which that book is filled. So far as I can remember it was all about the need for strict order, absolute obedience to the authorities, and so on. "You see," said Gogol, "I was
of the same opinion before! I expressed exactly the same convictions as now! Why, then, reproach me with betrayal, apostasy?
Me?" And that was said by the author of *The Government Inspector,* one of the most damning comedies that ever appeared on
the stage! Shchepkin and I said nothing. At last Gogol threw the
book down on the table and again began talking about art and
the theatre. He declared that he was dissatisfied with the performance of the actors in *The Government Inspector,* that they had
"lost the tone" and that he was willing to read them the whole
play from beginning to end. Shchepkin took him at his word and
immediately arranged when and where the reading should take
place. An old lady then called on Gogol. She had brought him a
piece of the holy bread. We took our leave.

Two days later the reading of *The Government Inspector* took
place in one of the drawing rooms of Gogol's house. I got permission to be present at this reading. The late Professor Shevyryov and, if I am not mistaken, Pogodin were also among those

present. To my great astonishment, not by any means all the actors who were in the cast of the play accepted Gogol's invitation. They took offence at the idea that Gogol seemed to want to teach them! Not a single actress turned up, either. As far as I could see, Gogol was hurt by this weak and unwilling response to his offer. . . . It is well known how chary he was of such favours. His face assumed a cold and gloomy expression. There was a suspicious gleam in his eyes. That day he certainly did look a sick man. He began to read and gradually grew animated. His cheeks coloured slightly, his eyes widened and brightened. . . . I heard him for the first and last time that day. Dickens, also an excellent reader, could be said to give a public performance of his novels; his reading was dramatic, almost theatrical: there were several first-class actors in his face alone who made you laugh and cry. Gogol, on the other hand, struck me by the extraordinary simplicity and restraint of his manner, by a sort of grave and at the same time naive sincerity; he did not seem to care whether there were any listeners or what they were thinking about. It seemed as though all Gogol was concerned about was how to convey his own impression more convincingly. The effect was quite remarkable, especially in the comic, humorous passages. It was impossible not to laugh—a good, healthy laughter; and the cause of all this merriment carried on undisturbed by the general hilarity and as though inwardly amazed at it, more and more absorbed in his reading, and only occasionally the barely perceptible crafty smile of the master played on his lips and around his eyes. With what a puzzled, astonished expression did Gogol utter the famous phrase of the Mayor about the two rats (at the very beginning of the play): "They came, they sniffed and they went away!" He even looked up at us slowly, as though asking for an explanation of such an astonishing occurrence.

It was only then that I realized how wrongly, how superficially *The Government Inspector* is usually performed on the stage, the actors being anxious only to get a quick laugh out of the audience. I sat there overcome by joyful emotion: it was a true festive occasion for me. Unfortunately, it did not last. Gogol had barely time to read through half of the first act when the door was flung open noisily and a very young, but already unusually tiresome author rushed across the room, with a quick smile and a nod of the head. Without uttering a word, he hastened to take a seat in the corner of the room. Gogol stopped, banged the bell on the table and said angrily to the footman who entered the room: "Didn't I tell you not to let anyone in?" The young writer stirred on his chair, but did not seem to be in the least embarrassed. Gogol took a sip of water and resumed his reading. But it was not the same thing at all. He began to hurry, to mumble, to swallow the words. Sometimes he left out whole sentences—and just waved his hand. The unexpected appearance of the young writer had disconcerted him; his nerves apparently could not stand the slightest shock. Only in the famous scene when Khlestakov starts telling lies did Gogol pluck up courage and raise his voice: he wanted to show the actor who played Khlestakov how one had to perform that really difficult scene. In Gogol's interpretation it seemed natural and truthful to me. Khlestakov is carried away by the strangeness of his position, by his surroundings and by his own frivolous nimble-mindedness; he knows that he is telling lies and—believes his own lies: it is a sort of ecstasy, a sort of inspiration, a story-teller's enthusiasm—it is not an ordinary sort of lie, not an ordinary sort of bragging. He was himself "carried away." "The petitioners are buzzing in the hall, thirty-five thousand couriers are driving at breakneck speed—and these fools here are listening, pricking up their ears, and look what a clever, amusing man of the world I am!" That was the impression produced by Khlestakov's monologue as read by Gogol. But, on the whole, the reading of *The Government Inspector* that day was, as Gogol himself expressed it, no more than a sketch, a mere hint of the real thing. And all because of the uninvited young writer who, not in the least abashed, stayed behind with the tired, pale-looking Gogol and even followed him to his study.

I took leave of Gogol in the entrance hall and never saw him again. But he was still destined to have an important influence on my life.

Towards the end of February of the following (1852) year, I was present at a morning meeting of the Society for Visiting the Poor, which was soon to be dissolved, in the hall of the Noblemen's Club. Suddenly I caught sight of Ivan Panayev rushing wildly about from one person to another and evidently imparting to everyone an unexpected, cheerless piece of news, for everyone at once looked surprised and sad. Panayev, at last, rushed up to me, and, saying with a faint smile in an unconcerned tone of voice: "Do you know, Gogol has died in Moscow. Yes, indeed. . . . Burnt all his papers and—died," and rushed off. There can be no doubt that, as a lover of literature, Panayev was inwardly grieved at such a loss—besides, he had a kind heart, but the pleasure of being the first to tell someone such a stunning piece of news (his unconcerned tone of voice was merely assumed for greater effect), that kind of pleasure, that kind of joy, overcame every other feeling in him. Rumours about Gogol's illness had been current in Petersburg for several days, but no one expected such an outcome. Under the first impression of this news I wrote the following short article:

A Letter from Petersburg [1]

Gogol is dead! What Russian heart will not be deeply moved by these words? He is dead. Our loss is so cruel, so sudden that we

---

[1] *Moscow News,* 13 March, 1852.

still cannot believe it. At a time when all of us could still hope that he would at last break his long silence, that he would gladden, exceed our impatient expectations, this fatal news came! Yes, he is dead, the man whom we now have the right, a bitter right conferred on us by his death, to call great; the man who by his name marked an epoch in the history of our literature; the man we are proud of as one of our glories! He is dead, struck down in the prime of life, at the height of his powers, without finishing the work he has begun, like one of the noblest of his predecessors. His loss renews our grief for those unforgettable bereavements, as a new wound awakens the pain of old ones. This is not the time nor the place to speak of his merits—that is the business of future criticism; let us hope that it will understand its task and appraise him with that impartial judgment, filled with respect and love, with which people like him are appraised before posterity; we do not feel like doing it now; all we want is to be the sounding board of that great grief which we feel everywhere around us; we do not want to appraise him, but to weep; we cannot speak calmly of Gogol now—the most beloved, the most familiar image becomes blurred in eyes filled with tears. . . . On the day Moscow is burying him we wish to hold out our hands to her from here—to unite with her in one feeling of general mourning. We were not able to have a last look on his lifeless face; but we send him our farewell greeting from afar, and lay down with most reverent feeling the tribute of our grief and our love on his fresh grave, on which we did not, like our Moscow colleagues, succeed in throwing a handful of our native soil! The thought that his remains lie in Moscow fills us with a kind of sorrowful satisfaction. Yes, let them lie there, in the heart of the Russia he knew so well and loved so well, loved so ardently that only thoughtless and short-sighted people do not feel the presence of that loving flame in every word uttered by him! But what is so hard to bear is the thought that the last and most mature works of his genius are irretrievably lost to us—and we hear with horror the cruel rumours of their destruction. . . .

We need hardly speak of those few people to whom our words will appear exaggerated or altogether misplaced. . . . Death has a purifying and reconciling force; slander and envy, hostility and misunderstanding—they all fall silent before the most ordinary grave; they will not break the silence before Gogol's grave. Whatever the place history finally allots to him, we are certain that no one will refuse to repeat after us: May he rest in peace, may the memory of his life be everlasting! Eternal glory to his name!

T-v.[1]

I sent this article to one of the Petersburg journals, but it was just then that the censorship had for some time been getting more and more severe. . . . Such-like *crescendos* happened quite often and—to an outside observer—as inconsequentially as, for instance, the increase in mortality during an epidemic. My article did not appear on any of the following days. Running across the editor of the journal in the street I asked him why he did not publish it. "You see the sort of climate it is," he replied, allegorically. "I'm afraid it can't be done." "But," I observed, "my article is a most innocent one." "Innocent or not," the editor replied, "the point is that we've been forbidden to mention Gogol's name. Zakrevsky went to his funeral wearing the ribbon of St. Andrew—that they cannot bear to think of here." Soon afterwards I received a letter from a friend in Moscow filled with reproaches. "Good Lord," he exclaimed, "Gogol has died and not a single

---

[1] Apropos of this article (someone said about it at the time quite rightly that there was no rich businessman about whose death the papers would not have written with greater warmth) I can recall the following: one very highly placed lady—in Petersburg—expressed the view that the punishment I incurred for this article was undeserved or, at least, too severe and cruel. In a word, she took my part very warmly. "But," someone objected, "you don't seem to realize that in his article he called Gogol a great man." "Impossible!" "I assure you." "Oh, in that case I've nothing more to say: *je regrette, mais je comprends qu'on ait dû sévir.*"

notice has appeared about him in the Petersburg papers! This silence is shameful!" In my reply I explained in somewhat harsh terms the reason for that silence and, to prove it, sent him my forbidden article as documentary evidence. He submitted it at once for examination to General Nazimov, the Inspector of Schools of the Moscow District, and received permission from him to publish it in *The Moscow News*. That happened in the middle of March and on April 16 I was arrested and kept imprisoned for a month at the police station for disobeying and breaking the censorship rules (the first twenty-four hours I spent in a cell talking to an exquisitely polite and educated police sergeant who told me about a walk he had had in the Summer Gardens and spoke about "the aroma of birds"), and then banished to my country estate. I have not the least intention of accusing the Government of the time: the Inspector of Schools of the Petersburg District, the late Mussin-Pushkin, represented the whole thing (for reasons unknown to me) as downright disobedience on my part; he did not hesitate to assure the higher authorities that *he had summoned me personally and handed me personally the Censorship Committee's prohibition to publish my article* (the prohibition by one censor could not, in view of the existing censorship regulations, prevent my submitting my article for the decision of another censor), *while I had never seen Mr. Mussin-Pushkin and had had no interview with him*. The Government could not suspect a high official and a trusted person of distorting the truth to such an extent! But it all turned out for the best: my arrest and my banishment to the country was of undoubted benefit to me: it brought me into contact with such sides of Russian life as would most certainly have escaped my attention under ordinary circumstances.

As I was finishing the last sentence I remembered that my first meeting with Gogol took place much earlier than I mentioned before. In fact, I was one of his students in 1835 when he lectured(!) on history to us at St. Petersburg university. His lecturing, to tell the truth, was highly original. In the first place, Gogol usually missed two lectures out of three; secondly, even when he appeared in the lecture room, he did not so much speak as whisper something incoherently and showed us small engravings of views of Palestine and other Eastern countries, looking terribly embarrassed all the time. We were all convinced that he knew nothing of history (and we were hardly wrong) and that Mr. Gogol-Janovsky, our professor (he appeared under that name on the list of lectures) had nothing in common with the writer Gogol, already familiar to us as the author of *Evenings on a Farm near Dikanka*. At the final examination on his subject he sat with his face tied up in a handkerchief, as though suffering from toothache, looking terribly depressed, and—never opened his mouth. Professor J. P. Shulgin put the questions to the students for him. I can still see, as though it were today, his thin, long-nosed face with the two ends of the black silk handkerchief sticking out like two huge ears. No doubt he realized very well how utterly comic and awkward his position was: he sent in his resignation that very year. That, however, did not prevent him from exclaiming: "Unrecognized I mounted the rostrum and unrecognized I descend from it." He was born to be the instructor of all his contemporaries, but not from a university chair.

In the foregoing (first) fragment of my reminiscences I mentioned my meeting with Pushkin. I may as well say a few words about a few other literary celebrities who are now dead but whom I was lucky enough to meet. I shall begin with Zhukovsky. While residing—shortly after 1812—in his village in the Belevsky district, he paid several visits to my mother, who was still unmarried at the time, at her Mtsensk estate. I have heard it even said that during one of his visits he took the part of a sorcerer in a theatrical performance and I have a vague recollection of having seen in the pantry of my mother's house the sorcerer's hat with golden stars which he had worn at that performance. Many years have passed since then and, I suppose, he had long forgotten the young lady he had happened to become acquainted with while passing through our village. When our family went to live in Petersburg —I was 16 then—my mother took it into her head to remind Zhukovsky of her existence. She embroidered a beautiful velvet cushion for his birthday and sent me to the Winter Palace with it. I had to introduce myself, tell him whose son I was and then give him her present. In the huge palace, which was quite unfamiliar to me at the time, I had to walk through long stone corridors and climb stone staircases, every now and then coming across motionless sentries, who also looked as though they were carved out of stone. At last I found Zhukovsky's apartment and was confronted by a six-foot flunkey with galoons along every seam of his red uniform and eagles on the galoons. By this time I was overcome with such panic that when I entered Zhukovsky's study, where I was shown in by the flunkey in the red uniform, and when I saw the dreamily affable but rather grave and somewhat astonished face of the poet staring at me from behind a tall bureau, I could not utter a sound in spite of all my efforts: my tongue, as the saying is, clove to my palate. Flushed with shame and with tears nearly starting to my eyes, I stood rooted to the spot in the doorway, holding out in both my hands, like an infant at a christening, the luckless cushion on which (I remember it as clearly as though it all happened yesterday) was embroidered a maiden in medieval dress with a parrot on her shoulder. My embarrassment, I suppose, aroused a feeling of compassion in Zhukovsky's kind heart. He went up to me, took the cushion quietly out of my hands, asked me to sit down, and spoke nicely to me.

I explained to him at last what it was all about and—took to my heels as soon as I decently could.

Already at that time Zhukovsky had lost his former importance as a poet in my eyes; but I was all the same glad of our meeting, unsuccessful though it had been. On returning home, I recalled with particular feeling his smile, the tender sound of his voice, his slow and pleasant gestures. All Zhukovsky's portraits are very much alike; his face was not one of those whose likeness is difficult to catch or which often change. In 1843, of course, there was no trace in him of the frail, romantic young man, in which guise the author of "The Singer in the Camp of Russian Warriors" [written in 1812 after the surrender of Moscow to Napoleon] appeared to our fathers. He had grown into a portly, almost stout man. His face, always a little puffy, of a rather milky hue, without wrinkles, exhaled tranquillity; he held his head a little on one side, as though listening to something and pondering; his thin, scanty hair lay in separate strands over his almost completely bald head; his dark, deep-set, slanting, Chinese-like eyes shone with gentle loving-kindness, and there was always a scarcely perceptible but sincere smile on his rather full, but finely drawn lips. His semi-oriental origin (his mother, of course, was a Turkish woman) could be detected in every feature of his face.

A few weeks later I was again taken to see Zhukovsky by Voin Ivanovich Gubaryov, an old friend of our family and a remarkable and typical representative of his time. A far from rich landowner of the Kromsk district, Oryol province, he was an intimate friend of Zhukovsky, Bludov and Uvarov in his early youth; in their circle he represented French philosophy, the sceptical encyclopaedic element, rationalism, in short, the eighteenth century. Gubaryov spoke an excellent French, knew Voltaire by heart and thought him to be the greatest man in the world; he scarcely read any other writer; his mentality was a purely French one, pre-revolutionary French, I hasten to add. I can still remember his almost unceasing loud and frigid laugh and uninhibited, slightly cynical, opinions and manners. His appearance alone condemned him to a lonely and independent life: he was a far from handsome, fat man, with an enormous head and a pockmarked face. His long life in the provinces left its mark on him at last, but he remained a "type" to the very end, and to the very end—beneath his worn Cossack coat of an impoverished landowner who walked about in tarred top-boots at home—he preserved his freedom and even his exquisite manners. I do not know why he was not successful and why he did not make a good career for himself as his friends did. I don't suppose he possessed the necessary perseverance or was sufficiently ambitious: ambition does not agree with the semi-indifferent and semi-ironic epicureanism he had adopted from his model Voltaire. He did not think he possessed any literary talent and fortune did not smile on him, so he just kept in the background, allowed himself to sink lower and lower, and grew into a lonely old bachelor. But it would have been very interesting to find out what the relations were of this inveterate Voltairean to his friend, the future ballad-writer and translator of Schiller, when both of them were still young! One could not think of a greater contradiction, but then life itself is nothing but a contradiction that has to be constantly overcome.

In Petersburg Zhukovsky remembered his old friend and did not forget what would please him most: he made him a present of a new, beautifully bound edition of the complete works of Voltaire. I am told that shortly before his death—and Gubaryov died a very old man—his neighbours used to see him in his tumbledown hovel sitting at a table on which lay the present of his famous friend. He carefully turned the gilt-edged pages of his favourite book and in the wilds of the steppes amused himself sincerely, as in the days of his youth, with the witticisms that had once upon a time amused Frederick the Great at Sans-Souci and Catherine the Great in Tsarskoye Selo. Another kind of intellect, another kind of poetry, another kind of philosophy did not exist for him. That, needless to say, did not prevent him from wearing round his neck a lot of little icons and amulets and—from being under the thumb of his illiterate housekeeper. . . . The logic of contradictions!

I never met Zhukovsky again.

I saw Krylov only once—at a party given by a high-ranking, but rather bad Petersburg author. He sat motionless for over three hours between two windows—and never uttered a word! He wore a capacious, threadbare frock-coat, a white necktie, and a pair of boots with tassels on his huge feet. He rested both his hands on his knees and never turned his colossal, heavy, majestic head even once; only his eyes rolled from time to time beneath his beetling brows. It was impossible to make out whether he was listening and taking everything in or whether he was simply sitting *like that* and "vegetating." There was not a trace of somnolence or attention on that vast, typically Russian face—only a great deal of intelligence and inveterate laziness, and occasionally a very crafty expression seemed about to appear on it, but could not—perhaps would not—break through all that senile fat. . . . Our host at last told him that dinner was served. "There is a sucking pig and horse-radish sauce for you, Ivan Andreyich," he observed fussily, as though carrying out some inescapable duty. Krylov gave him a half-friendly and half-ironic look. . . . "You didn't say a sucking pig, did you?" he seemed to utter inwardly. Then he rose heavily and, shuffling his feet heavily, went to take his place at table.

Lermontov, too, I saw only twice: at the house of Princess Sh[akhovskoy], a Petersburg high society woman, and a few days later at a New Year's fancy ball at the Noblemen's Club on the eve of 1840. At Princess Sh[akhovskoy]'s I, a very rare and unaccustomed visitor at high society parties, saw him only from a distance, observing the poet, who had become famous in so short a time, from a corner where I had secreted myself. Lermontov sat down on a low stool in front of a sofa on which, wearing a black gown, was sitting one of the society beauties of those days, the fair-haired Countess [Emilia] Mussin-Pushkin, who died young and who really was a strikingly beautiful girl. Lermontov wore the uniform of the Life Guards Hussar Regiment. He had removed neither his sword nor his gloves and, frowning and hunching his shoulders, gazed sullenly at the Countess. She only exchanged a few words with him, talking mostly to Count Sh[akhovskoy], also a Hussar officer, who was sitting beside him. There was something ominous and tragic in Lermontov's appearance: his swarthy face and large, motionless dark eyes exuded a sort of sombre and evil strength, a sort of pensive scornfulness and passion. His hard gaze was strangely out of keeping with the expression of his almost childishly tender, protruding lips. His whole figure, thick-set, bow-legged, with a large head on broad, stooping shoulders, aroused an unpleasant feeling; but everyone had at once to acknowledge its immense inherent strength. It is, of course, a well-known fact that he had to some extent portrayed himself in Pechorin. The words: "His eyes did not laugh when he laughed," from *A Hero of Our Time,* etc., could really have been applied to himself. I remember that Count Sh[akhovskoy] and the young Countess suddenly burst out laughing at something and went on laughing for some time; Lermontov, too, laughed, but at the same time he kept looking at them with a sort of offensive astonishment. For all that I could not help feeling that he was fond of Count Sh[akhovskoy] as a fellow-officer and that he was also well-disposed towards the Countess. There could be no doubt that, following the fashion of those days, he was trying to assume a Byronic air together with a number of other even worse eccentricities and whimsicalities. And he paid dearly for them!

At heart Lermontov was probably terribly bored; he felt stifled in the airless atmosphere where fate had forced him to live.

At the ball in the Noblemen's Club he was not given a moment's rest; women constantly pestered him, took him by the hand, one mask following another, while he practically never moved from his place, listening to their shrill voices in silence and looking sombrely at them in turn. For a moment I thought that I caught a beautiful expression of poetic inspiration on his face. Perhaps, the following lines occurred to him just then:

> *When the hands of the city-bred beauties*
> *That at the touch of a man's hand*
> *Long ceased to tremble, with bold assurance*
> *My cold hands touch . . . . etc.*

Let me incidentally say a few words about another dead author, though he belonged to *deis minorum gentium* and cannot possibly be put side by side with the writers mentioned above—namely, about M. N. Zagoskin. He was a good friend of my father's in the thirties when we lived in Moscow and when he visited us almost daily. His *Yury Miloslavsky* was the first powerful literary impression of my life. When the novel appeared I was at the boarding-school of a certain Weidenhammer; our Russian master, who was also our class supervisor, used to read it to us during breaks. With what devouring attention did we listen to the adventures of Kirsh, Miloslavsky's servant, of Alexey, of the highwayman Omlyasha! But—strange to say—while *Yury Miloslavsky* seemed to me the height of perfection, I regarded its author, M. N. Zagoskin, with utter indifference. This fact can be easily explained; the impression produced by Mikhail Zagoskin, far from increasing the feelings of worship and enthusiasm which his novel aroused in me, could only decrease them. There was nothing majestic about Zagoskin, nothing spell-binding, nothing that impresses itself on a youthful imagination; to tell the truth, he was even rather comical, and his rare good nature could hardly be appreciated by me for its true worth: *that* quality has no importance whatever in the eyes of thoughtless youth. The very figure of Zagoskin, the strange shape of his head, which looked almost as though it were flattened, his square face, protruding eyes under everlasting spectacles, his shortsighted and obtuse look, the extraordinary movements of his eyebrows, lips and nose when he looked surprised or just talked, his sudden exclamations, flourishes of hands, the deep cleft which divided his short chin in two—everything about him seemed eccentric, clumsy and ludicrous to me. He had, besides, three other rather comic weaknesses: he fancied himself extraordinarily strong; [1] he was convinced that no woman could resist him, and, finally (and that was particularly surprising in a rabid patriot like him) he had an unfortunate weakness for the French language, which he mangled mercilessly, constantly mixing up the singular and the plural and the genders, so much so that we nicknamed him *Monsieur l'article* in our house. For all that, it was impossible not to like Zagoskin for his golden heart and for the artless candour which strikes one in his works.

My last meeting with him was very sad. I called on him many years later in Moscow, shortly before his death. He no longer left his study and kept complaining of the constant aches and pains in all his limbs. He did not grow thin, but a deathly pallor covered his still full cheeks, making him look more cheerless than ever. He still kept raising his eyebrows and goggling at people; but the unintentional comicality of these mannerisms only deep-

---

[1] The legend of his strength even spread abroad. At a public meeting in Germany I heard to my great astonishment a ballad which described the arrival in the capital city of Muscovy of a strong man Rappo who, at one of his public performances, challenged all sorts of people and invariably defeated them; suddenly, one spectator, unable to bear the humiliation of his fellow-countrymen, rose from his seat—it was *der russische Dichter: stehet auf der Zagoskin!* (the accent on *kin.*) He wrestled with Rappo, and having defeated him, withdrew modestly and with dignity.

ened the feeling of pity aroused by the poor author's whole figure, which was clearly falling into decay before one's eyes. I spoke to him about his literary work, told him that in the Petersburg circles his literary merits were once more appreciated. I referred to the importance of *Yury Miloslavsky* as a folk tale. . . . Zagoskin's face brightened. "Thank you, thank you," he said to me, "and I thought that I had been forgotten, that our younger generation had trampled me into the mud and placed a huge tree-trunk on top. (Zagoskin did not speak French with me, and in Russian he liked to use forceful expressions.) Thank you," he repeated, pressing my hand not without agitation and feeling, as though I were responsible for the fact that he had not been forgotten.

I remember being at the time overwhelmed by rather bitter thoughts about literary fame. Inwardly I almost reproached Zagoskin with cowardice. "What is he so pleased about?" I thought. But, then, why should he not have been pleased? He heard from me that he was not altogether dead—and what can be more bitter than death? A literary celebrity may perhaps live so long that he will not experience even that trivial pleasure. A period of senseless eulogies will be followed by a period of no less senseless abuse and then—silent oblivion. . . . And who of us can claim the right not to be forgotten, the right to burden the memory of posterity with his name, for has not posterity its own needs, its own worries, its own aspirations?

But I am glad all the same to have given the excellent Zagoskin even that bit of ephemeral pleasure before the end of his life.

IV

A TRIP TO ALBANO AND FRASCATI

———◆———

Reminiscences of A. A. Ivanov

ON ONE OF THE MOST BEAUTIFUL DAYS of October 1857, an old hackney coach, its windows rattling quietly, rolled along the road from Rome to Albano.

On the box sat the driver with a morose face and huge side whiskers, by all signs a thorough-going coward and sensualist. In the carriage sat three Russian *forestieri:* the late painter Ivanov, V. P. Botkin [1] and myself. However, only Botkin and I could claim to be *"forestieri."* Ivanov, or, as he was known from the inn Falcone to the Café Greco, *il Signor Alessandro,* had by his dress and habits long become a native Roman.

It was a really marvellous day, a day that no pen or brush could possibly do justice to; it is a well-known fact that after Claude Lorraine no landscape painter could do full justice to the Roman landscape; the writers, too, found themselves incompetent for that task (one has only to recall Gogol's *Rome* and other works). I shall therefore merely say that the air was transparent and gentle, the sun shone dazzlingly but did not burn, a soft

---

[1] He, too, is dead now.

breeze blew through the open windows of our carriage, caressing our no longer youthful faces—and we drove along, surrounded by a sort of festive autumnal radiance, and with a festive and also, I suppose, autumnal feeling in our hearts.

The day before we had paid a visit to the Vatican with Ivanov. He was in wonderful form, neither shy nor oversensitive, and talked readily and a great deal. He told us about the different schools of Italian painting, of which he had made a most thorough and conscientious study; all his opinions were sound and full of respect for "the old masters." He worshipped Rafael. It is a well-known fact that at one time Ivanov was under the powerful influence of Overbeck, who had elucidated Rafael to him; but when Overbeck went further to Peruggino and his predecessors, Ivanov refused to follow him; Russian common-sense stopped him on the threshold of the artificial, ascetic, and symbolic world into which the German painter had sunk; for that reason the idealist Ivanov was always regarded by Overbeck as a crude realist. Ivanov greatly deplored the modern movement among our artists (one of them called Rafael in my presence an *ungifted* painter), and told us something about Bryulov and Gogol, to whom he always referred by his name and patronymic as Nikolai Vassilyevich. From his respectful but cautious remarks about our great writer we could conclude that he had made a thorough study of him. Gogol did not understand Ivanov at all, though he wrote in most flattering terms of his "Epiphany"; one must not forget that Gogol went into raptures over Bryulov's picture "The Last Days of Pompeii"; and to admire those two pictures at one and the same time means not to understand the art of painting. Ivanov recalled with particular sympathy the terrible impression the universal condemnation of his *Selected Passages from the Correspondence with my Friends* made on Gogol; of this and of the events of 1848 Ivanov spoke with a shudder. Perhaps he was wondering whether his picture, too, would be as violently abused;

and in the principles which all but triumphed in 1848 he for some reason saw the end and destruction of every kind of art.

Our conversation turned also on his picture. We had not yet seen it at the time, and he meant to open his studio for about three days, which he did a few weeks later. He kept saying that it was far from finished, and he told us a few interesting facts of the journey he had made to Germany to meet a certain famous German scholar [David Friedrich Strauss, the author of a life of Christ] whose views were identical with those he, Ivanov, wished to express in his picture. He intended to invite that scholar to Rome so that he should decide whether or not the picture conformed to those views.

According to Ivanov, Strauss probably took him for a madman, particularly as their conversation was conducted by Strauss in Latin and by Ivanov in Italian, for Ivanov knew no German; it must be explained, besides, that Ivanov had a very hazy notion of Latin and Strauss of Italian. I can still vividly remember Ivanov's naive, almost touching, astonishment when Botkin and I began to explain to him that even if Strauss had agreed to come to Rome or, to put it more exactly, even if he had been allowed to go there, he would not have been able to decide whether or not Ivanov had attained his object and expressed the doctor's ideas, for to do that one had to possess a special understanding of the art of painting, which Strauss could hardly be said to possess. He would quite likely have failed to recognize the expression of his own views in paint or, on the other hand, have recognized them where they had never been expressed.

"I see, I see," Ivanov kept repeating, grinning goodnaturedly, lisping and blinking. "This is very interesting [his favourite expression]. This has never occurred to me. . . ."

His long isolation from people, his life of complete seclusion, his constant concentration on one and the same idea, left a special mark on Ivanov; there was something mystical and childish about him, something wise and amusing at one and the same time, something pure, sincere, and secretive, even cunning. At the first glance one got the impression that his whole being seemed permeated by a sort of mistrust, by a sort of stern and sometimes ingratiating timidity; but when he got used to us—and that happened quite soon—his gentle soul seemed to open up. He would suddenly burst out laughing at the most ordinary joke, he would be astonished and bereft of speech by the most commonplace statement, he would be frightened a little by a somewhat sharply expressed opinion (I remember him once even giving a jump when he heard one of us declare that a certain Russian lady writer was a fool), and, suddenly, he would give utterance to a remark that was full of truth and mature thought, a remark revealing that quite an uncommon intelligence had been hard at work. Unfortunately, the education he had received was very superficial, which, indeed, is the case with the majority of our artists.

This shortcoming he tried to make good by assiduous work. He was very familiar with the ancient world, he had made a thorough study of the Assyrian antiquities (he wanted them for his future paintings); the Bible, and especially the Gospels, he knew almost by heart. He liked to listen rather than to speak, and in spite of that, it was a real pleasure to talk to him: so much conscientious and honest desire for truth was there in him. He was always the first to arrive at our parties and, as soon as a discussion arose, he followed the development of everyone's trend of thought with intense and patient attention. Among the Russians who were resident in Rome at the time was an excellent and far from stupid fellow, whose ideas, however, were not always thought out or well expressed; Ivanov was the last to give him up as hopeless. He was not interested either in literature or in politics; he was only interested in problems of art, morals and philosophy. Once someone brought him a sketch-book of rather good caricatures. Ivanov spent a long time examining them and, then, raising his head, said: "Christ never laughed." He was everywhere received with pleasure; one look at his face with its broad white forehead, kind, tired eyes, smooth, child-like cheeks, pointed nose and droll but pleasant mouth—aroused in everyone's heart an involuntary feeling of sympathy and affection. He was short, thick-set, broad-shouldered; his whole figure, from his small pointed beard to his chubby little hands with stubby fingers and his nimble legs with thick calves exhaled the breath of Russia, and even the way he walked was typically Russian. He was not vain, but he had a high opinion of his work: it was not for nothing that he put all his hopes and strength into it.

Our driver stopped at a bad hostelry to rest his horses and to have a drink of "folietta." We, too, got out and ordered some bread and cheese. The cheese was bad and the bread half-baked and sour, but we ate our meagre lunch with that joyous and bright feeling which is an intrinsic part of the beauty which seems to fill the Roman air at any time, but especially in the golden days of autumn. The innkeeper's daughter, a swarthy, black-eyed, barefooted little girl in a parti-colored skirt, looked calmly and even proudly at us from the stone threshold of *her* house, and her father, a good-looking man of about forty, in a worn velvet coat thrown over one shoulder, smiled majestically, flashing with the whites of his enormous black eyes, as he sat in the semi-darkness of his inn at a cheap table and listened condescendingly to our driver's complaints about the bad times, the dearth of foreigners, and so on. Ivanov, who was suddenly overwhelmed by a feeling of uneasy impatience, did not let him go on too long. We set off again.

Our conversation turned on the Vatican once more.

"We shall have to go there again tomorrow," observed Botkin to Ivanov, "and from there we'd like you to come and have dinner with us as you did yesterday."

Botkin and I dined every day at the Hotel d'Angleterre in the public dining-room at a general table.

"Dinner?" exclaimed Ivanov, turning pale suddenly. "Dinner?" he repeated. "No, thank you very much. It's a wonder I survived it yesterday."

We thought that he was hinting in jest at his eating too much at dinner the day before (he generally ate a lot and greedily), and tried to persuade him to change his mind.

"No, no," he kept saying, growing paler and paler and more and more excited. "I won't go. They'll poison me there."

"Poison you?"

"Yes, poison. Give me poison."

Ivanov's face assumed a strange expression, his eyes roved.

Botkin and I exchanged glances; we could not suppress a sudden feeling of horror.

"What are you saying, my dear Alexander Andreyich? How can they give you poison at the general table? They'd have to poison the whole dish. And who wants to murder you?"

"Well, there are such people who—who want my life. As for poisoning the whole dish, all he has to do is to put some poison —on my plate. . . . !"

"Who is—he?"

"Why, the waiter."

"The waiter?"

"Yes, he's been bribed. You don't know the Italians. They're terrible people, and they're very clever at this sort of thing. All he has to do is to take a pinch of poison out of the lapel of his frock-coat and just throw it in and—no one will be the wiser! They always used to poison me in whatever town I happened to be. There is only one honest waiter in Rome—on the ground floor in Falcone. I can still trust him."

I was about to object, but Botkin nudged me secretly with his knee.

"Well," said Botkin, "in that case what I propose is that you should come and have dinner with us tomorrow and every time we help ourselves to some food, we shall exchange plates with you."

Ivanov accepted this proposal, the pallor disappeared from his face, his lips ceased trembling and he looked reassured. Later we found out that after every good dinner he rushed home to take some emetic and drink milk.

Poor recluse! He paid dearly for his twenty years of seclusion.

Half an hour later we were in Albano. Ivanov became animated suddenly and rushed off to hire horses to take us to Frascati. Three badly saddled ancient jades were brought to us from different lanes. After haggling a long time with their owners, during which I had the occasion to marvel at Ivanov's iron perseverance, we at last agreed on the price, mounted our Rosinantes and set off in the direction of Frascati. We climbed up a mountain road along the so-called "gallery," lined by a whole row of splendid evergreen oak-trees. Each of these trees was several hundred years old, and Claude Lorraine and Poussin had admired their classic contours, in which strength and beauty mingled as in no other tree known to me. These oak-trees and the umbrella-like stone-pines, cypresses and olive trees go marvellously well together; they form part of that wonderfully harmonious chord which is such a predominant feature of the environs of Rome. Circular Albany Lake showed blue beneath us and a light mist rose over it, and around us, along the slopes of the mountains and along the valleys, near and far, divine colours spread before our eyes on a magically transparent canvas. . . . But I have promised not to indulge in descriptions. Mounting higher and higher, riding through genial, bright, yes—bright woodlands, on emerald green, summer-like, grass, we reached at last the little town of Rocca di Papa, clinging like a bird's nest to the top of a rock.

We dismounted in a small square opposite a church, built in

Lombard style with little flourishes on its façade, and sat down for a moment beside a well of silvery water, with the Papal crest and a Latin inscription on a half-broken column. Narrow streets, winding and steep like staircases, ran in every direction from the square. Ragged boys at once came running to have a look at us and to receive their customary tribute, a few "paoli"; women, mostly old women, poked their heads out of some windows; sounds of unmistakably guttural voices could be heard; in the distance there appeared in the middle of a narrow alleyway a beautiful tall and slender girl in an Albano costume and, after standing still picturesquely in the almost black shadow, falling from the stone walls, she turned round quietly and disappeared. A heavily laden donkey ambled past with a creaking of baskets, advancing carefully, its little hoofs clip-clopping on the big cobbles of the roadway; behind it marched importantly, just as if he were some consul, a stern-looking man in a blue, soiled cloak, hiding the lower part of his face, and a tall hat, full of holes, which I suppose, he never took off to anyone. Ivanov took a crust of bread out of his pocket, squatted down on the edge of the well and began to eat it, holding the reins of his horse in one hand and from time to time dipping the bread in the cold water. Every trace of worry disappeared from his face; it was radiant with the joy of peaceful artistic feelings; at that moment he wanted nothing in the world, and he seemed himself to be a worthy subject for an artist on that little square of the little town which was such a favourite spot for painters, before that dark church, behind which the lilac-grey mountains rose so imponderously and so high into the radiantly blue abyss of the sky.

Poor Ivanov! He should have lived for many, many years, and yet death was already lying in wait for him.

We mounted our horses again and rode away, this time all the way down the mountain. Ivanov became talkative. He told us all sorts of amusing Roman stories and laughed at them himself with a child-like laughter. On the road, walking towards us, we met a handsome young fellow of twenty-two, his hands tied behind him, accompanied by two mounted gendarmes.

"What has he done?" Ivanov asked one of them.

"Stabbed someone—*ha dato una coltellata,*" the gendarme replied unconcernedly.

I looked at the young fellow: he smiled, showing his large, white teeth, and nodded amicably to me.

A peasant woman, who was standing nearby behind a low wall, on which her goat had clambered, also smiled, showing us the same kind of dazzlingly white teeth. She looked at the prisoner, then at us, and smiled again.

"A happy people," observed Ivanov.

We arrived in Frascati rather late. The last train was due to leave in three quarters of an hour. We had just time to inspect the nearest villa with a beautiful garden. I forget what it was called. A few days before our trip to Albano, Ivanov and I went to the Tivoli and paid a visit to the Villa d'Este. We could not admire enough this, to my mind, most remarkable of all the huge, monumental, magnificent villas, not one of those which had inspired Tyutchev's lovely poem, but one of those which conjures up in your imagination the cardinals and the princes of the times of the Medici and the Farnese, brings back to your mind the poems of Ariosto and the Decameron, the paintings of Paolo Veronese with their splendour, their velvets and silks, with the strings of pearls on the necks of beautiful fair-haired women listening absently to the sounds of theorbos and flutes, with peacocks and dwarves, marble statues, Olympian gods and goddesses on gilt ceilings, grottoes, goat-legged satyrs and fountains. In Frascati we rushed hurriedly through the villa, looked at it from below, and walked down the cascading terraces of its artificial gardens. I remember we were particularly struck by the wonderful sunset we saw there. It poured with an unbearably intense glow, a blazing torrent of blood-red gold, through the vast square of a marble window at the end of a long, high corridor with light columns which appeared to be flying upwards.

For some time afterwards it seemed to me as though the hot reflection of that conflagration still lingered on my own face and on the faces of my companions.

In the train our compartment was shared by a young honeymoon couple, and once more we caught a glimpse of the heavy, pitch-black hair, of the sparkling eyes and teeth—all those features which, a little large and coarse in close proximity, bore the unmistakable stamp of grandeur, simplicity and a kind of wild grace. . . .

"I must show you Marianne [a famous model]," Ivanov observed suddenly in an undertone. . . .

He showed us her afterwards.

The eternal city soon received us in her bosom. We walked along the already darkened streets. Ivanov saw us off to the Piazza di Spagna, and we parted, carrying away in our minds the impression of a happily spent day.

About eight months later, on neither a hot nor a cold, but rather dull July day, I met Ivanov in the square of the Winter Palace in Petersburg, amid the constantly whirling clouds of clammy, dirty dust, which is one of the appurtenances of our northern capital. He returned my greeting with a worried look; he had just left the Hermitage; the sea-breeze lifted the skirts of his formal frock-coat; he screwed up his eyes and held on to his hat with two fingers; his picture was already in Petersburg and was beginning to stir up all sorts of harmful rumours. A few days later I left for the country and a fortnight later the news of his death reached me. . . . I recalled the almost superstitious horror with which he always referred to Petersburg and his impending journey there.

It is not my intention now to embark on a detailed analysis of the merits and demerits of Ivanov's famous picture; others have done it and, no doubt, will go on doing it much better than I. I merely want to say a few words about what I think of Ivanov's talent and what I understand its importance to be. The late A. S. Khomyakov published an article in *Russian Conversation,* written, as everything else that appeared under his name, charmingly and with conviction, but with which, I am afraid, I cannot agree. In his view, Ivanov was a pure and powerful artist, filled with religious feeling, which stemmed directly from Russian national life. Appearing on the scene at a time of unbelief and a general decline of art, he had drawn from the depth of his meek and deeply religious heart a new embodiment of Christian dogmas and, by doing so, laid the foundations of national Russian painting and was responsible for the regeneration of art in general. Such a view appears to be both gratifying and logically correct; but, unfortunately, it can hardly be said to be true. That Ivanov remained a Russian in all his aims and aspirations cannot be denied; but he was a Russian of his, that is to say, of our transitory period. Like all of us, he did not enter the promised land, either; he saw it from a distance, he had a presentiment of it, but he died without reaching its borders. He did not belong to the harmonious and original creative painters (we have not got them yet in Russia); his very talent, his talent as a painter, was rather weak and precarious, a fact that becomes clear to anyone who will take the trouble to look at his work attentively and without prejudice. There is everything in it: amazing hard work, an honest aspiration towards an ideal, careful thought—in a word, everything except the one thing that matters, namely creative power and free inspiration. Over Ivanov, too, the fatal law of the disintegration of the separate parts of which true talent is composed exercised its power, the law that still hangs heavy on Russian art. Had he had Bryulov's talent or had Bryulov had the soul and heart of Ivanov, what wonders should we not be witnessing! But what happened was that one of them could express everything he wanted, but had nothing to say, and the other could have said many things, but was tongue-tied. One painted flamboyant pictures with striking effects but without poetry and without any idea in it, and the other tried to depict a deeply felt, new and vital idea, but his execution was uneven, approximate, lacking in vitality. One, if I may put it that way, gave us a truthful representation of falsehood and the other gave us a false, that is, a weak and incorrect representation of truth. It is said that Ivanov copied the head of Apollo Belvedere and the head of the Byzantine Christ he had discovered in Palermo over thirty times and, gradually bringing them together, at last succeeded in painting his John the Baptist. . . . But true artists do not create that way! Still, if we are to choose between these two movements, it is better, a thousand times better, to follow Ivanov as long as a real leader has not yet appeared. An idea is endowed by special powers, it is felt and shines through a work of art even if the execution is unsatisfactory, especially if, like Ivanov, a man serves it selflessly and self-sacrificingly. There is no sacrifice in the world that has been in vain. Some people may say that Ivanov should not have undertaken something that was beyond his strength; they could point to the first sketches of his picture which are not so profound, but the execution of which is more natural and more alive. There is, of course, something abnormal, something tragic even, in the existence of this aspiration for the unattainable, but if this aspiration comes from a pure source, it can be of enormous benefit, even though it is not altogether successful, or even though it had failed to attain its end. A young man who finds himself under the influence of Bryulov is most likely by that very fact to be ruined as an artist (how many examples of that have we not seen!); on the other hand, a young man, who has understood and has grown to love the inner light that can be perceived in Ivanov's works, can develop and go far, if only nature has not denied him talent. Ivanov, the hard-working martyr, died half-way to his goal, enfeebled and unappreciated, but the path he followed led to truth, and his future heir, that "still unknown chosen one," will follow his path, the path he was the first to pave.

I can foresee another objection. People may say: why study Ivanov, an imperfect and obscure master, when there are great, indubitable, triumphant models? Why a hint when we can have a firmly expressed opinion? But, to begin with, Ivanov, as an original, typical Russian, is nearer and speaks more powerfully to young Russian hearts: he is dearer and more comprehensible to them; secondly, his great merit, his merit as an idealist and thinker, consists chiefly in the fact that he points out the models to us, leads us to them, awakens us, stirs us; he himself may not satisfy, but he does not suffer cheap satisfaction in others; in the fact that he forces his pupils to set themselves high and difficult tasks, and not to be satisfied with the masterly execution of some *raccourcis* and other tricks of painting technique which the followers of Bryulov are so fond of. From this point of view, even Ivanov's faults are more useful than many beautifully executed commonplaces.

This is not the place to enter into an analysis of what Ivanov's idea actually was; but I cannot finish my article without expressing the wish that his album of sketches from the life of Christ should be published. The album is now in the hands of his brother. In those remarkable drawings the fundamental idea that guided Ivanov is set out more clearly; in them he was not constrained by his brush, which he did not entirely master, particularly towards the end of his life when his eyes, strained by unbroken, strenuous work, began to fail him. In his picture, too, the figure of Christ is more successful than the others; it is particularly significant in the sketch owned by V. P. Botkin. Photographs of this sketch would be a real present to all the admirers of Alexander Ivanov, the kind, honest, unhappy Russian artist.

1861.

V

APROPOS OF *FATHERS AND SONS*

———————

I WAS SEA-BATHING AT VENTNOR, a small town on the Isle of Wight —it was in August, 1860—when the first idea occurred to me of *Fathers and Sons,* the novel which deprived me, forever I believe, of the good opinion of the Russian younger generation. I have heard it said and read it in critical articles not once but many times that in my works I always "started with an idea" or "developed an idea." Some people praised me for it, others, on the contrary, censured me; for my part, I must confess that I never attempted to "create a character" unless I had for my departing point not an idea but a living person to whom the appropriate elements were later on gradually attached and added. Not possessing a great amount of free inventive powers, I always felt the need of some firm ground on which I could plant my feet. The same thing happened with *Fathers and Sons;* at the basis of its chief character, Bazarov, lay the personality of a young provincial doctor I had been greatly struck by. (He died shortly before 1860.) In that remarkable man I could watch the embodiment of that principle which had scarcely come to life but was just beginning to stir at the time, the principle which later received the name of nihilism. Though very powerful, the impression that man left on

193

me was still rather vague. At first I could not quite make him out myself, and I kept observing and listening intently to everything around me, as though wishing to check the truth of my own impressions. I was worried by the following fact: not in one work of our literature did I ever find as much as a hint at what I seemed to see everywhere; I could not help wondering whether I was not chasing after a phantom. On the Isle of Wight, I remember, there lived with me at the time a Russian who was endowed with excellent taste and a remarkable "nose" for everything which the late Apollon Grigoryev called "the ideas" of an epoch. I told him what I was thinking of and what interested me so much and was astonished to hear the following remark: "Haven't you created such a character already in—Rudin?" I said nothing. Rudin and Bazarov—one and the same character!

Those words produced such an effect on me that for several weeks I tried not to think of the work I had in mind. However, on my return to Paris I sat down to it again—the *plot* gradually matured in my head; in the course of the winter I wrote the first chapters, but I finished the novel in Russia, on my estate, in July [1861]. In the autumn I read it to a few friends, revised something, added something, and in March, 1862, *Fathers and Sons* was published in *The Russian Herald.*

I shall not enlarge on the impression this novel has created. I shall merely say that when I returned to Petersburg, on the very day of the notorious fires in the Apraksin Palace, the word "nihilist" had been caught up by thousands of people, and the first exclamation that escaped from the lips of the first acquaintance I met on Nevsky Avenue was: "Look what *your* nihilists are doing! They are setting Petersburg on fire!" My impressions at that time, though different in kind, were equally painful. I became conscious of a coldness bordering on indignation among many friends whose ideas I shared; I received congratulations, and almost kisses, from people belonging to a camp I loathed, from enemies. It embarrassed and—grieved me. But my conscience was clear; I knew very well that my attitude towards the character I had created was honest and that far from being prejudiced against him, I even sympathised with him.[1] I have too great a respect for the vocation of an artist, a writer, to act against my conscience in such a matter. The word "respect" is hardly the right one here; I simply could not, and knew not how to, work otherwise; and, after all, there was no reason why I should do that. My critics described my novel as a "lampoon" and spoke of my "exasperated" and "wounded" vanity; but why should I write a lampoon on Dobrolyubov, whom I had hardly met, but whom I thought highly of as a man and as a talented writer? However little I might think of my own talent as a writer, I always have been, and still am, of the opinion that the writing of a lampoon, a "squib," is unworthy of it. As for my wounded vanity, all I can say is that Dobrolyubov's article on my last work before *Fathers and Sons—On the Eve* (and he was quite rightly considered as the mouthpiece of public opinion)—that that article, published in 1861, is full of the warmest and—honestly speaking—the most undeserved eulogies. But the critics had to present me as an offended lampoonist: *leur siège était fait,* and even this year I could read in Supplement No. 1 to *Cosmos* (page 96) the following lines: "At last, *everyone knows* that the pedestal on which Turgenev stood has been destroyed chiefly by Dobrolyubov. . . ." and further on (page 98) they speak of my "feeling of bitterness," which the critic, however, "understands and—perhaps even forgives."

---

[1] I should like to quote the following extract from my diary: "30 July, Sunday. An hour and a half ago I finished my novel at last. . . . I don't know whether it will be successful. *The Contemporary* will probably treat me with contempt for my Bazarov and . . . will not believe that while writing my novel I felt an involuntary attachment to him."

The critics, generally speaking, have not got quite the right idea of what is taking place in the mind of an author or of what exactly his joys and sorrows, his aims, successess and failures are. They do not, for instance, even suspect the pleasure which Gogol mentions and which consists of castigating oneself and one's faults in the imaginary characters one depicts; they are quite sure that all an author does is to "develop his ideas"; they refuse to believe that to reproduce truth and the reality of life correctly and powerfully is the greatest happiness for an author, even if this truth does not coincide with his own sympathies. Let me illustrate my meaning by a small example. I am an inveterate and incorrigible Westerner. I have never concealed it and I am not concealing it now. And yet in spite of that it has given me great pleasure to show up in the person of Panshin (in *A House of Gentlefolk*) all the common and vulgar sides of the Westerners; I made the Slavophil Lavretsky "crush him utterly." Why did I do it, I who consider the Slavophil doctrine false and futile? Because *in the given case life, according to my ideas, happened to be like that,* and what I wanted above all was to be sincere and truthful. In depicting Bazarov's personality, I excluded everything artistic from the range of his sympathies, I made him express himself in harsh and unceremonious tones, not out of an absurd desire to insult the younger generation (! ! !),[1] but simply as a result of my observations of my acquaintance, Dr. D., and people like him. "Life happened to be *like that,*" my experience told me once more, perhaps mistakenly, but, I repeat, not dishonestly. There was no need for me to be too clever about it; I just had to depict his character *like that.* My personal predilec-

---

[1] Among the multitude of proofs of my "spite against our youth" one critic cited the fact that I made Bazarov lose his game of cards to Father Alexey. "He simply doesn't know," the critic observed, "how most to hurt and humiliate him! He can't even play cards!" There can be no doubt that if I had made Bazarov win his game, the same critic would have exclaimed, "Isn't it abundantly clear? The author wants to suggest that Bazarov is a cardsharper!"

tions had nothing to do with it. But I expect many of my readers will be surprised if I tell them that with the exception of Bazarov's views on art, I share almost all his convictions. And I am assured that I am on the side of the "Fathers"—I, who in the person of Pavel Kirsanov have even "sinned" against artistic truth and gone too far, to the point of caricaturing his faults and making him look ridiculous! [1]

The cause of all the misunderstandings, the whole, so to speak "trouble," arose from the fact that the Bazarov type created by me has not yet had time to go through the gradual phases through which literary types usually go. Unlike Onegin and Pechorin, he had not been through a period of idealisation and sympathetic, starry-eyed adoration. At the very moment the *new* man—Bazarov —appeared, the author took up a critical, objective attitude towards him. That confused many people and—who knows?—that was, if not a mistake, an injustice. The Bazarov type had at

---

[1] Foreigners cannot understand the cruel accusations made against me for my Bazarov. *Fathers and Sons* has been translated several times into German. This is what one critic writes in analysing the last translation published in Riga (*Vossische Zeitung, Donnerstag, d. 10 Juni, zweite Beilage, Seite 3:* "Es bleibt für den unbefangenen . . . Leser schlechthin unbegreiflich, wie sich gerade die radicale Jugend Russlands über diesen geistigen Vertreter ihrer Richtung (Bazaroff), ihrer Ueberzeugungen und Bestrebungen, wie ihn T. zeichnete, in eine Wuth hinein erhitzen konnte, die sie den Dichter gleichsam in die Acht erklären und mit jeder Schmähung überhaüfen liess. Man sollte denken, jeder moderne Radicale könne nur mit froher Genungthuung in einer so stolzen Gestalt, von solcher Wucht des Charakters, solcher gründlichen Freiheit von allem Kleinlichen, Trivialen, Faulen, Schlaffen und Lügenhaften, sein und seiner Parteigenossen typisches Portrait dargestellt sehn."*
That is: "To an unprejudiced . . . reader it is utterly incomprehensible how radical Russian youth could work itself into such a fury over the spiritual representative of their movement (Bazarov), their convictions and their aspirations, as Turgenev depicted him, and at the same time send the author to Coventry and hold him up to execration. One might have supposed that every modern radical would be only too glad to recognise himself and his comrades in such a proud personality, endowed with such a strength of character, such utter freedom from everything that is trivial, vulgar and false."

least as much right to be idealized as the literary types that preceded it. I have just said that the author's attitude towards the character he had created confused the reader: the reader always feels ill at ease, he is easily bewildered and even aggrieved if an author treats his imaginary character like a living person, that is to say, if he sees and displays his good as well as his bad sides, and, above all, if he does not show unmistakable signs of sympathy or antipathy for his own child. The reader feels like getting angry: he is asked not to follow a well-beaten path, but to tread his own path. "Why should I take the trouble," he can't help thinking. "Books exist for entertainment and not for racking one's brains. And, besides, would it have been too much to ask the author to tell me what to think of such and such a character or what he thinks of him himself?" But it is even worse if the author's attitude towards that character is itself rather vague and undefined, if the author himself does not know whether or not he loves the character he has created (as it happened to me in my attitude towards Bazarov, for "the involuntary attraction" I mentioned in my diary is not love). The reader is ready to ascribe to the author all sorts of non-existent sympathies or antipathies, provided he can escape from the feeling of unpleasant "vagueness."

"Neither fathers nor sons," said a witty lady to me after reading my book, "that should be the real title of your novel and—you are yourself a nihilist." A similar view was expressed with even greater force on the publication of *Smoke*. I am afraid I do not feel like raising objections: perhaps, that lady was right. In the business of fiction writing everyone (I am judging by myself) does what he can and not what he wants, and—as much as he can. I suppose that a work of fiction has to be judged *en gros* and while insisting on conscientiousness on the part of the author, the other *sides* of his activity must be regarded, I would not say, with indifference, but with calm. And, much as I should like to please my critics, I cannot plead guilty to any absence of conscientiousness on my part.

I have a very curious collection of letters and other documents in connection with *Fathers and Sons*. It is rather interesting to compare them. While some of my correspondents accuse me of insulting the younger generation, of being behind the times and a reactionary, and inform me that they "are burning my photographs with a contemptuous laugh," others, on the contrary, reproach me with pandering to the same younger generation. "You are crawling at the feet of Bazarov!" one correspondent exclaims. "You are just pretending to condemn him; in effect, you are fawning upon him and waiting as a favour for one casual smile from him!" One critic, I remember, addressing me directly in strong and eloquent words, depicted Mr. Katkov and me as two conspirators who in the peaceful atmosphere of my secluded study, are hatching our despicable plot, our libellous attack, against the young Russian forces. . . . It made an effective picture! Actually, that is how this *plot* came about. When Mr. Katkov received my manuscript of *Fathers and Sons*, of whose contents he had not even a rough idea, he was utterly bewildered.[1] The Bazarov type seemed to him "almost an apotheosis of *The Con-*

---

[1] I hope Mr. Katkov will not be angry with me for quoting a few passages from a letter to wrote to me at the time. "If," he wrote, "you have not actually apotheosized Bazarov, I can't help feeling that he has found himself by some sort of accident on a very high pedestal. He really does tower above all those who surround him. Compared to him, everything is either rubbish, or weak and immature. Was that the impression one ought to have got? One can feel that in his novel the author wanted to characterize a principle for which he has little sympathy, but that he seems to hesitate in the choice of his tone and has unconsciously fallen under its spell. One cannot help feeling that there is something forced in the author's attitude towards the hero of his novel, a sort of awkwardness and stiffness. The author seems to be abashed in his presence, he seems not so much to dislike him as to be afraid of him!" Mr. Katkov goes on to express his regrets that I did not let Mrs. Odintsov treat Bazarov ironically, and so on—all in the same vein! It is clear, therefore, that one of the conspirators was not altogether satisfied with the other's work.

temporary Review," and I should not have been surprised if he had refused to publish my novel in his journal. *"Et voilà comme on écrit l'histoire!"* one could have exclaimed, but—is it permissible to give such a high-sounding name to such small matters?

On the other hand, I quite understand the reasons for the anger aroused by my book among the members of a certain party. They are not entirely groundless and I accept—without false humility—part of the reproaches levelled against me. The word "nihilist" I had used in my novel was taken advantage of by a great many people who were only waiting for an excuse, a pretext, to put a stop to the movement which had taken possession of Russian society. But I never used that word as a pejorative term or with any offensive aim, but as an exact and appropriate expression of a fact, an historic fact, that had made its appearance among us; it was transformed into a means of denunciation, unhesitating condemnation and almost a brand of infamy. Certain unfortunate events that occurred at that time increased the suspicions that were just beginning to arise and seemed to confirm the widespread misgivings and justified the worries and efforts of the "saviours of our motherland," for in Russia such "saviours of the motherland" had made their appearance just then. The tide of public opinion, which is still so indeterminate in our country, turned back. . . . But a shadow fell over my name. I do not deceive myself; I know that that shadow will not disappear. But why did not others—people before whom I feel so deeply my own insignificance—utter the great words: *Périssent nos noms, pourvu que la chose publique soit sauvée* . . . i.e. may our names perish so long as the general cause is saved! Following them, I too can console myself with the thought that my book has been of some benefit. This thought compensates me for the unpleasantness of undeserved reproaches. And, indeed, what does it matter? Who twenty or thirty years hence will remember all these storms in a teacup? Or my name—with or without a shadow over it.

But enough about myself, and besides it is time to finish these fragmentary reminiscences which, I am afraid, will hardly satisfy the reader. I just want to say a few parting words to my young contemporaries, my colleagues who enter upon the slippery career of literature. I have already said once and I am ready to repeat that I am not blinded about my position. My twenty-five-year-old "service to the Muses" has drawn to a close amid the growing coldness of the public, and I cannot think of any reason why it should grow warmer once more. New times have come and new men are needed; literary veterans, like the military ones, are almost always invalids, and blessed are those who know how to retire at the right time! I do not intend to pronounce my farewell words in preceptorial tones, to which, incidentally, I have no right whatever, but in the tone of an old friend who is listened to with half-condescending and half-impatient attention, provided he is not too longwinded. I shall do my best not to be that.

And so, my dear colleagues, it is to you that I am addressing myself.

Greif nur hinein ins volle Menschenleben!

I would like to say to you, quoting Goethe—

Ein jeder lebt's—nicht vielen ist's bekannt
Und wo ihr's packt—da ist's interessant!

[i.e. "put your hand right in (I am afraid I can't translate it any better), into the very depth of human life! Everyone lives by it, but few know it, and wherever you grasp it, there it is interesting!"] It is only talent that gives one the power for this "grasping," this "catching hold" of life, and one cannot acquire talent; but talent alone is not enough. What one needs is the constant communion with the environment one undertakes to reproduce; what one needs is truthfulness, a truthfulness that is inexorable in relation to one's own feelings; what one needs is freedom, absolute freedom of opinions and ideas, and, finally, what one needs is education, what one needs is knowledge! "Oh, we understand! We can see what you are driving at!" many will perhaps exclaim at this point. "Potugin's ideas! Ci-vi-li-za-tion, *prenez mon ours!* [It's an old, old story!]" Such exclamations do not surprise me, but they will not make me take back anything I have said. Learning is not only light, according to the Russian proverb, it is also freedom. Nothing makes a man so free as knowledge and nowhere is freedom so needed as in art, in poetry; it is not for nothing that even in official language arts are called "free." Can a man "grasp," "catch hold of" what surrounds him if he is all tied up inside? Pushkin felt this deeply; it is not for nothing that he said in his immortal sonnet, a sonnet every young writer ought to learn by heart and remember as a commandment—

> . . . . *by a free road*
> *Go, where your free mind may draw you.* . . .

The absence of such freedom, incidentally, explains why not a single one of the Slavophils, in spite of their undoubted gifts,[1] has ever created anything that is alive; not one of them knew how to remove—even for a moment—his rose-coloured spectacles. But the saddest example of the absence of true freedom, arising out of the absence of true knowledge, is provided by the last work of Count L. N. Tolstoy (*War and Peace*), which at the same time exceeds by its creative force and poetic gifts almost anything

---

[1] One cannot, of course, reproach Slavophils with ignorance or lack of education; but for the achievement of an artistic result one needs—to use a modern expression—the combined action of many *factors*. The factor the Slavophils lack is freedom; others lack education, still others talent, etc. etc.

that has appeared in our literature since 1840. No, without education and without freedom in the widest sense of the word—in relation to oneself and to one's preconceived ideas and systems, and, indeed, to one's people and one's history—a true artist is unthinkable; without that air, it is impossible to breathe.

As for the final result, the final appraisal of a so-called literary career—here, too, one has to remember the words of Goethe:

Sind's Rosen—nun sie werden blüh'n

—"if these are roses, they will bloom." There are no unacknowledged geniuses as there are no merits which survive their appointed time. "Sooner or later everyone finds his niche," the late Belinsky used to say. One has to be thankful if one has done one's bit at the right time and at the right hour. Only the few chosen ones are able to leave for posterity not only the content, but also the *form*, of their ideas and opinions, their personality, to which, generally speaking, the mob remains entirely indifferent. Ordinary individuals are condemned to total disappearance, to being swallowed up by the torrent; but they have increased its force, they have widened and deepened its bed—what more do they want?

I am laying down my pen. . . . One more last advice to young writers and one more last request. My friends, never try to justify yourselves (whatever libellous stories they may tell about you). Don't try to explain a misunderstanding, don't be anxious, yourselves, either to say or to hear "the last word." Carry on with your work—and in time everything will come right. At any rate, let a considerable period of time elapse first—and then look on all the old squabbles from an historical point of view, as I have tried to do now. Let the following example serve as a lesson to you: in the course of my literary career I have only once tried "to get the facts right." Namely, when *The Contemporary Review* began assuring its subscribers in its announcements that it had dispensed with my services because of the *unfitness* of my convictions (while, in fact, it was I who, in spite of their requests, would have nothing more to do with them—of which I have documentary proof), I could not resist announcing the real state of affairs in public and—of course, suffered a complete fiasco. The younger generation were more indignant with me than ever. "How did I dare to raise my hand against their idol! What does it matter if I was right? I should have kept silent!" I profited by this lesson; I wish you, too, should profit by it.

As for my request, it is as follows: guard our Russian tongue, our beautiful Russian tongue, that treasure, that trust handed down to you by your predecessors, headed again by Pushkin! Treat this powerful instrument with respect; it may work miracles in the hands of those who know how to use it! Even those who dislike "philosophic abstractions" and "poetic sentimentalities," even to practical people, for whom language is merely a means for expressing thoughts, a means to an end, just like an ordinary lever, even to them I will say: respect at least the laws of mechanics and extract every possible use from every thing! Or else, glancing over some dull, confused, feebly longwinded diatribe in a journal, the reader will perforce think that instead of a *lever* you are using some antedeluvian props—that you are going back to the infancy of mechanics itself. . . .

But, enough, or I shall become longwinded myself.

1868–69
Baden-Baden.

204

VI

THE MAN IN THE GREY SPECTACLES

From the Reminiscences of 1848

THE WHOLE OF THE WINTER of 1847–48 I spent in Paris. My lodgings were not far from the Palais-Royal and I used to go there almost every day to have a cup of coffee and read the newspapers. In those days the Palais-Royal was not the almost deserted place that it is today, though the days of its great and special glory had long passed, I mean the glory which made our veterans of 1814 and 1815 invariably ask anyone they met for the first time on his return from Paris: "Well, and how is our grand old Palais-Royal?" One day—it was at the beginning of February, 1848—I was sitting at one of the tables under the awning of the Café de la Rotonde. A tall, spare, sinewy man, whose black hair was going grey, and who wore a pair of rusty, steel spectacles with smoky-grey glasses on his aquiline nose, came out of the café, looked round, and, I suppose, seeing that all the seats under the awning were occupied, went up to me and asked my permission to sit down at my table. I did not mind, of course. The man in the grey glasses did not so much sit down as plump down into the chair, pushed his old top hat to the back of his head, and leaning his bony hands on his gnarled stick, ordered a cup of coffee, refusing the proffered newspaper with a scornful shrug. We exchanged a few insignificant phrases; I remember he muttered twice under his breath—"What a cursed—what a cursed time!" Then he hastily drained his coffee and was soon gone. But the impression left by him stuck in my mind for a long time.

He was most certainly a native of Southern France—of Provence or Gascony. His sun-tanned, wrinkled face, his sunken cheeks, toothless mouth and hollow, croaking voice, even his clothes, threadbare and soiled, as though not made for him—everything pointed to a restless, roving life. "He must have had a lot of experience," I thought to myself. "Knocked about the world. Been through the mill. It isn't only now that he is in such a 'mess'; he has probably spent all his life under some constraint and in servility. Where, then, did he get that apparent feeling of conscious superiority which could be seen in the expression of his face, in his every gesture, even in his shuffling, careless gait? Beggars, meek creatures, do not walk like that." I was particularly struck by his eyes—dark-brown with yellowish whites. He either opened them wide, looking straight before him with a dull, motionless stare, or narrowed them strangely, raising his beetling brows and glancing sideways over the rim of his glasses—and whenever he did that every feature of his face lit up with spiteful mockery. However, I did not think a lot of him that day: the expectation of the forthcoming banquet in aid of the reforms excited the whole of Paris—and I began reading the papers.

Next day I went again to have a cup of coffee in the Palais-Royal and I again met the man in the grey glasses. He was the first to greet me with a bow, as an old acquaintance. With a faint smile and no longer asking my permission, as though he felt that I would find a meeting with him agreeable, he sat down at my table, though none of the other tables was occupied, and at once began talking to me, without any ceremony and without looking in the least embarrassed.

A few moments passed. . . .

"You are a foreigner, aren't you? A Russian?" he asked suddenly, stirring his coffee slowly with his spoon.

"That I am a foreigner you could, I suppose, have guessed from my accent. But why do you think I am a Russian?"

"Why? You see, you said *pardon* just now. Like that—*pa-a-rdon,* drawing out the syllables. Only Russians draw the words out like that. However, I knew you were a Russian, anyway."

I was about to ask him to explain himself, but he started speaking again.

"You did well to come here just now. It's an interesting time for a tourist. You will see big things (*de grandes choses*)."

"What will I see?"

"Well, it's the beginning of February now. Before a month has passed, France will be a republic."

"A republic?"

"Yes. But don't be too quick to rejoice, if, that is, this does please you. Before the end of the year the Bonapartists will again be the masters [he used a much stronger expression] of the same old France."

When he mentioned that France would shortly become a republic, I did not of course believe a word of it. All I thought was: "Here's a man who wants to startle me, regarding me, no doubt, as an inexperienced Scythian." But Bonapartists? Why on earth Bonapartists? At that time, while Louis-Philippe was still on the throne, no one thought of the Bonapartists, at least no one spoke of them. I had not run across a hoaxer by any chance, had I? Or one of those rogues who are to be found in all cafés and hotels, sniffing out foreigners and usually ending by asking for a loan from them? But no! He did not look like one of them. . . . Besides, that unceremonious casualness of address, the unconcerned tone with which he uttered his paradoxes. . . .

"You don't think the king will agree to any reforms then?"

I asked after a short pause. "The demands of the opposition are not very great, are they?"

"Of course, of course (*Connu, connu. . . .),*" he said casually. "Extension of electoral rights, equality of opportunity, and so on and so forth. Words, words, words. There won't be any banquets, the king will make no concessions, nor will Guizot agree to any. However," he added, apparently noticing the far from favourable impression he made on me, "to the devil with politics! To be engaged in it is great fun, but to watch others engaged in it is stupid. Little dogs act like that, while the big ones—enjoy themselves. All that is left for the little dogs to do is to bark or yelp. Let's talk about something else."

I don't remember what exactly we talked about. . . .

"You are, of course, going to the theatre?" he asked again with the suddenness which I had already observed in him and which made me think that he was not listening to what one said to him. "All you Russians are great theatre-goers, aren't you?"

"Yes, I am."

"And I suppose you admire our actors?"

"Yes, some of them. . . . Especially those at the Théâtre Français. . . ."

"All our actors," he interrupted me, "are ruined by their good taste. It's their traditions, their schools—awful! They are all sort of eviscerated and frozen stiff. They remind me of the fish you have in Russian markets in winter. Not one of our actors will say 'I love you' on the stage without first spreading out his legs like a pair of compasses and rolling up his eyes languorously. And all for the sake of good taste! Real actors are to be found only in Italy. When I lived in Italy. . . . Incidentally, what's your opinion of the constitution which King Bomba has granted to his loyal subjects? He won't forgive them that favour of his for a long time—not for a long time! Well, when I lived in Naples there were wonderful actors in the people's theatre there—great

fellows! But, then, every Italian is an actor. It's in their nature
. . . and we merely talk about naturalness. In France no one even
in the Palais-Royal Theatre can compete with any itinerant
preacher. . . . *Per le santissime anime del Purgatorio!*" he exclaimed suddenly in a nasal, sing-song voice and, as far as I could
judge, in a pure Italian accent.

I laughed, and he, too, laughed soundlessly, opening his mouth
wide and looking askance at me over the rim of his glasses.

"But," I began, "Rachel—"

"Rachel," he repeated. "Yes, she certainly is a force. The
force and flower of the Jewish race which has now got possession
of the pockets of the whole world and will soon get possession of
everything else. He who has the pocket has the woman, and he
who has the woman has the man. (*Qui a la poche, a la femme; et
qui a la femme, a l'homme.*) Yes—Rachel! There's also that
Meyerbeer who keeps teasing and threatening us with his
Prophet. I shall give it—I shan't give it. . . . A clever fellow. In a
word, a Jew—a maestro, only not in the musical sense. However,
even Rachel has deteriorated lately. And it's all the fault of you
foreigners. There is an actress in Italy—her name is Ristori. I'm
told she's married some marquis and left the stage. She is excellent, except that she is a little affected."

"Have you lived in Italy long?" I asked.

"Yes. I have lived in all sorts of places."

"But you haven't lived in Russia, have you?"

"Are you fond of music too?" he asked, without answering my
question. "Do you go to the opera?"

"Yes, I'm fond of music."

"Oh? You are? Well, of course, you're a Slav and all Slavs are
melomanes. It's the worst art of all. When it doesn't appeal to
a man, it's boring, when it does, it's harmful."

"Harmful? Why harmful?"

"It's as harmful as excessively hot baths. Ask the doctors."

"I see! And what's your opinion of the other arts?"

"There is only one art—sculpture. That is cold, passionless, majestic, and arouses in man the idea, or, if you like, the illusion of immortality and eternity."

"And painting?"

"Painting? Too much blood, body, colours—too much sin. They paint naked women. A statue is never naked. Why excite a man's passions? Men are sinful as it is, sinful and criminal. They are all permeated with sin."

"All without exception? And all permeated?"

"All! You, me, even that fat bachelor with the good-natured face who is buying a doll as a present for somebody's else's, or, perhaps, his own, child. We are all guilty of some crime. Everyone has committed some crime in his life and no one has the right to say that there is no place for him on the vile seat in the dock."

"You ought to know," I could not help exclaiming.

"You're quite right. I ought to know better than anyone. *Experto credi* (instead of *crede*)—*Roberto*."

"Well, and literature? What is your opinion of literature?" I went on with my cross-examination. "If you're trying to mystify me," I thought, "why should not I make fun of you? It's you who've made a mistake in the Latin tag no one asked you to quote."

"Literature is not an art," he said in a casual tone of voice. "Literature must first of all—entertain. And it is only biography that is entertaining."

"Are you so fond of biographies?"

"I'm afraid you've misunderstood me. I mean those works in which the authors tell the readers all about themselves, in which they display themselves—to be laughed at, I mean. As a matter of fact, people cannot possibly know anything else properly—and not even that! That is why Montaigne is the greatest writer. There is no one like him."

"He has the reputation of being a great egoist," I observed.

"Yes, that's where his strength lies. He alone had the courage to be an egoist and—a laughing stock to the end. That is why he amuses me. I read one page, another and—laugh at him, at myself, and that is all there is to it!"

"Well, and the poets?"

"The poets are preoccupied with the music of words, with verbal music. And you know what I think of music."

"What, then, ought one to read? What, for instance, ought the ordinary common people to read? Or do you believe that the common people must not read?"

(I noticed a ring with a crest on one of the stranger's fingers. In spite of his miserable and ragged appearance, I thought that he must hold aristocratic views; and, perhaps, he was an aristocrat by birth himself.)

"On the contrary," he replied, "the common people must read; but what they read is of no importance. I'm told your peasants only read one book. *(Franzyl the Venetian,* it flashed across my mind.) If they finish reading one book, they will buy another one like it. And quite right, too. It adds to their importance in their own eyes and—prevents them from thinking. And those who go to church need not read at all."

"Do you consider religion to be as important as that?"

The stranger glanced at me over the rim of his glasses.

"I'm afraid I don't believe in God very much, sir, but religion is a matter of great importance. To serve it is perhaps almost the best vocation. Priests are fine fellows; they alone have an idea of the real meaning of power: to command with humility and—to obey with pride: that is the whole secret. Power—power—to possess power—there is no other happiness on earth!"

I was already becoming accustomed to the sudden changes in

our conversations, and merely tried not to lag behind my strange interlocutor. He, on the other hand, spoke with such an air as though all the axioms which he promulgated so confidently followed one from another logically and consistently, though you could not help feeling all the time that it made no difference to him whether you agreed with him or not.

"If," I began, "you are so fond of power and hold so high an opinion of the priesthood, why did you not follow the same path and become a priest?"

"Your observation is just, sir," he said, "but I was aiming higher. I wanted to found a religion of my own. And I tried to—er—during my sojourn in America. Still, I was not the only one who has had that intention. Lots of people go in for it there."

"You've been in America too?"

"I spent two years there. Perhaps you've noticed that I acquired the nasty habit of chewing tobacco there. I don't smoke and I don't take snuff—I chew. Sorry! (He spat.) So that's how it was. I tried to found a religion and had even thought of a myth—not a bad one, at that. Only to make it acceptable, one had to be a martyr, to shed one's blood. Without that cement, you can't lay any foundation. It's not like war: there it's much more profitable to shed someone else's blood. But to shed my own—no! I did not want to do that. No, sir!"

He was silent for a minute or two.

"You've just said that I was fond of power," he resumed. "You were quite right. For instance, I'm sure I shall be a king one day."

"A king?"

"Yes, a king—on some uninhabited island."

"A king—without subjects?"

"One can always find subjects. You have a proverb in Russia: "If I had a trough, and something in the trough, I'd find a pig, too." It is in the nature of men to obey. They'd swim across the

seas to my island for the purpose of finding a master to whose
rule they could submit. That's true."

"Why, you're a madman!" I thought to myself. "Is that why
you think," I said aloud, "that the French will submit to the
Bonapartists?"

"Yes, sir, for that very reason."

"But, my dear sir," I cried, "haven't the French got a king
and master now? Isn't, therefore, men's need which you spoke of
just now, their need to submit, satisfied already?"

The stranger shook his head.

"You see, the trouble is that Louis-Philippe, our present king,
doesn't feel himself to be king and master. However, we didn't
want to talk politics, did we?"

"Do you prefer philosophy?" I asked.

He spat out his chewed tobacco, American-fashion, a long distance away.

"Aha," he exclaimed, "so you want to speak ironically to me,
do you? Well, I don't mind philosophy; particularly as my philosophy is very simple and bears no resemblance whatever, for example, to German philosophy, which I don't know at all, but which
I hate as I do all Germans." The stranger's eyes blazed up suddenly. "I hate them because I am a patriot. You, too, as a Russian should hate them, shouldn't you?"

"But—I—"

"If not, it's the worse for you. You just wait—they'll show you
what they can do to you. I hate them, I am afraid of them," he
added, lowering his voice, "and one of my happiest memories is
that I had the good luck to shoot at them, at those Germans!"

"You did? Where was it?"

"Why, again in Italy. You see, I took part in—One moment,
though. We were, I believe, talking of philosophy. Let me tell
you, sir, that all my philosophy can be summed up as follows:

there are two misfortunes in a man's life: birth and death. The second misfortune is not so great—it can be voluntary."

"And what about life?"

"Well, you can't define it all at once. But note that in life there are only two good things, namely, when man assists in birth or—death, that is to say, either of the two misfortunes I have just mentioned. *Guerra, caza y amores,* the Spaniards say."

I happened to know that proverb. "You forget the second verse," I observed. *"Por un placer mil dolores."*

"Excellent! There you have the proof of the truth of my philosophy. However," he added, getting up quickly from his chair, "we've talked enough. Goodbye!"

"Wait a moment," I exclaimed. "I've been talking to you for about an hour and I don't know whom I have the honour—"

"You want to know my name? What for? I did not ask you for yours, did I? Neither did I ask you where you lived and I don't think it necessary to tell you where I live, in what hovel I'm staying. We meet here—well, that's all right, then! You did like my conversation, though, didn't you?" He narrowed his eyes ironically. "You like me, don't you?"

I felt a little disgusted. The fellow was a bit too unceremonious.

"I am interested in you, sir," I replied with deliberate emphasis, "but I do not like you."

"And I am not interested in you, but I do like you. That, I think, is sufficient for a relationship such as ours. If you like, you can call me—well, Monsieur François. And, if you don't mind, I shall call you Monsieur Ivan. . . . Almost every Russian is called Ivan, isn't that so? I found that out when I had the doubtful pleasure of being a tutor at one of your general's houses in one of your provinces. And what a damn fool that general was! And how miserably poor that province was! And now, goodbye, M. Ivan!"

He turned round and walked away.

"Goodbye, M. François," I called after him.

"I wonder what sort of man he is?" I asked myself on my way home. "What a strange fellow! Is he teasing me? Inventing all sorts of absurd stories? Or is he really convinced of what he was saying. What is he doing? What's his business? What is his past? Who is he? An unsuccessful writer, a journalist, a schoolmaster, a bankrupt businessman, an impoverished nobleman, a retired actor? And what is he trying to achieve now? And why did he choose me of all people as his confidant?"

I asked myself all those questions but, of course, could not answer them. But my curiosity was aroused, and it was not without some excitement that I went to the Palais-Royal next day. This time, however, I waited in vain for my eccentric; but on the following day he appeared again under the awning of the café.

"Ah, M. Ivan," he cried, as soon as he saw me, "good morning. Fate seems to have brought us together again. How are you?"

"I'm quite well, thank you. And how are you, M. François?"

"I'm quite well, too, thank you. *Ça boulotte.* Yesterday, however, I nearly kicked the bucket. Heart attack. . . . Smelled of death—horrible smell! But that's not important. Let's rather go and sit down in the park. It's too crowded here today. I can't stand people staring at me from all sides, or from behind. Besides, it's such a lovely day. . . ."

We went to the park and sat down. I remember that when he had to pay two sous for his chair, he took a tiny, flat, old purse out of his pocket, rummaged in it for a long time, and I don't think he had more than two sous in it. I waited for him to resume his paradoxes, but what happened was quite different. He began questioning me about various important Russian personages. I told him what I knew about them; but he wanted more details, more biographical data. It turned out that he knew

215

many things I did not suspect. He certainly was a well informed man.

Gradually our conversation turned to politics. It was, in fact, difficult to avoid discussing politics at a time when public opinion was in such a state of excitement. M. François mentioned, in passing and as though unwillingly, Guizot and Thiers. About Guizot he observed that France was so unlucky: she had only one man with a will of his own and he, too, seemed to have appeared at the wrong moment. He was sorry for Thiers, saying that his role was finished for a long time.

"Why," I cried, "it's only beginning! Think of the speeches he is making in the Chamber of Deputies!"

"New men will be rising now," he murmured, "and all those speeches are just empty sounds and nothing more. The man is sailing in a boat and is talking to the waterfall which will presently capsize his boat together with himself. However, I can see you don't believe me."

"Well," I went on, "do you really suppose that Odilon Barrot—"

At this point M. François glared at me and burst into loud laughter, tossing back his head.

"Boom-boom-boom," he said, mimicking the waiter, carrying his coffee cups in the Rotonde, "that's Odilon Barrot for you—boom-boom!"

"Oh yes," I said, not without vexation, "according to you, we're on the eve of a republic. These new men of yours won't be the Socialists, will they?"

M. François assumed a somewhat solemn pose.

"Socialism, sir, was born in our country, and it will die in France, too, if indeed it isn't dead already. Or it will be killed. It will be killed in two ways: either with mockery, for M. Considérant could hardly go on asserting with impunity that people will grow a tail with an eye at its end, or—like that!" He made a gesture with his hands as though aiming with a gun. "Voltaire used to say that the French had not got epic heads, and I venture to say that we have not got socialist heads."

"Abroad they have a different opinion of you."

"In that case all you gentlemen abroad are doing is to prove for the hundredth time that you don't understand us. At the present moment Socialism requires creative force. It will follow it to the Italians, to the Germans, to you, perhaps as well. But a Frenchman is an inventor. He invented almost everything. But he is not a creator. The Frenchman is sharp and narrow as a rapier, and so he penetrates into the essence of things, he finds out, he invents. . . . But to create one has to be broad and round."

"Like the English or your favourite Germans," I put in not without sarcasm.

But M. François ignored my taunting remark.

"Socialism! Socialism!" he went on. "It's not a French princi-ple. We have quite different principles. We have two of them. Two corner-stones: revolution and routine. Robespierre and M. Prudhomme—these are our national heroes."

"Really? And what about the military element? Which place does it occupy in your opinion?"

"Why, we are not a military nation at all. Are you surprised at that? We are a brave, a very brave people. Bellicose but not mili-tary. Thank God, we're worth more than that." He worked his jaws up and down. "Yes, that is so. And yet if we, the French, did not exist, there would have been no Europe."

"But there would have been America."

"No. For America is the same as Europe only inside out. The Americans have none of the foundations on which the edifice of a European State is built, and yet the result seems to be the same. Everything human is the same. You remember the ser-geant's instruction to the recruits: right about turn is the same thing as left about turn, only it's in the opposite direction. Well, so America, too, is the same as Europe—only left about turn. If,"

217

M. François went on after a short pause, "if France were Rome, then it would be nice if a Cataline were to appear just now! Now, sir, now when soon, very soon," he raised his voice, "you will see it, sir, the stones, the stones on our roads—here, near here, some-where very near from where we are sitting, will again taste blood! But we shall have no Cataline, and we shall have no Caesar, either—we shall still have the same Prudhomme with Robespierre. Incidentally, don't you agree, sir, that it is a pity Shakespeare did not write Cataline?"

"So you have a high opinion of Shakespeare in spite of the fact that he was a poet?"

"Yes, he was a man, a man born under a lucky star—a man of talent. He could see white and black at one and the same time, and this is rare, but what is rarer still, he was not for the white or for the black. And he wrote an excellent play, too—*Coriolanus!* One of his best plays."

I at once recalled my theory about M. François's aristocratic origin.

"I expect the reason why you like *Coriolanus* so much," I said, "is that in this tragedy Shakespeare speaks very disrespectfully, almost contemptuously, of the common people, the mob."

"No," retorted M. François, "I do not despise the mob. I do not generally despise the people. Before despising anybody, one ought to start with oneself, which, I am afraid, only happens to me at long intervals when," he added, lowering his voice and knitting his brows gloomily, "when I have nothing to eat. Despise the people? Whatever for? The people are just the same as the soil. If I want to, I plough it and it nourishes me; if I don't want to, I leave it lying fallow. It carries me and—I trample on it. It is true that sometimes it suddenly shakes itself like a wet poodle and overthrows everything we have built on it—all our card houses. But that does not really happen very often, I mean, these earthquakes. On the other hand, I know perfectly well that in the end it will swallow me. And the people, too, will swallow me. There is nothing to be done about that. But to despise the people? One can despise only what under other circumstances one must respect. And here there is no place for either feeling. Here one must know how to make use of things, to make use of everything—that's what one must know."

"But, if I may ask, did *you* know how to make use of everything?"

M. François sighed.

"No, I'm afraid I didn't."

"Didn't you?"

"I did not, I'm telling you. You look at me and, I suppose, you're thinking: "You are prophesying that there's going to be a revolution in France soon, so that will be the time for you to—to fish in troubled waters." But a pike does not fish in troubled waters. And I'm not even a pike!"

He turned sharply round on his chair and brought his fist down on its back.

"No, I did not know how to make use of things," he said, "or I shouldn't have appeared before you looking like this!" He pointed to his clothes with a cursory movement of the hand. "I shouldn't perhaps have made your acquaintance at all then, which," he added with an affected smile, "I should have regretted very much. And I shouldn't have lived there, in the attic where I'm living now. I should not have been able to repeat, as I got up in the morning and looked out at the sea of roofs and chimney pots of Paris, Tugurtha's words, *"Urbs venalis!"* H'm—yes! I should have been like this city myself. I shouldn't have been in my present condition. I shouldn't have been in want, I shouldn't have been so poor. . . ."

"This is when he's going to ask me for some money," I thought.

But he fell silent, dropped his head on his chest and began tracing in the sand with his stick. Then he again heaved a deep sigh, took off his glasses, took an old check handkerchief out of his back pocket, rolled it up into a ball and passed it twice across his forehead, lifting his elbow high.

"Yes," he said at last, almost inaudibly, "life is a sad business. A sad business, sir, that's what life is. I have one consolation, though. I mean that I shall die soon and—a violent death. . . ."

"So you won't be a king, will you?" it nearly escaped my lips, but I restrained myself.

"Yes," he repeated, "a violent death. But look at this," he went on, showing me his left hand, in which he held his glasses, with its palm upwards, and, without letting go of his handkerchief, he put the forefinger of his right hand on it—both were rather dirty, "look at this: do you see this line cutting across the line of life?"

"Are you a palmist?" I asked.

"Do you see this line?" he repeated insistently. "So I am right. And I'd like you to know beforehand, sir, that whenever you find yourself in some place where you are least likely to remember me, you will remember me all the same—I'd like you to know then that I shall not be alive."

He hung his head again, dropping his hand with the handkerchief on his knee. His other hand with the glasses drooped lifelessly. I took advantage of the fact that M. François's eyes were lowered and did not embarrass me, to scrutinize him more closely than before. He suddenly appeared to me to be such an old man, there was such fatigue in the droop of his back and shoulders and in the very position of his large flat feet in their patched boots; his lips were compressed so bitterly, his unshaven cheeks were so deeply sunken, his gaunt neck drooped so weakly, the strand of his greying hair hung so forlornly over his furrowed brow. . . .

"What an unhappy, pathetic man you are," I said to myself there and then, "unlucky in all your undertakings and enterprises, in your family and all sorts of other affairs. If you had been married, your wife would have deceived and left you, and if you have children, you don't know them and you don't see them. . . ."

A loud exclamation in Russian interrupted my thoughts. Someone was calling me. I turned round and within two feet of me saw Alexander Herzen, who lived in Paris at the time. I got up and went up to him.

"Who are you sitting with?" he began, without making any attempt at lowering his voice. "What a horrible fellow!"

"Why?"

"But, good Lord, he's a spy. I'm sure he's a spy."

"Do you know him?"

"I don't know him at all, but you've only to look at him. A spy all over. What do you want to make friends with him for? You'd better look out!"

I said nothing to Herzen. But as I knew very well that for all his brilliant and penetrating intellect, his ability to understand people, especially those he did not know too well, was rather weak, and as I remembered very well that at his hospitable and congenial table one sometimes came across highly objectionable people, people who aroused his trustful sympathy by a few words, but who afterwards turned out to be real secret agents, as he himself later on described in his memoirs—knowing all this, I did not pay much attention to his warning and, after thanking him for his friendly concern, returned to M. François, who was sitting, forlorn and motionless, as before.

"What I wanted to tell you," he began as soon as I resumed my seat beside him, "is that you Russians suffer from a very bad habit. You talk loudly among yourselves in Russian in the street, before strangers, before Frenchmen, as though you were quite sure no one would understand you. And this is not wise. You see, I, for instance, understood everything your friend said."

I blushed involuntarily. "Please, don't think . . ." I began. "Of course, my friend—"

"I know him," M. François interrupted me. "He's a fellow of infinite jest. But *errare humanum est.*" (M. François evidently liked to show off his knowledge of Latin.) "Judging by my appearance one can imagine all sorts of things about me. But, please, tell me even if I were what your friend called me, what could I get from spying on *you?*"

"Of course, of course, you're quite right," I exclaimed. M. François looked glumly at me. "Did you learn Russian while you were a tutor at the general's?" I asked quite irrelevantly, for I was anxious to dispel the unpleasant impression which Herzen's somewhat precipitate judgment could not but have produced.

M. François's face brightened. He even grinned and patted me on the knee as though wishing to make me feel that he understood and appreciated my intention. Then he put on his spectacles and picked up the stick he had dropped.

"No," he said, "I learned Russian long before that. I learned your language when I got to Siberia from America, from Texas by way of California. Yes, I was there, too, in your Siberia! And the wonderful things that happened to me there!"

"For instance?"

"I won't talk about Siberia for—for many reasons. I don't want to grieve or insult you. We'd better say nothing," he added in broken Russian. "Ha, ha! But just listen to what happened to me once in Texas."

And M. François began to tell me with a circumstantiality that was quite uncharacteristic of him how, wandering across Texas in winter, he on one occasion spent the night in the hut of a Mexican immigrant. On awakening at night, he saw his host sitting on his bed with a knife in his hand—*con una navaja.* The Mexican, a huge man, strong as an ox, was drunk and he told M. François that he intended to kill him because he, François, reminded him of one of his worst enemies. "Prove to me," said the Mexican, "that I have no right to amuse myself by bleeding you to death, like a boar, for I can do it all with impunity and no one will ever know what happened to you. And even if it became known, no one would hold me responsible for it, because no one in the whole world cares a damn about you. Well, prove it! We have plenty of time, thank God!" "And lying all night with a knife at my throat," M. François went on, "I was forced to prove to that drunken brute either by quoting texts from the Bible (which should have had an effect on him as a Catholic) or by bringing forward arguments of a general nature, such as that the pleasure of my death would give him would not be so great as to justify soiling his hands. . . . 'You'll have to bury my corpse,' I told him, 'even if only to make everything look tidy, and all this is just giving yourself a lot of trouble.' I was even forced to tell him fairy stories and even sing songs." "Sing with me," he bellowed. *"La muchacha-a-a!"* I sang and the sharp blade of the knife, *de cette diablesse de navaja,* was an inch from my throat. It ended by the musician falling asleep at my side with his matted, disgusting head on my chest."

M. François told me the whole of this story in a quiet voice, without hurrying, as though falling asleep. Then he suddenly glared at me and fell silent.

"Well, what did you do to him, the Mexican, I mean?" I asked.

"Why, I—er—made it impossible for him to play such stupid jokes on people again."

"You mean?"

"I mean, I took the knife from him and—having finished the business, went on my way. . . . I've had other nasty adventures, too. And mostly because of them, because of those cursed ones," he added, pointing a finger at a middle-aged, modestly dressed, woman who was passing by just then.

"Because of whom?"

"Because of those—petticoats," he explained what he meant. "Oh, women, women! It is they who clip your wings, it is they who poison your blood. However, goodbye. I suppose I must be boring you, and I don't want to bore anyone. Especially a man I don't happen to need."

He drew himself up proudly, got up and went away with barely a nod in my direction, brandishing his stick jauntily.

To tell the truth, I did not believe that Mexican story of his. It even lowered François in my estimation. And again it occurred to me that he was pulling my leg. But with what object? "A queer fellow! A queer fellow!" I repeated. I could not take him for a spy all the same, in spite of Herzen's assurances. What surprised me, though, was that not one of the many passers-by in the Palais-Royal spoke to him or recognized him. It was true he seemed to wink at some of them. . . . Or did I imagine that, too?

I forgot to say that M. François never smelled of drink. But, then, he did not perhaps have enough money to buy himself a drink. But no. He gave one the impression of a sober man.

Neither the next day nor on any of the following days did he make an appearance at the café and—little by little I forgot all about M. François.

Shortly before February 24 I left for Belgium, and the news of the revolution in France reached me in Brussels. I can remember that no one received any letters or journals from Paris for a whole day; crowds of people gathered in the streets and squares of Brussels; everything seemed to hold its breath in anxious suspense. On February 26, at six o'clock in the morning, I was still in bed —I was not asleep—when the door of my hotel room was suddenly flung open and someone shouted in a stentorian voice: "France has become a republic!" Not believing my ears, I leapt out of bed and rushed out of the room. One of the waiters of the hotel was running along the corridor and, opening the doors in turn on the right and left, shouted his amazing news into every room. Half an hour later I was dressed and packed, and on the same day was travelling by train to Paris. At the frontier the rails had been removed; my fellow-travellers and I got as far as Doué with difficulty in a hired carriage and towards the evening we arrived in Pontoise. . . . Near Paris the rails had also been removed. This is not the place to describe everything I had experienced, seen and heard during that journey. I remember that at one station an engine with a first-class carriage clattered past us with a terrific din: in this "special" train travelled "the special Commissar," Antoine Touré; the people travelling with him waved tricolour flags and shouted; the station personnel eyed with astonishment the huge figure of the Commissar, who was leaning out of the window with a hand raised high.

The years 1793, 1794 came involuntarily into one's mind. I remember, too, that before we reached Pontoise our train collided with another train coming from the opposite direction. There were wounded among the passengers, but no one paid any attention; everyone was wondering whether it would be possible to travel any further. And as soon as our train moved on again, everyone began talking with the same excitement, everyone except a grey-haired old man, who had been skulking in a corner ever since Doué and kept repeating in a whisper: "Everything's lost! Everything's lost!" I remember, too, that in the same compartment with me was the notorious Mrs. Gordon (a close friend and emissary of Louis Napoleon), who began suddenly to talk about the necessity of appealing to "the prince" because "the prince" alone could save everything. . . . At first no one understood what she was talking about; but when she uttered the name of Louis Napoleon, everyone turned away from her as from a mad woman. And yet the words uttered by M. François about the Bonapartists flashed across my mind—his first prophecy had come true, after all.

I will not enlarge on my first impressions on my arrival in Paris, at the sight of the tricoloured cockades, the armed workers removing the stones from the barricades, etc. The whole of my first day in Paris passed in a sort of daze. On the following day I went as usual to the Palais-Royal and asked the "citizen" waiter for a cup of coffee. Though I did not meet M. François there, I could see that his forecast about the bloodstained cobblestones in the streets surrounding the Palais-Royal had come true: the only fighting during the February revolution took place in the square which separates this building from the Louvre.

I did not run across M. François during the following days, either. I saw him for the first time on March 17, on the very day when a huge crowd of workers was marching to the Town Hall to protest to the provisional government against the famous demonstration of the so-called "bearskins" (the disbanded grenadiers and the *voltigeures* of the National Guard). He walked in the middle of the crowd, striding along and waving his arms, and he seemed to be shouting or singing; he had tied a red scarf round his waist and pinned a red cockade to his hat. Our eyes met, but he showed no signs of recognition, though he deliberately turned full-face towards me: "See? Yes! It's me!" and shouted louder than ever, opening his dark mouth wider than it was necessary. Another time I saw him at the theatre. Rachel was singing the Marseillaise in her sepulchral voice. He was sitting in the stalls, where the members of the claques ordinarily sat. In the theatre he neither shouted nor applauded; but, his hands folded on his breast, gazed with sombre attention at the singer, when, wrapping round her the folds of the banner she had seized, she called upon the citizens "to arms" and "to the shedding of impure blood." I cannot say for certain whether or not I saw him on May 15 among the crowds of people marching past the Madeleine to storm the Chamber of Deputies; but I seemed to catch sight of someone resembling him in the first ranks of the demonstrators, and was it not his voice—his peculiar dull and hollow voice—that I heard shouting "Long live Poland!?"

But at the beginning of June, namely on the fourth of that month, M. François suddenly appeared before me in the same café at the Palais-Royal. He bowed to me, even shook hands with me (which he never did before), but did not sit down at my table, as though ashamed of his completely tattered clothes and his battered hat; besides, he was devoured—at least so it seemed to me—by nervous, restless impatience. His face looked haggard, his lips and cheeks kept spasmodically twitching; his inflamed eyes could hardly be seen behind his glasses, which he kept adjusting and pushing up his nose with all his five fingers. This time I could see that what I had long suspected was true: the glasses of his spectacles were ordinary glasses and he did not need them really: that was why he so often looked over their rims. The spectacles were a kind of mask for him. The anxiety, that peculiar anxiety of a homeless and starving tramp, was apparent in his whole figure. The almost beggarly appearance of this enigmatic man puzzled me. If he really was a secret agent, then why was he so poor? If he was not a secret agent, then what was he? How was one to explain his behaviour?

I began speaking to him about his prophecies.

"Yes, yes," he muttered with feverish haste, "it's all an old story now—de l'histoire ancienne. But aren't you going back to your Russia? You're not staying here, are you?"

"Why shouldn't I stay here?"

"Well, it's your funeral. You see, we shall soon be at war with you."

"With us?"

"Yes, with you, with the Russians. We shall soon be wanting glory, glory! War with Russia is inevitable!"

"With Russia? Why not with Germany?"

"First with Russia. However, this is all in the future. You're young—you'll live to see it. As for the republic," he went on with a wave of the hand, "it's finished. C'est fichu!"

"The national workshops! The national workshops!" he exclaimed with sudden animation. "Have you been there? Have you seen them? Have you seen how they are transferring earth from one place to another in wheelbarrows? That's where it will all start. There's going to be bloodshed, a lot of bloodshed! A whole sea of blood. What a situation! To be able to foresee it all and not to be able to do anything about it! ! To be a nobody, a nobody! To embrace everything," he spread out his arms with the battered sleeves—the ring on his forefinger was still there, "and to grasp nothing," he clenched his fists, "not even a piece of bread! Tomorrow's elections are also rather important," he added quickly, as though forcing himself not to dwell on the feelings he had just expressed.

M. François told me the names of the deputies who, according to him, would be certain to be elected in Paris; told me the number of votes—in round figures—which each of them would receive. Among the names mentioned by M. François, was the name of Cossidière, who, he claimed, would be at the head of the poll.

"Notwithstanding the 15th May?" I asked.

"Perhaps you think that I said it because he was the prefect of police?" replied M. François with a bitter smile.

But he at once recollected himself and again began talking of the elections. Louis Napoleon was also on the lists of the elected deputies. "He will be the last one, *à la queue*," remarked M. François, "but that, too, is good enough. When climbing a staircase one must first step over the lowest steps before getting to the highest."

The same evening I gave all those names and figures to Alexander Herzen and I remember well his astonishment when next day all M. François's predictions came true word for word.

"How do you know all this?" Herzen kept asking me.

I told him the source of my information. "Oh," he exclaimed, "that bastard!"

But to return to our conversation in the café. About that time the name of Proudhon was often repeated among the names of the prospective deputies. I mentioned it. According to M. François, Proudhon, too, appeared in the lists of elected deputies, though, at the bottom, which, however, also came true. But it seemed that M. François did not attach any great importance to him, nor to Lamartine and Ledru-Rollin. He spoke with contempt of all these personages, with a touch of pity of Lamartine, with a touch of spite for Proudhon, that "sophist in clogs" (*ce sophiste en sabots*), and as for Ledru-Rollin he just called him: "*Ce gros bête de Ledru,*" and kept referring again and again to the national workshops. Our whole conversation, however, did not last long, not more than a quarter of an hour. M. François did not sit down and kept looking round as though expecting someone. I did, incidentally, recall his red cockade and said: "So you do appear to be a Republican after all!"

"What kind of a Republican am I?" he interrupted me. "What made you think that? That's all right for the greengrocers (*pour les épiciers*). They still believe in the principles of 1789, universal brotherhood, progress—whereas I—"

But here M. François suddenly fell silent and looked round. I, too, looked round. An old man in a workman's smock and with a long white beard was signalling to him with a hand. He replied with the same wave of the hand and ran up to him.

Both disappeared.

After our meeting at the café I saw M. François three times more. Once—from a distance—in the Luxembourg Gardens. He stood beside a poorly dressed young girl, who was imploring him about something tearfully, pressing his hands and putting them to her lips. . . . But he kept refusing her requests gloomily, stamping impatiently and, suddenly pushing her away with an elbow, pulled his hat over his forehead and walked away. She ran off in the opposite direction, looking utterly lost. Our second meeting was much more significant. It took place on June 13, on the very day when there appeared on the Place de la Concorde for the first time a crowd of Bonapartists, whom Lamartine pointed out to the Chamber of Deputies and who were soon dispersed by the military. In one of the corners formed by the wall of the Tuileries Gardens, I saw a man in the motley dress of a charlatan, standing on a two-wheeled barrow and distributing leaflets. I took one of them: it contained a highly laudatory biography of Louis Napoleon. That man, a Breton, with a huge mane of long hair combed upwards, I had seen often before in suburban squares and boulevards: he sold a tooth elixir, an ointment against rheumatism and all sorts of other nostrums. While I was turning the pages of the pamphlet someone touched me on the shoulder. M. François! His toothless mouth was dilated in a smile and he looked at me ironically over the rims of his glasses.

"It's starting! This is when it's starting!" he said, shuffling strangely from foot to foot and rubbing his hands. "This is when! That's the apostle, the bringer of glad tidings! Do you like him?"

"This hairy charlatan?" I exclaimed. "This clown? Why, you're pulling my leg!"

"Yes, indeed, a charlatan!" retorted M. François. "That's how it should be. Extraordinary hair, bangles on his arms, tights with spangles. . . . That's exactly what's needed! What one must do is to strike the imagination! A legend, sir! It's a legend one requires! A miracle! An advertisement! A stage effect! At first a man will be surprised and then—he will respect you. Respect you? Why, he'll believe you, believe you! And you, sir, please remember the real thing is only just starting now. . . . And when the Red Sea (*la mer rouge*) is crossed—"

But just then the square was filled by a crowd of people running away from the soldiers' bayonets, and we became separated.

The last time I saw M. François was also from a distance—during the terrible June days. He wore the uniform of a National

Guardsman from the provinces, holding a rifle at the ready, and I cannot describe in words the expression of cold cruelty on his face.

Since then I never met M. François again. At the beginning of 1850 I happened to find myself in the Russian Church at the wedding of an acquaintance of mine, and suddenly, goodness only knows why, I began to think about M. François. It occurred to me that as his other prophecies had come true, so he might again have proved himself to be a prophet and was really no longer alive. A few years later, though, I was able to convince myself of his death. Behind the counter of one shop, I noticed a woman in whom after some hesitation I recognized the young girl who had been weeping so bitterly in the Luxembourg Gardens in front of M. François. I decided to remind her of that scene. At first she looked perplexed, but as soon as she realized what I was driving at, she became terribly excited, went pale and coloured in turn, and asked me not to insist on asking her any more questions.

"Tell me at least whether that man is dead or not."

The woman looked intently at me.

"He died the death he deserved. . . . He was a wicked man. Still," she added, "he was also very, very unhappy."

I could get nothing more out of her and the real identity of M. François has remained a mystery to me.

There are certain sea birds which appear only during a storm. The English call them stormy petrels. They fly low as the dark descends, just above the crests of the raging waves, and—vanish as soon as the weather clears again.

VII

MY MATES SENT ME!

———◆———

*An episode from the history of the Events
of June, 1848, in Paris*

THE *fourth* OF THE NOTORIOUS DAYS of June 1848 came, one of
the days which are written in blood in the annals of French history. . . .

I lived at the time in a no longer existing house on the corner
of the Rue de la Paix and the Boulevard des Italiens. From the
very beginning of June there was a smell of gun-powder in the
air. Everyone felt that a decisive clash was inevitable, and after
the meeting of the delegates of the national workshops a few days
after their dissolution with Marie, the member of the Provisional
Government, who in his address to them unthinkingly uttered the
word "slaves" (*esclaves*) which they interpreted as a reproach and
an insult—after that meeting the only question was not how many
days, but how many hours remained to that unavoidable and inevitable clash. *Est-ce pour aujourd'hui?* (Is it going to be today?)
—with such words people greeted each other every morning.

"*Ça a commencé!* (It's started!)," the laundress, who had brought
my washing, said to me on the morning of Friday, 23rd June.

According to her, a large barricade had been erected across the boulevard, not far from the Saint-Denis Gates. I went over there at once.

At first there was nothing in particular that I could see. The same crowds of people in front of the open cafés and shops, the same street traffic of carriages and omnibuses. The faces seemed a little more excited, the conversations a little louder and—strange to say—more gay, and that was all. But the further I went, the more did the appearance of the boulevard change. Carriages became less frequent, the omnibuses disappeared completely; the shops and cafés were being hastily closed or were closed already; there were many fewer people in the street. On the other hand, all the windows of the houses were open from top to bottom and a great number of people, mostly women, children, maids and nursemaids, were crowded in those windows and even in the doorways. They were all talking, laughing, not shouting but calling to one another, looking round, waving their hands—as though in expectation of some pageant. A light-hearted, festive curiosity seemed to have taken possession of all those crowds of people. Ribbons of many colours, kerchiefs, caps, white, pink, blue dresses shimmered and glittered in the bright summer sunshine, rose and rustled in the light summer breeze—just like the leaves on the "trees of freedom," the poplars planted everywhere. "Will they really be fighting and shedding blood here now, in five or ten minutes?" I thought. "Impossible! It's a comedy that's going to be performed here. There can be no question of tragedy—as yet!"

But there, in front of me, running aslant the whole width of the boulevard, the uneven line of the barricade—about eight feet high—came into sight. In the middle of it, surrounded by other tricolour and gold embroidered flags, a small red flag fluttered—to the right and left—with its ominous, pointed tongue. A few workers could be seen behind the ridge of heaped up grey stones. I moved a little nearer. The space just in front of the barricade was almost deserted, about fifty—no more—men walking to and fro in the roadway. (The roads were not macadamized in those days.) The workers exchanged jokes with the spectators in the street who came up to them; one of them, with a white, soldier's sword-belt round his waist, held out an uncorked bottle and a half-filled glass to them, as if inviting them to come up and have a drink; another, next to him, with a double-barrelled gun over his shoulder, yelled in a drawn-out voice: "Long live the national workshops! Long live the democratic and Socialist republic!" Beside him stood a tall, black-haired woman in a striped dress, also with a sword-belt and a revolver thrust in it; she alone did not laugh, her large, dark eyes were fixed in front of her as though deep in meditation. I crossed the street to the left and, together with five or six idlers like myself, took up a sheltered position along the wall of the house where the straight line of the boulevard was beginning to be broken, which was, and, indeed, still is, occupied by the Jouvin glove factory. The windows of the house were shuttered. I still could not believe, in spite of the forebodings and expectations of the last few days, that the affair would take a serious turn.

Meanwhile the sound of drums drew nearer and louder. From early morning this peculiar threefold drum-beat—*le rappel*—to summon the National Guard could be heard in the streets. And presently, gently rising and stretching out, like a long, black worm, there appeared on the left side of the boulevard, about twenty feet from the barricade, a column of the civil guard, its bayonets glittering above it like thin, scintillating needles; a few officers rode at its head. The column reached the opposite side of the boulevard and, after occupying it entirely, turned round to face the barricade and stopped dead, steadily increasing in size from behind and getting denser and denser. In spite of the arrival of such a considerable number of people, everything grew much quieter around; voices were hushed, bursts of laughter became less frequent and shorter; it was as though a haze had fallen over all sounds. An empty space suddenly appeared between the barricade and the National Guard, with two or three small, slightly spinning columns of dust whirling along over it and—looking round apprehensively, a little black-and-white dog walked about on thin legs in it. Suddenly—it was difficult to say whether from the front or from behind, from above or from below—there came a short, loud report; it was more like the sound of an iron bar falling heavily on the ground than like a shot, and immediately after this sound there came a strange, breathless silence. Everything seemed to have been hushed in expectation—the very air seemed to grow tense with suspense—and, suddenly, over my very head there came an unbearably loud rattle and roar, like the instantaneous tearing of a huge canvas. . . . That was the insurgents firing through the Venetian blinds of the top floor of the Jouvin factory they had occupied. My fellow-spectators and myself at once ran along the houses of the boulevard (I remember I still had time to notice in the empty space in front of the barricade a man on all fours, a cap with a red pompom, and the black-and-white dog spinning round in the dust) and, reaching a small lane, immediately turned into it. We were joined by a dozen or two other spectators, one of whom, a young man of twenty, had his leg shot through. On the boulevard behind us there was a continuous crackle of shots. We crossed into another street, the Rue d'Echiquier, if I am not mistaken. At one end of it I could see a low barricade. A twelve-year-old boy was jumping about on top of it, pulling faces and brandishing a Turkish sword; a fat national guardsman, as white as a sheet, ran past me, stumbling and moaning at every step, crimson drops of blood dripping on to the ground from the sleeve of his uniform.

The tragedy had begun—and one could no longer doubt its seriousness, though hardly anyone suspected even at that moment what dimensions it would reach.

It was not my business to fight either on the one side or the other: I went back home.

The whole day passed in indescribable apprehension. It was hot and close. . . . I did not leave the Boulevard des Italiens, which was thronged with all sorts of people. The most improbable rumours were in the air, constantly giving place to more fantastic ones. Towards nightfall one thing became absolutely clear: almost half of Paris was in the hands of the insurgents. Barricades appeared everywhere—especially on the other side of the Seine; the soldiers occupied strategic points and made ready for a fight to a finish.

Next day, from early morning, the appearance of the boulevard —and, generally, of the whole of Paris unoccupied by the insurgents—changed as if by the wave of a magic wand. Cavaignac, the G.O.C. of the Paris army, issued an order imposing a curfew, prohibiting every kind of traffic or any movement in the streets. The national guardsmen, Parisian as well as provincial, drawn up on the pavements, guarded the houses in which they were quartered; the regular army, the *garde mobile,* was fighting; foreigners, women, children and invalids were confined to their houses, the windows of which had to be wide open to prevent any ambush. The streets became instantly deserted. Only from time to time would a post office van or a doctor's carriage drive through the streets to be continually stopped by the sentries and the drivers asked to show their passes; or a battery would rumble heavily through the streets on its way to the fighting, or a platoon of soldiers would march by, or an aide-de-camp or an orderly would gallop past. The days that followed were dreadfully depressing; those who have not lived through them can have no true conception of what it was like. The Frenchmen, of course, felt frightened: they could well have imagined that their country and its whole social structure was being destroyed and was facing total annihilation; but the feeling of depression that seized upon the foreigner, condemned to a life of forced inactivity, was, if not more terrible, certainly more wearisome than their indignation and despair. The heat was oppressive; it was impossible to go out; the hot air poured unchecked through the open windows; the sun blazed blindingly; every occupation, reading, writing, was out of the question. . . . Five times, ten times a minute the guns roared; occasionally there came the rattle of rifle fire, the confused din of battle. . . . The streets were deserted; the incandescent cobble-stones of the road turned yellow, the incandescent air shimmered in the sunshine; along the pavements were lines of embarrassed faces, the motionless figures of the national guardsmen—and not a single ordinary living sound! There was a lot of empty space all around, but you felt hemmed in as in a grave or a prison.

After twelve o'clock—new sights; stretchers with killed and wounded. . . . A grey-haired man was carried past with a face as white as the pillow on which it lay: it was the fatally wounded deputy Charbonnel. . . . Heads were silently bared before him, but he did not see those signs of mournful respect: his eyes were closed. Then a crowd of prisoners went by: they were led by members of the *garde mobile,* all young fellows, almost children, who were not regarded with any confidence at first, but who fought like lions. . . . Some of them carried on their bayonets the blood-stained caps of their fallen comrades or flowers which women had thrown from windows to them. *"Vive la république!"* the national guardsmen kept shouting from the two sides of the boulevard, and drew out the last syllable somehow strangely and cheerlessly: *"Vive la mob-i-ile!"* The prisoners walked along without raising their eyes and clinging to one another like sheep: a disordered crowd, gloomy faces, many of them in rags, without caps; some had their hands tied. And the cannonade went on without interruption. The heavy monotonous roar of the barrage seemed to hang in the air; it hung over the city together with the acrid haze of the heat. . . . Towards evening, I could hear some new sounds from my room on the fourth floor: other sharp, fan-like salvoes, much nearer and of shorter duration, broke the monotonous roar of the gunfire. . . . That, as I was told, was the execution of the insurgents in the different *mairies*.

And so it went on, hour after hour, hour after hour. . . . It was impossible to sleep even at night. You tried to go out on the boulevard, walk even as far as the first street to find out what was happening or just for a breath of fresh air. . . . You were stopped at once and asked who you were, where you came from, where you lived and why you were not in uniform. And learning that you were a foreigner, they looked at you suspiciously and ordered you back home. On one occasion a provincial national guardsman (they were the most zealous ones) even insisted on arresting me because—I was wearing my morning tunic. "You put it on," he shouted like one in a frenzy, "because you thought it would make it easier for you to get in touch with the rebels! Who knows," he went on, "perhaps you are a Russian agent and you have gold in your pockets for the purpose of fomenting our troubles (*pour fomenter nos troubles*)!" I suggested that he should examine my pockets, but—that made him even angrier. Russian gold, Russian agents together with lots of other absurd cock-and-bull stories seemed to have become an obsession with all those excited, confused and bewildered people. . . .

I repeat: it was a dreadfully trying time.

Three days of this, I can honestly say, torture passed; the fourth day (26th June) came. The news from the parts of the city where the fighting was taking place reached us rather quickly, passing from one person to another along the pavement. So, for instance, we knew already that the Pantheon had been captured, that the whole left bank of the Seine was in the hands of the army, that General Bréa had been executed by the insurgents, that the Archbishop Offre of Paris had been fatally wounded, that only the suburb of Saint Antoine was still holding out. I remember we read Cavaignac's proclamation, appealing for the last time to the feeling of patriotism that remained in the most hardened hearts. . . . An orderly, a Hussar officer, suddenly galloped along the boulevard and, forming a circle the size of an apple with the fingers of his right hand, shouted: "That's the sort of bullets they are firing at us!"

In the same house where I had rooms and on the same landing lived the well-known German poet Herwegh, whom I knew very well. I used to visit him frequently, just to unburden my heart a little, to get away from myself, from the gnawing, aching boredom of inaction and solitude.

I was sitting in his room on the morning of June 26—he had just had his breakfast. Suddenly his manservant came in with a very worried face.

"What's the matter?"

"A 'blouse' is asking to see you sir."

"A 'blouse'? What 'blouse'?"

"A man in a blouse, a workman, an old man, sir. He asked for citizen (*citoyen*) Herwegh. Shall I let him in?"

Herwegh exchanged glances with me. "Yes," he said, "let him in."

The manservant went out, muttering to himself: "A man in— a blouse!" He was horrified. But it was not so long, a few days after the February revolution, that a blouse had been considered the most fashionable, decent and safe dress! It was not so long since that I had seen with my own eyes at a free performance specially given for the common people at the Théâtre Français, many of the most exquisite dandies of the so-called beau-monde wearing white and blue blouses, out of which peeped rather strangely their starched collars and *jabots*. But other times, other manners. At the time of the June fighting in Paris the blouse had become the symbol of rejection, the mark of Cain, arousing a feeling of horror and fury.

The manservant returned and with a silent shudder showed in a man who had followed him into the room, a man who really was wearing a blouse, a tattered, dirty blouse. The trousers and shoes of that man were soiled and patched, his neck was wrapped in a red rag, and his head was covered with a cap—a cap of grey-ing-black, matted hair that hung down to his eyebrows. A long aquiline nose and two small, dull, inflamed, aged eyes peeped out from under it. His cheeks were sunken, his face was covered with wrinkles, deep as scars, his mouth was wide and twisted, his chin unshaven, his hands red and dirty, and his back bent in that peculiar way that revealed the strain of prolonged and overpow-ering work. . . . There could be no doubt: before us stood one of those numerous hungry and obscure toilers with whom the lower strata of civilized societies swarm.

"Which one of you is citizen Herwegh?" he asked in a hoarse voice.

"I'm Herwegh," replied the German poet, not without some embarrassment.

"Are you expecting your son and his nurse from Berlin?"

"As a matter of fact I am. . . . But how do you know? He should have left four days ago, but I thought. . . ."

"Your boy arrived yesterday. But as the railway station in Saint Denis is in our hands," (at these words Herwegh's servant nearly jumped with fright) "and we can't send him here, he was taken to one of our women—here, on this bit of paper, is his address, and I was told by my mates to come to tell you about it, so that you shouldn't be worried. His nurse is with him. It's a nice place —they will be well fed there. And there's no danger, either. When it's over, you can go and fetch him—here, the address is on this bit of paper. Good-bye, citizen."

The old man went to the door.

"Wait, wait!" Herwegh cried.

The old man stopped, but did not turn round to us.

"Have you come here only for the purpose of reassuring me, a man unknown to you, about my son?"

The old man raised his bent head.

"Yes. My mates sent me."

"Just for that?"

"Yes."

Herwegh threw up his hands in astonishment. "But, good Lord, I—I—I don't know what to say. How on earth did you manage to get here? You must have been stopped at every crossing!"

"Yes, I was."

"Did they ask you where you were going? For what purpose?"

"Yes. They kept looking at my hands to see if there were any traces of gunpowder on them. One officer even threatened to shoot me."

Herwegh was struck dumb with amazement; the servant, too, stared open-eyed at him. *"C'est trop fort!"* he muttered unconsciously with pale lips.

"Good-bye, citizen," the old man said in a clear voice, as though having made up his mind to go.

"Wait—wait—let me thank you," Herwegh said, rushing up to him and detaining him.

He began fumbling in his pockets.

The old man pushed him away with his wide, unbending hand.

"Don't trouble, citizen. I won't take any money."

"Well, let me offer you—er—some lunch then—a glass of wine, perhaps—or something. . . ."

"Thank you, I won't refuse that," said the old man after a short pause. "I haven't had a bite for two days almost."

Herwegh at once sent his servant for some lunch and, meanwhile asked his visitor to sit down. The old man sank heavily into a chair, put both his hands on his knees and dropped his eyes. . . .

Herwegh began to question him, but the old man replied unwillingly and in a sullen tone of voice. It was evident that he was very tired, though he felt neither excitement nor fear, resigning himself to whatever might befall him. Besides, he was not particularly keen on carrying on a conversation with a "bourgeois." At lunch, however, he cheered up a little. At first he ate and drank greedily, then he relaxed a little and began to talk.

"In February," he declared, "we promised the provisional government to wait for three months. Well, the three months passed and we were still as badly off as ever. More so, in fact. The provisional government deceived us. It made many promises, but kept none. It did nothing for the workers. We'd spent all our money on food, there was no work, nothing to do. Some republic! Well, so we made up our minds to fight. We were done for, anyway."

"But," Herwegh observed, "what benefit could you expect from such a crazy insurrection?"

"We were done for, anyway," repeated the old man.

He wiped his lips carefully, folded his napkin, thanked Herwegh and got up.

"Are you going?" cried Herwegh.

"Yes. I have to go back to my mates. What have I got to stay here for?"

"But they are sure to stop you on your way back and, perhaps, really shoot you!"

"Perhaps. What about it? As long as I live, I shall have to get bread for my family, and where can I get it? And if I'm killed, people won't leave orphans without care and protection. Goodbye, citizen."

"At least tell me your name! I should like to know the name of the person who did so much for me!"

"There's no need whatever for you to know my name. To

tell you the truth, what I did, I didn't do for you. My mates told me to do it. Good-bye."

So the old man went away, accompanied by the manservant.

On that day the uprising was finally crushed. As soon as it was possible to go about the city, Herwegh found the woman who had given shelter to his son at the address left by the old man. Her husband and son had been taken prisoner; another of her sons had been killed on the barricades; her nephew had been executed. She, too, refused to accept any money; but, pointing to the two little girls running about in the room, the daughters of her killed son, she said: "If I should have to ask something for them at some future time, I hope your boy will remember them."

We never found out what happened to the old man who had visited Herwegh. It was impossible not to admire his action and the unconscious, almost majestic, simplicity with which he had accomplished it. It evidently never occurred to him that he was doing anything extraordinary, that he was sacrificing himself. But it is impossible not to admire the people who sent him, either, those who at the height of the desperate fighting could remember the worry and anxiety of a "bourgeois" they did not know and took care to set his mind at rest. It is true that twenty-two years later men like these set Paris on fire and shot their hostages; but he who has even a little knowledge of the human heart will not be shocked by these contradictions.

1868.

VIII

THE EXECUTION OF TROPMANN

────────◆────────

I

IN JANUARY OF THE CURRENT YEAR (1870), while dining in Paris at the house of an old friend of mine, I received from M. Du Camp, the well-known writer and expert on the statistics of Paris, quite an unexpected invitation to be present at the execution of Tropmann—and not only at his execution: it was proposed that I should be admitted to the prison itself together with a small number of other privileged persons. The terrible crime committed by Tropmann has not yet been forgotten, but at that time Paris was interested in him and his impending execution as much as, if not more than, the recent appointment of the pseudo-Parliamentarian ministry of Olivier or the murder of Victor Noir, who fell at the hand of the afterwards surprisingly acquitted Prince P[ierre] Bonaparte. In the windows of all the photographers' and stationers' shops were exhibited whole rows of photographs showing a young fellow with a large forehead, dark eyes and puffy lips, the "famous" Pantin murderer (*de l'illustre assassin de Pantin*), and already for some evenings running thousands of workmen had gathered in the environs of the Roquette prison in the vain expectation of the erection of the guillotine, and dispersed only after midnight. Taken by surprise by M. Du Camp's proposal, I accepted it without giving it much thought. And having promised to arrive at the place fixed for our meeting—at the statue of Prince Eugene, on the boulevard of the same name, at 11 o'clock in the evening—I did not want to go back on my word. False pride prevented my doing so. . . . And what if they should think that I was a coward? As a punishment of myself—and as a lesson to others—I should now like to tell everything I saw. I intend to revive in my memory all the painful impressions of that night. It will not be only the reader's curiosity that will be satisfied: he may derive some benefit from my story.

II

A small crowd of people was already waiting for Du Camp and me at the statue of Prince Eugene. Among them was M. Claude, the police commissioner of Paris (*chef de la police de sûreté*), to whom Du Camp introduced me. The others were, like myself, privileged visitors, journalists, reporters, etc. Du Camp had warned me that we should probably have to spend a sleepless night in the office of the prison governor. The execution of condemned criminals takes place in winter at seven o'clock in the morning; but one has to be at the prison before midnight or one might not be able to push one's way through the crowd. There is only about half a mile from the statue of Prince Eugene to the Roquette prison, but so far I could see nothing in any way out of the ordinary. There were just a few more people on the boulevard than usual. One thing, though, one could not help noting: almost all the people were going—and some, especially women, running along—in the same direction: besides, all the cafés and pot-houses were ablaze with lights, which is very rare in the remote quarters of Paris, especially so late at night. The night was not foggy, but dull, damp without rain, and cold without frost, a typical French January night. M. Claude said that it was time to go, and off we went. He preserved the imperturable cheerfulness of a man of affairs in whom such events did not arouse any feelings, except perhaps the desire to have done with his sad duty as soon as possible. M. Claude was a man of about fifty, of medium height, thick-set, broad-shouldered, with a round, closely cropped head and small, almost minute, features. Only his forehead and chin, and the back of his head, were extraordinarily broad; his unflinching energy came out in his dry and even voice, his pale, grey eyes, his short, strong fingers, in his muscular legs, and in all his unhurried but firm movements. He was said to be an expert at his profession, who inspired mortal terror in all thieves and murderers. Political crimes were not part of his duties. His assistant, M. J. . . . , whom Du Camp also greatly admired, looked like a kindly, almost sentimental man and his manners were much more refined. With the exception of these two gentlemen and perhaps Du Camp, we all felt a little awkward—or did it only seem to me to be so?—and a little ashamed, too, though we walked along jauntily—as though on a shooting expedition.

The nearer we came to the prison, the more crowded the streets became, though there were no real crowds as yet. No shouts could be heard, nor even any too loud conversations; it was evident that the "performance" had not yet commenced. Only the street urchins were already weaving round us; with their hands thrust in the pockets of their trousers and the peaks of their caps pulled over their eyes, they sauntered along with that special lolling, flitting gait, which can only be seen in Paris and which in the twinkling of an eye can be changed into a most quick run and the leaps of a monkey.

"There he is—there he is—it's him!" a few voices shouted around us.

"Why," Du Camp said to me suddenly, "you have been mistaken for the executioner!"

"A lovely beginning!" I thought.

The Paris executioner, *Monsieur de Paris,* whose acquaintance I made during that same night, is as tall and as grey as I.

But soon we came to a long, not too wide, square, bounded on two sides by two barrack-like buildings of grimy aspect and crude architecture: that was Roquette Square. On the left was the prison for young criminals *(prison des jeunes détenus)* and on the right—the house of the condemned prisoners *(maison de dépôt pour les condamnés),* or Roquette Prison.

III

A squad of soldiers was drawn up four deep right across the square, and about two hundred feet from it, another squad was also drawn up four deep. As a rule, no soldiers are present at an execution, but this time, in view of Tropmann's "reputation" and the present state of public opinion, excited by Noir's murder, the government thought it necessary to take special measures and not to leave the preservation of law and order to the police alone. The main gates of Roquette prison were exactly in the centre of the empty space, closed in by the soldiers. A few police sergeants walked slowly up and down before the gates; a young, rather fat police officer in an unusually richly embroidered cap (as it appeared the chief inspector of that quarter of the city) rushed upon our group with such insolence that it reminded me of the good old days in my beloved country, but recognizing his superiors, he calmed down. They let us into the small guard-room beside the gates with immense precautions, hardly opening the gates, and—after a preliminary examination and interrogation, took us across two inner courtyards, one large and another small, to the governor's lodgings. The governor, a tall, stalwart man, with a grey moustache and imperial, had the typical face of a French infantry officer, an aquiline nose, immobile, rapacious eyes and a tiny skull. He received us very politely and benignly; but even without his being aware of it, every gesture of his, every word of his, at once showed that he was "a reliable fellow" (*un gaillard solide*), an utterly loyal servant, who would not hesitate to carry out any order of his master. Indeed, he had proved his zeal in action: on the night of the *coup d'état* of December 2nd, he occupied with his battalion the printing works of the *Moniteur*. Like a real gentleman, he put the whole of his apartment at our disposal. It was on the second floor of the main building and consisted of four fairly well furnished rooms; in two of them a fire was lit in the fireplace. A small Italian greyhound with a dislocated leg and a mournful expression in her eyes, as though she, too, felt to be a prisoner, limped about, wagging her tail, from one rug to another. There were eight of us visitors; some of them I recognized from their photographs (Sardou, Albert Wolf), but I did not feel like talking to any of them. We all sat down on chairs in the drawing-room (Du Camp had gone out with M. Claude). It goes without saying that Tropmann became the subject of conversation and, as it were, the centre of all our thoughts. The prison governor told us that he had been asleep since nine o'clock in the evening and that he slept like a log; that he seemed to have guessed what had happened to his request for a reprieve; that he had implored him, the governor, to tell him the truth; that he kept insisting stubbornly that he had accomplices whom he refused to name; that he would probably lose his nerve at the decisive moment, but that he ate with appetite, did not read books, etc., etc. For our part, some of us wondered whether one ought to give credence to the words of a criminal who had proved himself to be an inveterate liar, went over the details of the murder, asked ourselves what the phrenologists would make of Tropmann's skull, raised the question of capital punishment—but all this was so lifeless, so dull, so platitudinous, that even those who spoke did not feel like carrying on.

To talk of something else was rather embarrassing—impossible; impossible out of respect for death alone, for the man who was doomed to die. We were all overwhelmed by a feeling of irksome and wearisome—yes, wearisome-uneasiness: no one was really bored, but this dreary feeling was a hundred times worse than boredom! It seemed as though there would be no end to the night! As for me, there was one thing I was sure of, namely that I had no right to be where I was, that no psychological or philosophic considerations excused me. M. Claude came back and told us how the notorious Jude had slipped through his fingers and how he was still hoping to catch him if he was still alive. But suddenly we heard the heavy clatter of wheels and a few moments later we were informed that the guillotine had arrived. We all rushed out into the street—just as though we were glad of the news!

IV

Before the prison gates stood a huge, closed van, drawn by three horses, harnessed one behind the other; another, two-wheeled van, a small and low one, which looked like an oblong box and was drawn by one horse, had stopped a little further off. (That one, as we learned later, was to convey the body of the executed man to the cemetery immediately after the execution.) A few workmen in short blouses were to be seen round the vans, and a tall man in a round hat, white necktie and a light overcoat thrown over his shoulders, was giving orders in an undertone. . . . That was the executioner. All the authorities—the prison governor, M. Claude, the district police inspector, and so on, were surrounding and greeting him. *"Ah, Monsieur Indric! bon soir, Monsieur Indric!"* (His real name is Heidenreich: he is an Alsatian.) Our group, too, walked up to him: *he* became for a moment the centre of our attention. There was a certain strained but respectful familiarity in the way he was treated by everybody. "We don't look down upon you for you are, after all, a person of importance!" Some of us, probably just to show off, even shook hands with him. (He had a pair of beautiful hands of remarkable whiteness.) I recalled a line from Pushkin's *Poltava:—*

The executioner . . . .
Playing with his white hands . . . .

M. Indric carried himself very simply, gently and courteously, but not without a touch of patriarchal gravity. It seemed that he felt that we regarded him that night as only second in importance after Tropmann, and, as it were, his first minister.

The workmen opened the big van and began taking out of it all the component parts of the guillotine, which they had to put up within fifteen feet of the prison gates.[1] Two lanterns began moving to and fro just above the ground, lighting up the polished cobblestones of the roadway with small, bright circles of light. I looked at my watch—it was only half past twelve! It had grown much duller and colder. There was already a great number of people about—and behind the lines of the soldiers, bordering the empty space in front of the prison, there rose the uninterrupted and confused din of human voices. I walked up to the soldiers: they stood motionless, drawing closer a little and breaking the original symmetry of their ranks. Their faces expressed nothing but cold and patiently submissive boredom; and even the faces I could discern behind the shakos and uniforms of the soldiers and behind the three-cornered hats and tunics of the policemen, the faces of the workmen and artisans, expressed almost the same thing, only with the addition of a sort of indefinable irony. In front, from behind the massively stirring and

---

[1] The readers who wish to acquaint themselves not only with all the particulars of the "execution" but also with everything that comes before it, should consult M. Du Camp's excellent article: *La Prison de la Roquette* in the *Revue des deux Mondes*, No. 1, 1870.

pressing crowd, one could hear exclamations, like: *Ohé Trop-mann! Ohé Lambert! Fallait pas qu'y aille!* Shouts, shrill whistles. One could clearly make out some abusive argument about a place, a fragment of a cynical song came creeping along like a snake—and there was a sudden burst of loud laughter, instantly caught up in the crowd and ending with a roar of coarse guffaws. The "real business" had not yet begun; one could not hear the anti-dynastic shouts everyone expected, nor the all too familiar menacing reverberations of the Marseillaise.

I went back to the place near the slowly growing guillotine. A certain gentleman, curly-headed and dark-faced, in a soft, grey hat, probably a lawyer, was standing beside me haranguing two or three other gentlemen in tightly buttoned up overcoats, waving the forefinger of his right hand forcefully up and down, trying to prove that Tropmann was not a murderer, but a maniac. *"Un maniaque! Je vais vous le prouver! Suivez mon raisonnement!"* he kept saying. *"Son mobile n'était pas l'assassinat, mais un orgueil que je nommerais volontiers démesuré! Suivez mon raison-nement!"* The gentlemen in the overcoats "followed his reason-ing," but, judging by their expressions, he scarcely convinced them; and the worker who sat on the platform of the guillotine looked at him with undisguised contempt. I returned to the prison governor's apartment.

V

A few of our "colleagues" had already gathered there. The courteous governor was regaling them with mulled wine. Again they started discussing whether Tropmann was still asleep, what he ought to be feeling and whether he could hear the noise of the people in spite of the distance of his cell from the street, and so on. The governor showed us a whole heap of letters addressed to Tropmann, who, as the governor assured us, refused to read them. Most of them seemed to be full of silly jokes, but there were also some that were serious, in which he was conjured to repent and confess everything; one Methodist clergyman sent a whole theological thesis on twenty pages; there were also small notes from ladies, who even enclosed flowers—marguerites and immortelles—in some of them. The prison governor told us that Tropmann had tried to get some poison from the prison pharmacist and wrote a letter asking for it, which the pharmacist, of course, at once forwarded to the authorities. I could not help feeling that our worthy host was rather at a loss to explain to himself the interest we took in a man like Tropmann who, in his opinion, was a savage and disgusting animal, and almost ascribed it to the idle curiosity of civilian men of the world, the "idle rich." After a little talk we just crawled off into different corners. During the whole of that night we wandered about like condemned souls, *"comme des âmes en peine,"* as the French say; went into rooms, sat down side by side on chairs in the drawing room, inquired after Tropmann, glanced at the clock, yawned, went downstairs into the yard and into the street again, came back, again sat down. . . . Some told drawing room stories, exchanged trivial personal news, touched lightly on politics, the theatre, Noir's murder; others tried to crack jokes, to say something witty, but, somehow, it did not come off at all and—provoked a sort of unpleasant laughter, which was cut short immediately, and a sort of false approbation. I found a tiny sofa in the first room and, somehow or other, managed to lie down on it. I tried to sleep but, of course, did not sleep. I did not doze off for one moment.

The distant hollow noise of the crowd was getting louder, deeper and more and more unbroken. At three o'clock, according to M. Claude, who kept coming into the room, sitting down on a chair, falling asleep at once and disappearing again, summoned by one of his subordinates, there were already more than twenty-five thousand people gathered there. The noise struck me by its resemblance to the distant roar of the sea: the same sort of unending Wagnerian *crescendo,* not rising continuously, but with huge intervals between the ebb and flow; the shrill notes of women's and children's voices rose in the air like thin spray over this enormous rumbling noise; there was the brutal power of some elemental force discernible in it. It would grow quiet and die down for a moment, then the hubbub would start again, grow and swell, and in another moment it seemed about to strike, as though wishing to tear everything down, and then it would again retreat, grow quiet, and again swell—and there seemed to be no end to it. And what, I could not help asking myself, did this noise signify? Impatience, joy, malice? No! It did not serve as an echo of any separate, any human feeling. . . . It was simply the rumble and the roar of some elemental force.

VI

At about three o'clock in the morning I must have gone out for the tenth time into the street. The guillotine was ready. Its two beams, separated by about two feet, with the slanting line of the connecting blade, stood out dimly and strangely rather than terribly against the dark sky. For some reason I imagined that those beams ought to be more distant from each other; their proximity lent the whole machine a sort of sinister shapeliness, the shapeliness of a long, carefully stretched out swan's neck. The large, dark-red wicker basket, looking like a suitcase, aroused a feeling of disgust in me. I knew that the executioners would throw the warm and still quivering dead body and the cut off head into that basket. . . . The mounted police (*garde municipale*), who had arrived a little earlier, took up their position in a large semi-circle before the façade of the prison; from time to time the horses neighed, gnawed at their bits and tossed their heads; large drops of froth showed up white on the road between their forelegs. The riders dozed sombrely beneath their bearskins, pulled over their eyes. The lines of the soldiers, cutting across the square and holding back the crowds, fell back further: now there were not two hundred but three hundred feet of empty space before the prison. I went up to one of those lines and gazed for a long time at the people crammed behind it; their shouting actually was elemental, that is, senseless. I still remember the face of a workman, a young fellow of about twenty: he stood there grinning, with his eyes fixed on the ground, just as though he were thinking of something amusing, then he would suddenly throw back his head, open his mouth wide and begin to shout in a drawn-out voice, without words, and then his head would again drop and he would start grinning again. What was going on inside that man? Why did he consign himself to such a painfully sleepless night, to an almost eight-hour long immobility? My ears did not catch any snatches of conversation; only occasionally there came through the unceasing uproar the piercing cry of a hawker selling a leaflet about Tropmann, about his life, his execution and even his "last words." . . . Or, again, an argument broke out somewhere far away, or there would be a hideous burst of laughter, or some women would start screaming. . . . This time I heard the Marseillaise, but it was sung only by five or six men, and that, too, with interruptions. The Marseillaise becomes significant only when thousands are singing it. *A bas Pierre Bonaparte!* someone shouted at the top of his voice. . . . Oo—oo—ah—ah! the crowd responded in an incoherent roar. In one place the shouts assumed the measured rhythm of a polka: one—two—three—four! one—two—three—four —to the well-known tune of *des lampions!* A heavy, rank breath of alcoholic fumes came from the crowd: a great deal of wine had been drunk by all those bodies; there were a great many drunken men there. It was not for nothing that the pot-houses glowed with red lights in the general background of this scene. The night had grown pitch-dark; the sky had become totally overcast and turned black. There were small clumps on the sparse trees, looming indistinctly out of the darkness like phantoms: those were street urchins who had climbed up on the trees and were sitting among the branches, whistling and screeching like birds. One of them had fallen down and, it is said, was fatally injured, having broken his spine, but he only aroused loud laughter, and that, too, for a short time.

On my way back to the prison governor's apartment, I passed the guillotine and saw on its platform the executioner surrounded by a small crowd of inquisitive people. He was carrying out a "rehearsal" for them; threw down the hinged plank, to which the criminal was fastened and which, as it fell, touched with its end the semi-circular slot between the beams; he let fall the knife, which ran down heavily and smoothly with a rapid, hollow roar, and so on. I did not stop to watch this "rehearsal," that is to say, I did not climb on to the platform: the feeling of some unknown transgression committed by myself, of some secret shame, was growing stronger and stronger inside me. . . . It is perhaps to this feeling that I must ascribe the fact that the horses, harnessed to the vans and calmly chewing the oats in their nose-bags, seemed to me at that moment to be the only innocent creatures among us all.

Once more I went back to the solitude of my little sofa and once more I began to listen to the roar of the breakers on the sea-shore. . . .

VII

Contrary to what is generally asserted, the *last* hour of waiting passes much more quickly that the first and, more especially, than the second or third. . . . So it happened this time. We were surprised at the news that it had struck six and that only one hour remained to the moment of execution. We had to go to Tropmann's cell in exactly half an hour: half past six. All traces of sleep at once disappeared from all the faces. I don't know what the others felt, but I felt terribly sick at heart. New figures appeared: a priest, a small, grey-haired little man with a thin little face flashed by in his long, black cassock with the ribbon of the Légion d'Honneur and a low, wide-brimmed hat. The prison governor prepared a sort of breakfast for us, *une collation;* huge cups of chocolate appeared on the round table in the drawing-room. . . . I did not even go near it, though our hospitable host advised me to fortify myself, "because the morning air might he harmful." To take food at that moment seemed—disgusting to me. Good Lord, a feast at such a time. "I have no right," I kept saying to myself for the hundreth time since the beginning of that night.

"Is *he* still asleep?" one of us asked, sipping his chocolate.

(They were all talking of Tropmann without referring to him by name: there could be no question of any other *him.*)

"Yes, he's asleep," replied the prison governor.

"In spite of this terrible racket?"

(The noise had, in fact, grown extraordinarily loud and turned into a kind of hoarse roar; the menacing chorus, no longer crescendo, rumbled on victoriously, gaily.)

"His cell is behind three walls," replied the prison governor.

M. Claude, whom the prison governor evidently treated as the most important person among us, looked at his watch and said: "Twenty past six."

We must, I expect, have all shuddered inwardly, but we just put on our hats and set off noisily after our guide.

"Where are you dining today?" a reporter asked in a loud voice.

But that struck us all as a little too unnatural.

VIII

We went out into the large prison courtyard; and there, in the corner on the right before a half-closed door, a sort of roll-call took place; then we were shown into a tall, narrow and entirely empty room with a leather stool in the centre.

"It is here that *la toilette du condamné* takes place," Du Camp whispered to me.

We did not all get in: there were only ten of us, including the prison governor, the priest, M. Claude and his assistant. During the next two or three minutes that we spent in that room (some kind of official documents were being signed there) the thought that we had no right to do what we were doing, that by being present with an air of hypocritical solemnity at the killing of a fellow human being, we were performing some odious, iniquitous farce—that thought flashed across my mind for the last time; as soon as we set off, again after M. Claude, along the wide stone corridor, dimly lit by two night-lights, I no longer felt anything except that now—now—this minute—this second. . . . We rapidly climbed two staircases into another corridor, walked through it, went down a narrow spiral staircase and found ourselves before an iron door. . . . Here!

The warder unlocked the door cautiously. It opened quietly—and we all went in quietly and in silence into a rather spacious room with yellow walls, a high barred window and a crumpled bed on which no one was lying. . . . The steady light of a large night lamp lit up all the objects in the room quite clearly.

I was standing a little behind the rest and, I remember, screwed up my eyes involuntarily; however, I saw at once, diagonally opposite me, a young, black-haired, black-eyed face, which, moving slowly from the left to right, gazed at us all with huge round eyes. That was Tropmann. He had woken up before our arrival. He was standing before the table on which he had just written a farewell (though rather trivial) letter to his mother. M. Claude took off his hat and went up to him.

"Tropmann," he said in his dry, soft, but peremptory voice, "we have come to inform you that your appeal for a reprieve has been dismissed and that the hour of retribution has come for you."

Tropmann turned his eyes on him, but they were no longer "huge"; he looked calmly, almost somnolently, and did not utter a word.

"My child," the priest exclaimed dully, going up to him from the other side, *"du courage!"*

Tropmann looked at him exactly as he had looked at M. Claude.

"I knew he wouldn't be afraid," said M. Claude in a confident tone, addressing us all. "Now when he has got over the first shock *(le premier choc)*, I can answer for him."

(So does a schoolmaster, wishing to cajole his pupil, tell him beforehand that he is "a clever fellow.")

"Oh, I'm not afraid *(Oh! je n'ai pas peur!)*," said Tropmann, addressing M. Claude again, "I'm not afraid!"

His voice, a pleasant, youthful baritone, was perfectly even.

The priest took a small bottle out of his pocket.

"Won't you have a drop of wine, my child?"

"Thank you, no," Tropmann replied politely, with a slight bow.

M. Claude addressed him again.

"Do you insist that you are not guilty of the crime for which you've been condemned?"

"I did not strike the blow! *(Je n'ai pas frappé!)*"

"But—? the prison governor interjected.

"I did not strike the blow!"

(For some time past Tropmann, as everyone knows, had

asserted, contrary to his former depositions, that he did take the Kink family to the place where they had been butchered, but that they were murdered by his associates, and that even the injury on his hand was due to his attempt to save one of the small children. However, he had told as many lies during his trial as very few criminals have done before him.)

"And do you still assert that you had accomplices?"

"Yes."

"You can't name them, can you?"

"I can't and I won't. I won't," Tropmann raised his voice and his face flushed. It seemed as though he were going to be angry.

"Oh, all right, all right," M. Claude said hurriedly, as though implying that he had put his questions only as a formality and that there was something else that had to be done now. . . .

Tropmann had to undress.

Two warders went up to him and began taking off his prison strait-jacket *(camisole de force)*, a kind of blouse of coarse bluish cloth, with belts and buckles behind, long sewn-up sleeves, to the ends of which strong pieces of tape were fastened near the thighs by the waist. Tropmann stood sideways, within two feet of me. Nothing prevented me from scrutinizing his face carefully. It could have been described as handsome but for the unpleasantly full lips, which made his mouth protrude a little too much and turn upwards funnel-like, just as with animals, and behind his lips were two rows of bad, sparse, fan-like teeth. He had thick, slightly wavy, dark hair, long eyebrows, expressive, protruding eyes, a wide clear forehead, a regular, slightly aquiline nose, little curls of black down on his chin. . . . If you happened to meet such a man outside prison and not in such surroundings, he would, no doubt, have made a good impression on you. Hundreds of such faces were to be seen among young factory workers, pupils of public institutions, etc. Tropmann was of medium height and of a youthfully thin and slender build. He looked to me like an overgrown boy, and, indeed, he was not yet twenty. He had a natural, healthy, slightly rosy complexion; he did not turn pale even at our entrance. . . . There could be no doubt that he really had slept all night. He did not raise his eyes and his breathing was regular and deep, like a man walking up a steep hill. Once or twice he shook his hair as though wishing to dismiss a troublesome thought, tossed back his head, threw a quick glance at the ceiling and heaved a hardly perceptible sigh. With the exception of those, almost momentary, movements, nothing in him disclosed, I won't say, fear, but even agitation or anxiety. We were all, I am sure, much paler and more agitated than he. When his hands were released from the sewn-up sleeves of the strait-jacket, he held up this strait-jacket in front of him, on his chest, with a pleased smile, while it was being undone at the back; little children behave like that when they are being undressed. Then he took off his shirt himself, put on another clean one, and carefully buttoned the neckband. . . . It was strange to see the free, sweeping movements of that naked body, those bare limbs against the yellowish background of the prison wall. . . .

Then he bent down and put on his boots, knocking loudly with his heels and soles against the floor and the wall to make sure his feet got into them properly. All this he did cheerfully and without any sign of constraint—almost gaily, just as though he had been invited to go for a walk. He was silent and—we were silent. We merely exchanged glances, shrugging our shoulders involuntarily with surprise. We were all struck by the simplicity of his movements, a simplicity which, like any other calm and natural manifestation of life, amounted almost to elegance. One of our colleagues, who met me by accident later during that day, told me that all during our stay in Tropmann's cell, he had kept imagining that it was not 1870 but 1794, that we were not ordinary citizens but Jacobins, and that we were taking to his execution not a common murderer but a marquis-legitimist, *un ci-devant, un talon rouge, monsieur!*

It has been observed that when people sentenced to death have their sentences read out to them, they either lapse into complete insensibility and, as it were, die and decompose beforehand, or show off and brazen it out; or else give themselves up to despair, weep, tremble and beg for mercy. . . . Tropmann did not belong to any of these categories—and that was why he puzzled even M. Claude himself. Let me say, by the way, that if Tropmann had begun to howl and weep, my nerves would certainly not have stood it and I should have run away. But at the sight of that composure, that simplicity and, as it were, modesty —all the feelings in me—the feelings of disgust for a pitiless murderer, a monster who cut the throats of little children while they were crying, *Maman! Maman!*, the feeling of compassion, finally, for a man whom death was about to swallow up, disappeared and dissolved in—a feeling of astonishment. What was sustaining Tropmann? Was it the fact that though he did not show off, he did "cut a figure" before *spectators*, gave us his last performance? Or was it innate fearlessness or vanity aroused by M. Claude's words, the pride of the struggle that had to be kept up to the end—or something else, some still undivined feeling? . . . That was a secret he took to the grave with him. Some people are still convinced that Tropmann was not in his right mind. (I have mentioned earlier the lawyer in the white hat, whom, incidentally, I never saw again.) The aimlessness, one might almost say, the absurdity of the annihilation of the entire Kink family serves to a certain extent as a confirmation of that point of view.

IX

But presently he finished with his boots and—straightened out, shook himself—ready! *Again* they put the prison jacket on him. M. Claude asked us to go out and—leave Tropmann alone with the priest. We did not have to wait even two minutes in the corridor before his small figure with his head held up fearlessly appeared among us. His religious feelings were not very strong and he probably carried out the last rite of confession before the priest, absolving his sins, just as a rite. All of our group with Tropmann in the centre at once went up the narrow spiral staircase, which we had descended a quarter of an hour before, and—disappeared in pitch darkness: the night lamp on the staircase had gone out. It was an awful moment. We were all rushing upstairs, we could hear the rapid and harsh clatter of our feet on the iron steps, we trod on each other's heels, we knocked against each other's shoulders, one of us had his hat knocked off, someone behind me shouted angrily: *"Mais sacrédieu!* Light a candle! Let's have some light!"* And there among us, together with us, in the pitch darkness was our victim, our prey—that unhappy man —and who of those who were pushing and scrambling upstairs was he? Would it not occur to him to take advantage of the darkness and with all his agility and the determination of despair to escape—where? Anywhere, to some remote corner of the prison —and just knock his head against a wall there! At least, he'd have killed himself. . . .

I do not know whether these "apprehensions" occurred to anyone else. . . . But they appeared to be in vain. Our whole group with the small figure in the middle emerged from the inside recess of the staircase into the corridor. Tropmann evidently belonged to the guillotine—and the procession set off towards it.

X

This procession could be called a flight. Tropmann walked in front of us with quick, resilient, almost bounding steps; he was obviously in a hurry, and we all hurried after him. Some of us, anxious to have a look at his face once more, even ran ahead to the right and the left of him. So we rushed across the corridor and ran down the other staircase, Tropmann jumping two steps at a time, ran across another corridor, jumped over a few steps and, at last, found ourselves in the tall room with the stool which I have mentioned and on which "the toilet of the condemned man" was to be completed. We entered through one door, and from the other door there appeared, walking importantly, in a white necktie and a black "suit," the executioner, looking for all the world like a diplomat or a protestant pastor. He was followed by a short, fat old man in a black coat, his first assistant, the hangman of Beauvais. The old man held a small leather bag in his hand. Tropmann stopped at the stool. Everyone took up a position round him. The executioner and his old assistant stood to the right of him, the prison governor and M. Claude to the left. The old man unlocked the key of the bag, took out a few white raw-hide straps, some of them long and some short, and kneeling with difficulty behind Tropmann, began hobbling his legs. Tropmann accidentally stepped on the end of one of those straps and the old man, trying to pull it out, muttered twice: *"Pardon, monsieur"* and, at last, touched Tropmann on the calf of the leg. Tropmann at once turned round and with his customary polite half-bow raised his foot and freed the strap. Meanwhile the priest was softly reading prayers in French out of a small book. Two other assistants came up, quickly removed the jacket from Tropmann, tied his hands behind him and began tying the straps round his whole body. The chief executioner gave orders, pointing here and there with a finger. It seemed that there were not enough holes in the straps for the tongues to go through: no doubt, the man who made the holes had a fatter man in mind. The old man at first searched in his bag, then fumbled about in all his pockets and, having felt everything carefully, at last drew out from one of them a small, crooked awl with which he began painfully to bore holes in the straps; his unskilful fingers, swollen with gout, obeyed him badly, and, besides, the hide was new and thick. He would make a hole, try it out—the tongue would not go through: he had to bore a little more. The priest evidently realised that things were not as they should be, and glancing stealthily once or twice over his shoulder, began to draw out the words of the prayers, so as to give the old man time to get things right. At last the operation during which, I frankly confess, I was covered with cold sweat, was finished and all the tongues went in where required. But then another one started. Tropmann was asked to sit down on the stool, before which he was standing, and the same gouty old man began cutting his hair. He got out a pair of small scissors and, twisting his lips, carefully cut off at first the collar of Tropmann's shirt, the shirt he had only just put on and from which it would have been so easy to tear off the collar beforehand. But the cloth was coarse and all in pleats and it resisted the none too sharp blades. The chief executioner had a look and was dissatisfied: the space left by the cut off piece was not big enough. He indicated with his hand how much more he wanted cut off and the gouty old man set to work again and cut out another big piece of cloth. The top and the back was uncovered —the shoulder-blades became visible. Tropmann twitched them slightly: it was cold in the room. Then the old man started on the hair. Putting his puffy left hand on the head of Tropmann, who at once bent it down obediently, he began cutting the hair with his right. Thick strands of wiry, dark-brown hair slid over the shoulders and fell on the floor; one of them rolled up to my boot. Tropmann kept bending his head in the same obedient manner; the priest dragged out the words of the prayers even more slowly. I could not take my eyes off those hands, once stained with innocent blood, but now lying so helplessly one on top of the other—and particularly that slender, youthful neck. . . . In my imagination I could not help seeing a line cut straight across it. . . . There, I thought, a five-hundred-pound axe would in a few moments pass, smashing the vertebrae and cutting through the veins and muscles, and yet the body did not seem to expect anything of the kind: it was so smooth, so white, so healthy. . . .

I could not help asking myself what that so obediently bent head was thinking of at that moment. Was it holding on stubbornly and, as the saying is, with clenched teeth, to one and the same thought: "I won't break down!" Were all sorts of memories of the past, probably quite unimportant ones, flashing through it at that moment? Was the memory of the face of one of the members of the Kink family, twisted in the agony of death, passing through it? Or was it simply trying not to think—that head, and was merely repeating to itself: "That's nothing, that doesn't matter, we shall see, we shall see . . ." and would it go on repeating it till death came crashing down upon it—and there would be nowhere to recoil from it? . . .

And the little old man kept on cutting and cutting. . . . The hair crunched as it was caught up by the scissors. . . . At last this operation, too, was at an end. Tropmann got up quickly, shook his head. . . . Ordinarily, the condemned prisoners who are still able to speak at this moment address the governor of the prison with a last request, remind him of any money or debts they may leave behind, thank their warders, ask that a last note or a strand of hair should be sent to their relatives, send their regards for the last time—but Tropmann evidently was not an ordinary prisoner: he scorned such "sentimentalities" and did not utter a single word. He was silent. He waited. A short tunic was thrown over his shoulders. The executioner grasped his elbow. . . .

"Look here, Tropmann (*Voyons, Tropmann!*)," M. Claude's voice resounded in the death-like stillness, "soon, in another minute, everything will be at an end. Do you still persist in claiming that you had accomplices?"

"Yes, sir, I do persist (*Oui, monsieur, je persiste*)," answered Tropmann in the same pleasant, firm baritone voice, and he bent forward slightly, as though courteously apologising and even re-gretting that he could not answer otherwise.

"*Eh bien! Allons!*" said M. Claude, and we all set off; we went out into the large prison courtyard.

XI

It was five to seven, but the sky hardly grew lighter and the same dull mist covered everything, concealing the contours of all ob-jects. The roar of the crowd encompassed us by an unbroken, ear-splitting, thunderous wave as soon as we stepped over the threshold. Our small group, which had become thinner, for some of us had lagged behind, and I too, though walking with the others, kept myself a little apart, moved rapidly over the cobbled roadway of the courtyard straight to the gates. Tropmann minced along nimbly—his shackles interfered with his walk—and how small he suddenly appeared to me, almost a child! Suddenly the two halves of the gates, like some immense mouth of an animal, opened up slowly before us—and all at once, as though to the accompaniment of the great roar of the overjoyed crowd which had at last caught sight of what it had been waiting for, the monster of the guillotine stared at us with its two narrow black beams and its suspended axe.

I suddenly felt cold, so cold that I almost felt sick; it seemed to me that this cold, too, rushed at us into the courtyard through those gates; my legs gave way under me. However, I cast another glance at Tropmann. He suddenly recoiled, tossing back his head and bending his knees, as though someone hit him in the chest. "He's going to faint," someone whispered in my ear. . . . But he recovered himself immediately and went forward with a firm step. Those of us who wanted to see how his head would roll off rushed past him into the street. . . . I had not enough courage for that; with a sinking heart I stopped at the gates. . . .

I saw the executioner rise suddenly like a black tower on the left side of the guillotine platform; I saw Tropmann, separated from the huddle of people below, scrambling up the steps (there were ten of them—as many as ten!); I saw him stopping and turning round; I heard him say: *"Dites à Monsieur Claude!"* [1] I saw him appear above and two men pouncing on him from the right and the left, like spiders on a fly; I saw him falling forward suddenly and his heels kicking. . . .

But here I turned away and began to wait, the ground slowly rising and falling under my feet. . . . And it seemed to me that I was waiting a terribly long time.[2] I managed to notice that at Tropmann's appearance the roar of the crowd seemed suddenly to roll up into a ball and—a breathless hush fell over everything. . . . Before me stood a sentry, a young red-cheeked fellow. . . . I just had time to see him looking intently at me with dull perplexity and horror. . . . I even had time to think that that soldier probably hailed from some god-forsaken village and came from a decent, law-abiding family and—and the things he had to see now! At last I heard a light knocking of wood on wood—that was the sound made by the top part of the yoke with the slit for the passage of the knife as it fell round the murderer's head and kept it immobile. . . . Then something suddenly descended with a hollow growl and stopped with an abrupt thud. . . . Just as though a huge animal had retched. . . . I cannot think of any better comparison. I felt dizzy. Everything swam before my eyes. . . .

---

[1] I did not hear the rest of the sentence. His last words were: *Dites à Monsieur Claude que je persiste,* that is to say, tell M. Claude that I persist in claiming that I had accomplices. Tropmann did not want to deprive himself of this last pleasure, this last satisfaction: to leave the sting of doubt and reproach in the minds of his judges and the public.

[2] As a matter of fact, only *twenty* seconds passed between the time Tropmann put his foot on the first step of the guillotine and the moment when his dead body was flung into the prepared basket.

Someone seized me by the arm. I looked up: it was M. Claude's assistant, M. J. . . . , whom my friend Du Camp, as I learnt afterwards, had asked to keep an eye on me.

"You are very pale," he said with a smile. "Would you like a drink of water?"

But I thanked him and went back to the prison courtyard, which seemed to me like a place of refuge from the horrors on the other side of the gates.

XII

Our group assembled in the guard-house by the gates to take leave of the prison governor and wait for the crowds to disperse. I, too, went in there and learnt that, while lying on the plank, Tropmann suddenly threw his head sideways convulsively so that it did not fit into the semicircular hole. The executioners were forced to drag it there by the hair, and while they were doing it, Tropmann bit the finger of one of them—the chief one. I also heard that immediately after the execution, at the time when the body, thrown into the van, was being driven rapidly away, two men took advantage of the first moments of unavoidable confusion to force their way through the lines of the soldiers and, crawling under the guillotine, began wetting their handkerchiefs in the blood that had dripped through the chinks of the planks. . . .

But I listened to all that talk as though in a dream. I felt very tired—and I was not the only one to feel like that. They all looked tired, though they all obviously felt relieved, just as if a load had been removed from their backs. But not one of us, *absolutely no one looked like a man who realized that he had been present at the performance of an act of social justice:* everyone tried to turn away in spirit and, as it were, shake off the responsibility for this murder.

Du Camp and I said goodbye to the prison governor and went home. A whole stream of human beings, men, women and children, rolled past us in disorderly and untidy waves. Almost all of them were silent; only the labourers occasionally shouted to one another: "Where are you off to? And you?" and the street urchins greeted with whistling the "cocottes" who drove past. And what drunken, glum, sleepy faces! What an expression of boredom, fatigue, dissatisfaction, disappointment, dull, purposeless disappointment! I did not see many drunks, though: they had either been picked up already or quieted down themselves. The workaday life was receiving all these people once more into its bosom —and why, for the sake of what sensations, had they left its rut for a few hours? It is awful to think what is hidden there. . . .

About fifty yards from the prison we hailed a cab, got into it, and drove off.

On the way Du Camp and I discussed what we had seen and about which he had shortly before (in the January issue of *Revue des deux Mondes* already quoted by me) said so many weighty, sensible things. We talked of the unnecessary, senseless barbarism of all that medieval procedure, thanks to which the criminal's agony went on for half an hour (from twenty-eight minutes past six to seven o'clock), of the hideousness of all those undressings, dressings, hair-cutting, those journeys along corridors and up and down staircases. . . . By what right was all that done? How could such a shocking routine be allowed? And capital punishment itself—could it possibly be justified? We had seen the impression such a spectacle made on the common people: and, indeed, there was no trace of the so-called instructive spectacle at all. Scarcely one thousandth part of the crowd, no more than fifty or sixty people, could have seen anything in the semi-darkness of early morning at a distance of 150 feet and through the lines of soldiers and the cruppers of the horses. And the rest? What benefit, however small, could they have derived from that drunken, sleepless, idle, depraved night? I remembered the young labourer, who had been shouting senselessly and whose face I had studied for several minutes. Would he start work today as a man who hated vice and idleness more than before? And what about me? What did I get from it? A feeling of involuntary astonishment at a murderer, a moral monster, who could show his contempt for death. Can the law-giver desire such impressions? What "moral purpose" can one possibly talk about after so many refutations, confirmed by experience?

But I am not going to indulge in arguments: they would lead me too far. And, anyway, who is not aware of the fact that the question of capital punishment is one of the most urgent questions that humanity has to solve at this moment? I will be content and excuse my own misplaced curiosity if my account supplies a few arguments to those who are in favour of the abolition of capital punishment or, at least, the abolition of public executions.

Weimar, 1870.

IX

ABOUT NIGHTINGALES

I AM SENDING YOU, my dear S.T., as a lover of and expert on all sorts of sports, the following story about nightingales, their songs, how to keep them, the method of catching them, written down by me from the words of an experienced old huntsman, a house serf. I have tried to preserve all his expressions and his manner of speech.

The best nightingales were always thought to be those in the Kursk province; but more recently they grew not so good; and today the best nightingales are thought to be those which are caught near Berdichev, on the frontier; there, about ten miles behind Berdichev, is a forest, known as Treyatsky; there are excellent nightingales there. The time to catch them is the beginning of May. They are to be found mostly in bird-cherry thickets or small woods, as well as in the marshes where such woods grow; the marsh nightingales be the most expensive ones. They arrive on the 20th of April (three days before St. George's Day); at first they sing softly, but by the month of May they're already going strong and are singing for all they're worth. You must go and listen to them at sunrise and sundown and at night, but best of all at sunrise and sundown; sometimes you have to spend a whole night in the marsh. A mate of mine and myself nearly froze to death in a marsh one night: it was freezing at night and by daybreak there was ice as thick as a pancake on the water; I was wearing an old summer coat, very threadbare it was, too; I only saved myself by curling up between two hillocks, taking off my coat, wrapping it over my head and breathing on my belly under my coat; my teeth chattered a whole day afterwards. To catch nightingales isn't very difficult: first you must listen carefully and make quite sure you knows the place where he is, then you clears the ground proper-like under the bush, puts down your trap and fastens down the hen by tying her legs, and you hides yourself and starts blowing your pipe: there's a special pipe made for it, something like a penny whistle. The trap is made out of a net with two little loops, one of the loops has to be dug firmly into the ground and the other must be just pushed in, and you then tie a string to it; when the nightingale flies down to the hen, you just pull out the string and the trap will be sprung. Some nightingales are very eager and they come down from the tree like a bullet as soon as they catches sight of the hen; others are more careful; they first flies down a bit lower, spying out the land, as you might say—wants to make sure it's his hen. It's best to catch such a one with a net. Your net must be about thirty-five feet and you puts it over a bush or dry mullen-pinks—and be careful you don't get it tangled up; as soon as the nightingale comes down, you just gets up and drives it into the net; for you see, he always flies low, and so he'll get caught in the meshes. If you wants to catch a nightingale with a net, you can do it without a hen bird, just with the little pipe. When you catch it, tie up the ends of his wings at once to make sure he don't struggle, and put him quickly in a small box, covered on top and underneath with cloth. Caught nightingales must be fed on ants' eggs, not too much each time but often; they soon get used to it and begin to peck. It won't be amiss to put live ants into the box: some marsh nightingales don't know nothing about ants' eggs, they never seen them, well, and when the ants starts carrying their eggs about, the nightingales gets excited-like and begins to catch 'em.

Here (in the Mtsensk, Chernsky and Belevsky districts) the nightingales are a poor lot and they sing badly. You can't understand nothing of it, they mixes up all their tunes, they warbles, they are in a devil of a hurry; or the worst thing of all they starts trilling—trrr—and suddenly—wee! He gives a loud squeak as if he's drowning. Aye, that's really horrible, that is! You just spits with disgust and walks away. Makes you feel real bad. A good nightingale must sing very clearly, he mustn't mix up his different tunes—and as for the tunes of a nightingale's song, there be altogether ten of 'em:

First: Chucking: chuck-chuck-chuck-chuck-chuck.

Second: Yaffle-yaffle-yaffle, like a woodpecker.

Third: Shot—sounds like dropping a lot of shot on the ground.

Fourth: Ripple—trrrrrr. . . .

Fifth: Plen-plen-plen-plen—very distinctly.

Sixth: Devil's pipe—drawn out like: ho-ho-ho-ho-ho, then briefly: too!

Seventh: Cuckoo's flight. A very rare tune: I've only heard it twice and both times in the Timsk district. A cuckoo cries like that when she starts flying. A strong, piercing whistle.

Eighth: A gosling: ga-ga-ga-ga. . . . In the Malo-Arkhangelsk nightingales this phrase comes out beautifully.

Ninth: A woodlark's knocking. Like a woodlark—a kind of round whistling—whew-whew-whew—

Tenth: Begins so: tee-wheet—tenderly, like a robin. This is not a tune really, but nightingales usually start like that. With a good, musical nightingale—it's sometimes also this way: he starts—tee-wheet, and then—took! This is known as a push-off. Then again: tee-wheet—took—took! Twice like that and at half beat—that's much better; the third time: tee-wheet and then suddenly: chrr—

chrr—chrr, either like shot or like a ripple—you can hardly keep on your feet—it knocks you over! Such a nightingale is called a half-beat or push-off. A good nightingale keeps every tune of his song long, clear and strong; the clearer the longer. A bad one is in a hurry: finished one tune, knocked it off, and away he goes to start another, and—makes an unholy mess of it. Aye, a fool's bolt is soon shot. But a good one—no! He sings sensibly as he ought. When he starts off on some tune, he won't give it up so quickly —not till he's got you under its spell good and proper. Some even goes round and round—goes on for ever, it seems; for instance, he starts one tune—shot, let's say, just as though very low down, then up and up, just as though he's putting a circle round you, aye, goes over and over like a carriage wheel. I've heard such a one at the house of a Mtsensk merchant. That was a nightingale, that was. Been sold for 1200 roubles in Petersburg, he has!

According to what I hears sportsmen say, it's difficult to distin-guish a good nightingale from a bad one. Many can't distinguish a cock from a hen. Many a hen is more handsome than a cock. One can distinguish a young bird from an old one, though. A young nightingale, when you spreads out his wings, has spots on the feathers and he's much darker; an old one is more grey. Choose a nightingale with large eyes, a thin beak, and make sure he is broad-chested and stands high on his feet. The nightingale that had been sold of 1200 roubles was of medium height. S—— bought him near Kursk from a boy for twenty copecks.

If properly kept, a nightingale can live for five winters. In winter he has to be fed on black-beetles or dried ants' eggs; only the eggs must be fetched not from a pine but from a deciduous wood, or he might get constipated from the resin. A nightingale must not be hung over a window but in the middle of the room, and the cage must have a soft, cotton or linen, ceiling.

Their most common illness is when they suddenly starts sneez-ing. That's a bad illness. If a bird gets over it, he's sure to die next winter. I tried putting some snuff in their food—with good results.

They starts singing at Christmas—or a little before, at first softly; beginning with Lent, from March, in their true voice, and they stops with St. Peter's Day (29th June). They usually starts very tenderly, very mournfully with: plen-plen-plen. . . . Not too loudly, but you hears it all over the room. It has such a pleasant ring—like bits of glass—turns your heart over. Even after a long time—as soon as I hears it, it goes through me, makes my hair stand on end. Moves me to tears. Aye, you goes out and you cries there as you stand.

Young nightingales ought to be caught before the end of June. You must find out when the old birds are bringing them food. I sometimes sits watching three, four hours or half a day, but I makes a note of the place. They build their nests on the ground —of dry grass and leaves. There's a clutch of five fledglings in the nest, sometimes fewer. You takes the fledglings and puts them in a trap, and you'll catch the old ones at once too. You must catch the old ones to feed the young. You puts the whole family in the box, throws in lots of ants' eggs and lets ants in too. Then the old ones will start feeding their young straight away. Then you must cover the cage, and when the young ones start feeding themselves, take away the old ones. The young nightingales you gets out of their nest before the end of June are more likely to survive and they'll start singing earlier. The young must be taken from a long, loud-voiced nightingale. They do not hatch in a cage. In the woods a nightingale stops singing as soon as his brood is hatched, and about the end of June he moults. He'll sing a tune in flight and that's all. He only whistles. He sings only when he's sitting; in flight, when he is diving after a hen, he warbles.

It is a good thing to put a cage with young birds near a cage with older ones, so that they should learn to sing. They should be hung next to each other. And here you have to look sharp: if the young bird sits quiet-like, without moving or uttering a sound and listening while the old bird's singing, he'll be all right and in two weeks he'll perhaps be ready; but the one who doesn't keep silent and keeps warbling after the old 'un, will, if you're lucky, start singing proper-like next year, and even that is doubtful. Some sportsmen bring their young nightingales secretly in their hats to an inn where there is a good nightingale; they have a cup of tea or a pint of beer themselves while the young birds are learning. That's why it's best to cover the cage with the young 'uns when you brings them to an old 'un.

The Russian merchants are the greatest nightingale fanciers: they don't mind paying a thousand for a bird. The Belevsky merchants used to give me and my mate 200 roubles—and the horse and cart was theirs. They would send me off to Berdichev; I had to bring back two pairs of good nightingales, and if I caught more, even as much as fifty, they was mine.

I had a mate who was mad on nightingales and I used to go with him a lot. He was very shortsighted, but that did not matter to him. Once he heard a marvellous nightingale near Lebedyan. He comes and tells me all about him, and he be shaking all over with eagerness. He started catching him, and he was sitting on a tall aspen. However, he came down, my mate chased him into the net, and he struck against the net and hung on it. My mate starts taking him, I suppose his hands must have shook, for the nightingale darted between his legs and flew away singing. My mate just yelled blue murder. Afterwards he swore he felt distinctly someone pulling the nightingale out of his hands by force. Well—I don't know—everything's possible. Then he started luring him again, but no luck! The bird must have got a fright. It sang no more. My mate went looking for him for ten days, and what do you think? There was not a sound out of that nightingale—he was gone, and that was that. Well, sir, my mate nearly went off his head. Aye, I had to drag him back home. He'd fling his hat on the ground and start beating his forehead with his fist. Or he'd stop dead and holler: "Dig me a hole in the ground, I want to hide myself away deep in the earth, that's where a blind, clumsy fool like me should be!" Aye, that's what it feels like sometimes!

It happens that people try to get good nightingales away from one another by getting to the right place earlier. But you must know how to do it, and you can't do it without luck, either. It also happens that they tries to get you away from the right place by witchcraft. In that case, all you have to do is to say a prayer. Once I was frightened to death. I was sitting near a wood at night, listening to nightingales, and it was a real dark night, pitch-dark. . . . And suddenly it seemed to me that it was no longer a nightingale's songs that I heard, but that something was a-roaring, just as though it was coming straight at me. . . . I nearly died of fright, I can tell you. I jumped up and ran as fast as my legs would carry me. . . . The peasants don't interfere with you—they don't care a hang, they even laugh at you. A peasant is a coarse fellow. A nightingale or a chaffinch—it's all one to him. They have no understanding for this sort of thing. All they knows is to plough and lie on the stove with a woman. I have told you everything now, sir.

Village Spasskoye,
6 November, 1854.

X

PÉGAS

Sportsmen often love to boast about their dogs and to extol their qualities: this also is a sort of indirect self-glorification. But there is no doubt that among dogs, as among men, there are clever and foolish ones, talented and untalented ones, and there are among them even animals of genius, even eccentrics; [1] and the diversity of their qualities, both "physical and mental," their temperament and habits, will not yield anything to the diversity observed in the human race. Indeed, it can be said without fear of contradiction that as a result of his long companionship with man, a companionship that goes back to prehistoric times, the dog has become infected with him, both in the good and bad sense of the word: his own normal order of life has certainly been disturbed and undergone a change, as his appearance itself has been disturbed and changed. The dog has become more subject to disease, more nervous, and his expectation of life has decreased; but he has become more intelligent, more impressionable and more quick-witted; his mental outlook has widened. Envy, jealousy and—a capacity for friendship; desperate bravery,

---

[1] In the spring of 1871 I saw in a circus in London a dog performing the part of a clown, showing quite an undoubted flair for comedy.

devotion to the point of self-sacrifice and—ignominious cowardice and fickleness; suspiciousness, spitefulness and—good nature, cunning and straightforwardness—all these qualities manifest themselves—sometimes with astonishing force—in the dog that has been re-educated by man and that deserves more than the horse to be called the noblest of all man's conquests, according to the well-known expression of Buffon.

But enough of philosophizing: let the facts speak for themselves.

Like many another "inveterate" sportsman, I've had many dogs, bad, good and excellent—I even had one that was positively mad and that committed suicide by jumping out of the dormer window of a drying-room on the fourth floor of a paper mill. But the best hound that I ever possessed was undoubtedly a long-haired, black woolly dog with yellow spots, called "Pégas." I bought him near Karlsruhe from a gamekeeper (*Jagdhüter*) for 120 guldens, about eighty silver roubles. I was several times offered a thousand francs for him. Pégas—(he is still alive, though at the beginning of the present year he suddenly lost almost all of his scent, his hearing, his eyesight and is altogether in a sorry state)—Pégas is a big dog with a wavy coat of hair, and an astonishingly intelligent and proud face. He is not of an entirely pure breed: he is a mixture of an English setter and a German sheep-dog; his tail is thick, his forelegs too fleshy and his hindlegs a little too skinny. He was quite extraordinarily strong and a mighty fighter: he must have several canine souls on his conscience, not to mention cats. . . .

To start with his faults in hunting: there are not many of them and it will not take me long to enumerate them. He was afraid of heat, and when there was no water near he got into the state when a dog is said to be "dying for a drop"; he was also a little slow and heavy in search of game; but as he had a simply fabulous scent—I have never seen or met anything like it—he still

279

found the game quicker and oftener than any other dog. His pointing used to astonish everyone—and never, *never* did he make a mistake. "If Pégas points, there must be game," was a generally accepted axiom among all our fellow-sportsmen. He never chased after a hare or any other game; but not having received a correct and strict English training, he rushed to pick up the game immediately after a shot was fired without waiting for the word of command—a bad fault! He immediately recognized by its flight whether a bird was wounded or not and if, after following it with his eyes, he ran after it, raising his head in a special way, it was a sure sign that he would find it and bring it. At the height of his powers and abilities, not one bird that had been hit escaped him: he was the most wonderful retriever one could imagine. It is difficult to enumerate the pheasants he had retrieved from the bramble thickets which abound in almost all German woods, or partridges who had run almost half a mile from the spot where they had fallen, or hares, wild goats, foxes. Sometimes he would pick up the scent two, three or four hours after the animal had been wounded. One had only to say to him *Cherche, verloren!* (search, lost!) and he at once went loping first to one side, then another and, coming across the track of the animal, followed it at a spanking pace. One minute, two minutes passed and the hare or wild goat was already screeching between his teeth, or he would be running back with the booty in his mouth.

Once, at a hare chase, Pégas performed such a wonderful trick that I would have hesitated to tell about it if I had not a dozen witnesses to back me up. The chase through the woods had come to an end and the huntsmen gathered in a clearing near the edge of the wood. "I have wounded a hare just at this spot," one of my fellow-huntsmen told me and he put the usual request to me: to let Pégas follow its scent. I must observe that no dog except mine, *l'illustre Pégas,* was taken on these hunting expeditions. In such cases, dogs are only a nuisance: they get excited themselves and excite their owners—and by their own movements give warning to the game and drive it away. The beaters keep *their* dogs on a leash. As soon as the chase started and the cries were heard, my Pégas was transformed into a statue; he looked attentively in the direction of the thicket in the woods, raising and dropping his ears imperceptibly. He even stopped breathing; the animal might run across under his very nose and his sides would just quiver or he would lick his nose—that was all. Once a hare ran literally over his paws. All Pégas did was to pretend to bite it. But to return to my story.

I gave the order: *Cherche, verloren!* and he went off. A few minutes later we heard the scream of the caught hare—and there was the beautiful figure of my dog rushing back straight towards me. (He never gave up his booty to anyone else.) Suddenly, twenty feet from me, he stopped, put the hare on the ground, and off he went again! We all exchanged astonished glances. "What's the meaning of this?" I was asked. "Why did Pégas not bring the hare up to you? He has never done anything like that before." I did not know what to say, for I could not understand it myself— when suddenly there was another scream of a hare in the woods —and Pégas again came running through the thicket with *another* hare between his teeth! He was greeted with loud and unanimous applause.

Only huntsmen can appreciate how keen must be the scent of a dog and how great his intelligence and perspicacity if he is capable—with a killed and still warm hare in his mouth—to scent, while running at full speed and in the sight of his master, another wounded hare and to grasp the fact that it is the scent of *another* one and not of the hare he held between his teeth.

Another time he was taken to pick up the scent of a wounded wild goat. The hunt was taking place on the bank of the Rhine. He ran up to the bank, rushed off to the right, then to the left and, probably realizing that a wild goat could not be lost though he had lost its scent, jumped into the water, swam across the Rhine (which, opposite the Grand Duchy of Baden is divided into many branches) and, getting out on a little island overgrown with reeds, lying opposite, caught the wild goat there.

I can also remember a winter hunt on the summits of the Schwarzwald. There was deep snow everywhere, the trees were covered with hoar-frost, a thick mist hung over everything, concealing the contours of objects. The huntsman next to me fired and when, after the beaters had done their work, I went up to him, he told me that he had fired at a fox and probably wounded it, because it waved its brush. We let Pégas follow its trail and he at once disappeared in the white haze which surrounded us. Five, ten, fifteen minutes passed. . . . Pégas did not come back. My friend must have hit the fox, for if it had not been wounded and Pégas had been sent off on a wild goose chase, he would have returned at once. Suddenly we heard an indistinct barking in the distance: it seemed to reach us from another world. We at once went in the direction of the barking: we knew that if Pégas was not able to bring back the game, he stood barking over it. Led by the infrequent, desultory sounds of his bass voice, we moved carefully through the mist, as though in a dream, hardly seeing where we put down our feet. We were going up hill and down dale, walking through the damp, cold mist with snow up to our knees; icicles kept falling down on us as we brushed aside the branches. . . . It was like a journey through fairy-land. Each one of us looked like a ghost to everyone else, and everything around had a ghost-like appearance. At last something dark loomed in front of us at the bottom of a hollow. It was Pégas. Sitting on his hind legs, he hung his head and, as they say, "looked glum"; in front of his very nose, in a deep hole between two granite slabs, lay the dead fox. It had crawled there before it died and Pégas could not get it out. That was why he let us know about it by his barking. He had a bad scar over his right eye; it was from the deep wound another fox had inflicted on him after he had found it alive six hours after it had been hit by a bullet—and with whom he had fought a deadly battle.

I also remember another case. I was invited to a shooting party in Offenburg, a town not far from Baden. The shooting rights of that particular district were owned by a whole crowd of sportsmen from Paris: there was a large number of game, especially pheasants, in it. I, of course, took Pégas with me. There were altogether fifteen of us. Many had excellent, mostly English, thoroughbred gundogs. As we passed from one beat to another, we formed a single file on a road skirting a wood; to our left was a huge, empty field; in the middle of it—and about fifty feet away from us—was a small heap of Jerusalem artichokes (*topinambour*). Suddenly my Pégas raised his head, sniffed the air and went straight towards that distant heap of dried-up stalks standing erect in the field. I stopped and invited my fellow-sportsmen to follow my dog, for "there's sure to be something there." Meanwhile, the other dogs gathered round and began running round Pégas, sniffing the ground, but they scented nothing; but he, not in the least disconcerted, kept walking along as though following a straight line. "I expect a hare must be hiding somewhere in the field," one Parisian remarked to me. But I could see by my dog's bearing and by the way he walked that it was not a hare and invited them all again to follow him. "Our dogs can scent nothing," they replied in one voice, "yours must be mistaken." (They did not know Pégas in Offenburg at that time.) I let it pass, cocked my double barrelled shotgun and went after Pégas, who was glancing at me from time to time over his shoulder, and at last reached the heap of Jerusalem artichokes. "What if nothing happens?" I asked myself. "We'll make fools of ourselves, Pégas and I." But at that very moment a whole dozen cock-pheasants rose into the air with an ear-splitting noise, and to my great delight I shot down a brace, which did not always happen to me, for I am an indifferent shot. "That's put you in your place, my Parisian gentlemen—you and your thoroughbred dogs!" With the dead pheasants in my hands I returned to my fellow-sportsmen. . . . . Compliments were showered on me and on Pégas. I suppose I must have looked pleased, but he—why, he just looked as if nothing had happened, he did not even put on an air of modesty.

I can state without exaggeration that Pégas again and again picked up the scent of partridges at a distance of a hundred or two hundred feet. And how well he thought out everything in spite of his somewhat lazy search! Just like an experienced strategist. He never dropped his head, sniffing at the trail, shamefully snorting and pushing down his nose; he always acted by sniffing the air, *dans le grand style,* as the French say. I did not have to budge from my place: all I had to do was to watch him. I was greatly amused when I happened to go out shooting with someone who did not know Pégas. Within hardly half an hour I would hear him exclaim: "What a dog! Why, he's a professor!"

He caught my meaning at once; a look was enough for him. That dog was the cleverest animal I had ever come across. That on one occasion, having missed me, he left Karlsruhe, where I was spending the winter, and four hours later was discovered at my old lodgings in Baden-Baden, is perhaps nothing extraordinary; but the following incident shows what an intelligent animal he was. A mad dog happened to be at large in the environs of Baden-Baden and had bitten someone; the police at once issued an order that all dogs without exception should wear muzzles. In Germany such orders were instantly obeyed; and Pégas found himself wearing a muzzle. He resented it extremely; he kept complaining—that is, sitting down opposite me, barking or offering me his paw, but there was nothing to be done, the order had to be obeyed. One morning my landlady came into my room and told me that, taking advantage of a minute when he was free, Pégas had buried his muzzle! I could not believe it. But a few moments later my landlady again ran into my room and whispered to me to follow her quickly. I went out on the front steps —and what did I see? Pégas with the muzzle in his mouth was walking stealthily, as though on tiptoe, across the yard and, having got into the shed, began digging a hole with his paws, and then carefully buried his muzzle in it! There could be no doubt that he thought to get rid of the hateful constraint in this way.

Like almost all dogs, he could not bear beggars or badly dressed people (women and children he never touched), and the main thing was that he did not allow anyone to take anything away; the sight of a bundle over the shoulder or in the hand aroused his suspicions—and then woe to the back of the trousers of the suspicious character and—in the last resort—woe to my purse! I had to pay a lot of money in damages for him! Once I heard a terrible uproar in my front garden. I went out and saw on the other side of the gate a badly dressed man with torn "unmentionables" and in front of the gate Pégas in the attitude of a conqueror. The man complained bitterly about Pégas and kept shouting, but the masons, who worked on the opposite side of the street, told me with a loud laugh that that man had picked an apple from a tree in the front garden—and only then had he been attacked by Pégas.

He had—why conceal it?—a dour and stern character; but he was greatly, even tenderly, devoted to me.

Pégas's mother was famous in her time, too, and she also was of a very stern character; she showed no affection even for her master. His brothers and sisters were also distinguished by their talents; but of his numerous progeny not one could even remotely compare with him.

Last year (1870) he was still at the top of his form, though he began to show signs of fatigue; but this year everything has changed suddenly. I suspect he has suffered something like the softening of the brain. Even his intelligence forsook him, and yet it was impossible to say that he was too old.

He is only nine. It was pitiful to see this truly great dog transformed into an idiot; at a shoot he would begin searching senselessly, that is to say, running forward in a straight line, with his tail and head hanging down. Or he would stop dead suddenly and look at me intently and dully, as though asking me what he should do and what had happened to him! *Sic transit gloria mundi!* He still lives with me *en pension,* but it is no longer the former Pégas—it is a pitiful wreck of his former self! I took leave of him not without a feeling of sadness. "Goodbye," I thought, "my incomparable dog! I shall never forget you, and I shall never have such a friend as you!"

I don't suppose I shall go hunting any more, either.

Paris, December, 1871.

XI

PERGAMOS EXCAVATIONS

A Letter to the Editor of European Herald

... ALLOW ME to have two or three pages of your journal so that I can share with your readers the deep impression made on me by the marble high reliefs of the best Attic sculpture (3rd century B.C.) discovered in Pergamos (not in ancient Troy) and now acquired by the Prussian Government. I saw them during my recent visit to Berlin. Pergamos was the capital of a small kingdom in Asia Minor, at first conquered, like the whole Greek world, by Rome and then destroyed by the incursion of the barbarians. The existence of these friezes, erected by some reigning emperor of the Attala dynasty and considered by the ancients to be one of the wonders of the world, was not, of course, unknown to scholars, especially German scholars; they are mentioned in the preserved works of one rather obscure writer of the second century; but the honour of discovering these magnificent relics belongs to Humann, the German consul in Smyrna, and the merit of acquiring them for Germany belongs to the Prussian Government, with the energetic assistance of the Crown Prince. The whole thing was done very cleverly and in secret; engineers and learned professors were sent in good time, a plot of land was bought near the village of Bergam, under which all these treasures were hidden; the *firman* of the Sultan for the ownership of the discovered marbles and not of their photographs only (as is the case with the Greek government) was very successfully obtained, again, in good time, and in the end Prussia—for some paltry 130,000 marks —can be proud of a conquest which will bring her more glory than the conquest of Alsace-Lorraine and, I daresay, it will prove to be more durable.

These marbles were part of the front or frieze of a huge altar dedicated to Zeus and Pallas Athene (their figures are one and a half times life size) that stood before the palace or temple of Attalos. They were found at a rather small depth and, though broken into pieces (more than 9,000 separate pieces have been collected, some of them, it is true, three and a half square feet or more), the chief figures and groups have been preserved, and the marble had not been subject to the destructive influences of the open air and other violent causes from which the remains of the Parthenon had suffered so much. All these fragments have been carefully numbered and loaded on two ships, and transferred from Asia Minor to Trieste (two other boats are still on the way with the remnants of four colossal statues and architectural parts), then sent by rail to Berlin. Now they occupy several halls in the Museum; they are laid out on the floor and are gradually being put together in their original order under the supervision of a committee of professors and with the assistance of a whole company of expert Italian modellers. Luckily, the major groups suffered comparatively less than the smaller groups—and the public, which is permitted to view them once a week from the top of small platforms surrounding the marbles, can already form an opinion of what an amazing spectacle these high reliefs will present when put up vertically in a specially erected building where they will appear before the astonished gaze of the present-day generation in all their two-thousand-year-old—nay, more—their immortal beauty.

These high-reliefs (many of the bodies are so convex that they stand out completely from the back wall, which scarcely touches their limbs on one side) represent the battle between the gods and the titans or the giant sons of Ge (the earth). I can't help observing, incidentally, how lucky a people must be to possess such poetic religious legends, filled with such profound meaning, as did the Greeks, those aristocrats of the human race. The victory is without a doubt won by the gods, who represent light, beauty and reason; but the dark, savage forces of the earth are still offering resistance—and the battle is not over. The middle of the frieze is occupied by Zeus (Jupiter), who strikes down with a thunderbolt, in the shape of an inverted sceptre, a giant, who falls headlong, with his back to the spectator, into the abyss; on the other side, another giant rises, with a furious face, evidently one of the chief fighters, and, straining every nerve, shows such contours of muscles and torso as would have delighted Michelangelo. The goddess of Victory hovers over Zeus, spreading her eagle wings and raising aloft the palm leaf of triumph; the god of the sun, Apollo, in a long light *khiton,* through which his divine, youthful limbs can be clearly seen, rushes along in his chariot, drawn by two steeds, as immortal as he; Eos (Aurora) precedes him, sitting sideways on another steed, a wavy cloak slung across her chest and, turning to her god, urges him to drive on with a wave of her bare arm; the steed under her also—and as though consciously—turns round his head; under the wheels of Apollo's chariot a crushed giant is dying—and it is impossible to put into words the moving and tender expression with which approaching death brightens up his heavy features; his drooping, weakened, dying arm is by itself a miracle of art, and it is worth while going to Berlin for the sole purpose of admiring it. Further on Pallas (Minerva), seizing a winged giant by the hair and dragging him along on the ground with one hand, throws a long spear with the other, while her serpent, the serpent of Pallas, twining round the conquered giant, drives its fangs into him. Incidentally, almost all the giants terminate not in feet but in serpents' bodies—not tails, but bodies, whose heads also take part in the fighting; Zeus's eagles turn on them—one serpent's wide-open mouth, caught in an eagle's claws, has been preserved. There Cibella (Demeter), the mother of the gods, hurries along on a lion, the fore-part of which is unhappily missing (a great many fragments of marble had been burnt by the barbarians for lime); a human foot pushes convulsively against the lion's belly, and by its strikingly realistic truth, forms a complete contrast to the ideally beautiful foot which undoubtedly belongs to a god, who sets it victoriously on a dead giant. Bacchus—Dionysios, Diana—Artemis, Hephaestos—Vulcan are also among the victorious fighters; there are others, so far nameless gods, nymphs, satyrs—altogether about forty figures and all of them above human height! The figure of Ge (Earth), the mother of the giants, is most striking; summoned by the destruction of her sons, she rises out of the soil up to her waist. . . . The lower part of her face is missing (the heads of Zeus and Pallas, alas, have also disappeared), but the majestic, infinite sorrow that emanates from her brow, her eyes, her eyebrows, from the whole of her colossal head—has to be seen . . . one cannot even hint at it. All these—sometimes radiant, sometimes stern, living dead, triumphant, perishing figures, these intertwining, scaly, serpentine coils, these outspread wings, these eagles, these steeds, weapons, shields, these flying garments, these bodies, the most beautiful human bodies in every kind of position, incredibly brave, melodiously shapely—all these most diverse expressions of faces, supreme movements of limbs, this triumph of malice, and despair, and divine gaiety and divine cruelty—all that heaven and earth—why, it is a world, a whole world, and its revelation sends a cold shiver of delight and passionate reverence through one's veins. And one thing more: at the sight of all these irrepressibly fine wonders, what becomes of all our accepted ideas about Greek sculpture, its severity, serenity, about its confinement within the borders of its particular art, of its classicism—all those ideas which have been inculcated on us as indubitable truths by our instructors, theoreticians, aesthetes, by the whole of our training and scholarship? It is true that, for instance, we were told apropos Laocoon or the dying gladiator or, finally, the Farnesian Bull, that in ancient art there were traces of what later on was called romanticism and realism; we were referred to the Rhodes School of Sculpture, even to the Pergamene school; but it is pointed out at once that all these works of art were already showing certain signs of decadence, bordering, in the Farnesian Bull for instance, on rococo; people talked of the frontiers between painting and sculpture and the violation of these frontiers, but how can one talk of decadence in face of this Battle of the Gods and the Giants, which by its origin belongs to the last era of Greek sculpture—the first century after Phidias? And how can this Battle be put under any heading? The realism, if we are to use this word, the realism of certain details is amazing; the realism that finds expression in the footwear, folds of clothes, the flow of tresses, even the whorl of hair over the horses' hoofs, a realism which most modern Italian sculptors won't surpass, and they are masters at this sort of work! "Romanticism," of course, in the sense of freedom of bodily movements, poses, subject matter, which would have been termed "échevelé" by a French pedant; but all these realistic details disappear to such an extent in the general impression—the whole of this stormy romanticism is so permeated by a high sense of order and a cleverly and perfectly expressed highly artistic idea, that all that remains for epigones like us is to bow our heads and learn, learn again, reviewing everything that we have hitherto considered as the fundamental truth of our judgments and our conclusions. I repeat, this Battle of the Gods is truly a revelation, and when this altar is put up, all artists, all true lovers of beauty will have to go and worship it.

I have mentioned only in passing the thousands of small fragments which are lying on the floors of the halls and which are being gradually put back in their right place as far as possible. Walking round these, you are constantly amazed by some exquisite shoulder or part of a hand or foot, or a piece of wavy tunic, or simply by some architectural ornament. . . . There is, by the way, a small, fully preserved yellow marble head of a woman whose size does not fit any goddess. . . . I forgot to mention that at the sides of this huge altar there were low reliefs of a smaller size. The expression of this exquisite head is so utterly modern that one really can't help feeling that it had read Heine and known Schumann. . . .

However, this will suffice. I should like to add one word, though: on leaving the Museum I thought: "How lucky I am that I did not die before this last impression, that I saw it all!" I venture to express the hope that others, too, will think the same after spending an hour or two in contemplation of the Pergamene Marbles of The Battle between the Gods and the Giants.

Petersburg, March 18, 1880.

XII

THE QUAIL

I was ten when what I am now going to tell you happened to me.

It was summer. I lived at the time with my father on a farm in the South of Russia. The farm was surrounded by several miles of steppe. There was no wood or stream anywhere near; the flat steppe was intersected here and there by shallow ravines, overgrown with bushes and stretching away in the distance like long, green serpents. Little streams trickled at the bottom of these ravines; somewhere beneath a steep slope springs could be seen with water as pure as tears; little paths led to them and near the water, in the damp mud, trails of birds and small animals crisscrossed each other. They needed good water as much as people.

My father was a passionate sportsman; and as soon as he got a free moment and the weather was fine, he would take his shotgun, put his hunting bag over his shoulder, call his old dog Trezor and go off to shoot partridges and quail. He scorned hares, leaving them to the huntsmen with packs of dogs, whom he called "borzoi-breeders." We had no other game, except that in the autumn there was usually an incursion of woodcock. But there was a great number of quail and partridges, especially partridges. Near the ravines one often found little circular holes in the dry dust, the places where the partridges were cleaning themselves. Old Trezor would immediately point, his tail trembling and the skin on his forehead furrowing, while my father turned pale, and cautiously cocked his gun. He often took me with him. . . . And I did enjoy it tremendously! I shoved my trousers into the boot-tops, put a flask over my shoulder and imagined myself a sportsman! I was dripping with sweat, small pebbles got into my boots, but I did not feel any fatigue and did not lag behind my father. And when I heard a shot and saw a bird fall, I skipped about and even yelled—I was so happy! The wounded bird struggled and flapped her wings on the grass or between Trezor's teeth, blood poured from her, but I felt happy all the same and had no feeling of pity at all. What would I not have given to be able to fire a gun myself and kill partridges and quail! But my father told me that I would not have a gun before I was twelve; and even then he would give me only a one-barrelled gun and would let me fire only at larks. We had thousands of larks near our farm; on a nice, sunny day hundreds of them flew weaving in the clear sky, rising higher and higher and ringing like little bells. I looked upon them as my future booty and took aim at them with a little stick which I carried over my shoulder instead of a gun. It is very easy to hit them when they hover about four or six feet above the ground, quivering before suddenly diving into the grass. Sometimes, far out in the field, bustards were standing in the stubble or the winter corn; wouldn't it be wonderful, I thought to myself, if I could kill such a huge bird? Why, I would be the happiest man in the world if I could only do that! I would point them out to my father, but he would reply that a bustard was a very wary bird and never let a man come near it. Once, however, he did try to steal up to a solitary bustard, thinking that it must have been wounded and lagged behind the flock. He ordered Trezor to follow him and told me to stay where I was; he loaded his gun with grape-shot, turned round once more to see if Trezor was following him, even spoke sternly to him, whispered to him: "Heel! Heel!" and bending double, crawled not straight, but sideways in the direction of the bustard. Though Trezor did not bend double, he, too, walked along in a most remarkable fashion: almost bandy-legged, with his tail between his legs and biting his lower lip. I could not restrain myself and followed my father and Trezor almost on all fours. But the bustard did not let us get even three hundred paces near it; at first it ran off, then it flapped its wings and flew away. Father fired and just followed it with his eyes. . . . Trezor leapt forward, but he, too, just looked at the sky. . . . I, too, looked and—felt so disgusted! Couldn't the bustard really have waited a little longer? The grape-shot would have got it for sure then!

One day father and I went shooting—it was on the eve of St. Peter's Day. At that time, at the beginning of July, young partridges are still too small and father did not want to shoot them. He went to the small oak bushes growing near a field of rye where there were always quail to be had. It was not convenient to cut the grass there and it remained very high for a long time. There were lots of flowers there: vetch, clover, harebells, forget-me-nots, wild pinks. Whenever I went there with my sister or with one of our maids, I always gathered a whole armful of them; but when I went there with my father, I never picked any flowers, for I regarded that occupation as undignified for a sportsman.

Suddenly Trezor pointed; my father shouted: "Take it!" and a quail leapt out from under Trezor's very nose and—flew away. Only she flew away in a very peculiar way: she turned somersaults, twisted round in the air, fell on the ground, just as though she had been wounded or had a broken wing. Trezor rushed after her as fast as he could, which he did not usually do when a bird flew properly. My father could not even fire, for he was afraid to hit the dog. All of a sudden I saw Trezor leap forward and catch the quail. He caught her and brought her to my father. My father took her and put her on the palm of his hand, with her little tummy upwards. I ran up. "What was the matter?" I asked. "Was she wounded?" "No," replied my father, "she was not wounded. I expect she must have a nest with little chicks somewhere near here and she deliberately pretended to be wounded so that the dog might think that it could catch her easily." "Why did she do that?" I asked. "Why," replied my father, "to lead the dog away from her chicks. She would have flown properly afterwards. Only this time she made a mistake. She pretended a little too well and Trezor caught her." "So she isn't wounded?" I asked again. "No, of course not, but I don't think she's going to live. Trezor must have crushed her between his teeth." I moved closer to the quail. She lay motionless on my father's hand with her little head hanging down, and looked at me sideways with one of her small brown eyes. And suddenly I felt so sorry for her! It seemed to me that she was looking at me and thinking: "Why should I have to die, why? Haven't I done my duty? Haven't I tried to save my little ones by leading the dog away from them as far as possible? And now I've been caught! I am a poor thing! A poor thing!" It was injust! Unjust!

"Daddy," I said, "perhaps she won't die. . . ." And I wanted to stroke the quail on the head. But my father said to me, "No! Watch, in a moment her legs will stretch out, she will tremble all over, and her eyes will close." And so it happened. When her eyes were closed, I burst out crying. "What's the matter?" my father asked and laughed. "I'm sorry for her," I said. "She was only doing her duty and she was killed! That is unjust!" "She was trying to be a little too clever," my father said. "Only Trezor was cleverer than she." "Wicked Trezor!" I thought, and my father, too, seemed to me to be unkind this time. What sort of cleverness was it? It was just love for her little babies and not cleverness! If she had been ordered to pretend in order to save her children, then Trezor should not have caught her! My father was about to put the quail into his hunting bag, but I begged him to give her to me. I held her carefully in both my hands, breathed on her—wouldn't she come to life? But she did not stir. "You're wasting your time, old fellow," my father said. "You won't bring her back to life. You see how her head is drooping." I raised her head gently by the beak, but as soon as I took away my hand, it fell down again. "Are you still sorry for her?" my father asked. "But who is going to feed her little ones?" I asked in turn. My father looked intently at me. "Don't worry," he said, "the cock-quail, their father, will feed them. Wait a moment," he added. "Isn't Trezor pointing again? I wonder if it's the nest. Yes, so it is."

And so it was. Two paces from Trezor's face, four little chicks lay snugly, close together in the grass. They were clinging to one another, stretching out their necks and breathing ever so quickly and all together, just as though they were quivering! They were already covered with feathers, there was no sign of any down on them, only their little tails were still short. "Daddy, Daddy," I shouted at the top of my voice, "call Trezor off or he'll kill them too!"

My father called Trezor back and sat down under a bush a little further away to have his lunch. But I remained near the nest. I did not want to eat. I took out a clean handkerchief and put the quail on it. "Look," I said to the little birds, "here's your mother. She sacrificed her life for you!" The little birds went on breathing rapidly as before, with all their bodies. Then I went up to my father. "Could you make me a present of this sweet little quail?" I asked him. "Yes, you can have her. But what are you going to do with her?" "I'm going to bury her!" "Bury her?" "Yes, near her nest. Give me your knife, please. I'm going to dig a little grave for her." My father looked surprised. "So that her children can visit her grave?" he asked. "No," I replied, "but I should like to, all the same. She'll be happy lying

297

there near her nest!" My father uttered no word. He took out his knife and gave it to me. I at once dug a little hole, kissed the quail on her breast, put her in the hole and covered it with earth. Then I cut two twigs with the same knife, peeled the bark off them, put them together in the form of a cross, tied them round with a blade of grass and pushed it into the grave.

Shortly afterwards my father and I walked away from that place, but I kept looking back at it. . . . The cross was a white one and could be seen from far away.

At night I dreamed that I was in heaven and—what do you think? My sweet little quail was sitting on a little cloud, looking as white as that little cross! And on her head she wore a little golden crown, and that seemed to have been given her as a reward for having suffered for her children!

Five days later my father and I came again to that same place. I even found the grave because of the little cross which had grown yellow but had not fallen down. But the nest was empty. There was not a trace of the little birds. My father assured me that their father must have taken them away, and when, a few paces from that spot, an old cock-quail suddenly flew out of a bush, he did not fire at him. . . . And I thought: "No, my father is a kind man!"

But the surprising thing about it is this: from that day my passion for hunting completely disappeared and I no longer thought of the time when my father would make me a present of a gun! However, when I grew up, I also began shooting; but I never became a real sportsman. There was one more thing that cured me of it.

One day a friend and I were out black-cock shooting. We found a brood. The hen rushed out, we fired and hit her; but she did not fall down but flew off further together with her chicks. I was about to follow them, but my friend said to me: "Much better to sit down here and try to decoy them. . . . They'll soon be back here again." My friend was very good at imitating the call of the black-grouse. We sat down and he began to whistle. And to be sure: first one young bird replied to his call, then another, and suddenly we heard the hen herself clucking very tenderly and very near. I raised my head and saw her coming towards us through the tangle of the long grass, hurrying, hurrying, with blood dripping from her chest! Her mother's heart, it seems, could not bear the thought that her chicks were in peril! I suddenly felt that I was a wicked murderer myself and I got up and clapped my hands. The grey hen flew away at once and the young birds, too, fell silent. My friend got very angry. He thought I was mad. . . . "You've spoilt the whole shoot," he declared.

But after that day I found it harder and harder to kill and shed blood.

XIII

A FIRE AT SEA

———————◆———————

It happened in may 1838.

With a great many other passengers I was on board the steamer *Nicholas I,* plying between Petersburg and Lubeck. Since the railways could hardly be said to exist at that time, all travellers chose to go by sea. For this reason many of them took their own carriages with them to continue their journey in Germany, France, and so on.

As far as I can remember, we had twenty-eight carriages on our ship. There were about two hundred and eighty passengers on board, including some twenty children.

I was very young then and, being a good sailor, was very much taken up with all the new impressions. There were several ladies on board, quite remarkably beautiful or good-looking, most of them, alas, now dead.

This was the first time my mother had allowed me to travel alone, and I had to promise her to behave myself and, above all, not to touch cards. . . . And it was precisely that promise that was to be broken first of all.

That evening the main saloon was crowded with people among whom there were several well-known Petersburg gamblers. They used to play faro every evening and the ringing of gold, which was to be seen much more frequently in those days than now, was quite deafening.

One of these gentlemen, seeing that I kept myself to myself and not knowing the reason for it, asked me quite unexpectedly to join his game; when, with the naivety of my nineteen years, I explained to him why I abstained, he burst out laughing and, turning to his friends, exclaimed that he had discovered a real treasure—a young man who had never touched cards and who, as a result, was quite certain to have the most fabulous, most unheard-of luck, real beginner's luck!

I don't know how it happened, but ten minutes later I was sitting at the card table engrossed in the game and with my hands full of cards and—playing, playing recklessly.

And I must confess the old saw turned out to be quite right: money flowed towards me in streams; two small heaps of gold rose on the table at either side of my trembling, perspiring hands. The gambler who had inveigled me into the game kept encouraging me and egging me on. . . . To tell the truth, I was beginning to think that I'd leave the table a rich man!

Suddenly the door of the saloon was flung wide open and a lady, looking beside herself, burst in, screamed in a strangled voice, "Fire!" and collapsed in a dead faint on the sofa. This produced a most violent commotion. No one remained in his place. Gold, silver, banknotes rolled and scattered in all directions, and we all made a dash for the door. How was it that we had not noticed before this the smoke that was already filling the saloon? I simply cannot understand it. The campanion-way was full of it. Here and there a deep red glow, as of burning coal, flared up. In a twinkling everyone was on the deck. Two great pillars of smoke, through which tongues of flame flickered, rose on either side of the funnel and along the masts. Bedlam broke loose and from then on it never ceased. The pandemonium was quite unbelievable. One felt that the desperate instinct of self-preservation had seized upon each of those human beings and not least upon me. I remember grasping a sailor by the arm and promising him ten thousand roubles in my mother's name if he succeeded in saving me. The sailor, who quite naturally could not take these words seriously, freed himself from my hold; and, indeed, I did not myself insist, realizing that there was no sense in what I was saying. Still, there was even less sense in what I saw around me. It is quite true that nothing can compare with the tragedy of a shipwreck or a fire at sea except its comedy. For instance, a rich landowner, seized with panic, was crawling on the deck, prostrating himself frantically; but when the water, which was being poured in vast quantities into the coal holds, for a moment allayed the fury of the flames, he drew himself up to his full height and shouted in a voice of thunder: "Men of little faith, did you really think that our God, our Russian God, would forsake us?" But that very instant the flames leapt higher and the poor man of much faith again began crawling on all fours and prostrating himself. An army general with a sullenly forlorn look kept shouting: "We must send a courier to the Emperor! When there was a mutiny in the military settlements a courier was sent to him. I was there, I was there myself, and this saved at least some of us!" Another gentleman with an umbrella in his hands began jabbing ferociously at a cheap oil portrait tied to its easel which stood near him among the baggage. With the tip of his umbrella he pierced five holes in it: through the eyes, nose, mouth and ears. This act of destruction he accompanied with the exclamation: "What's the use of all this now?" And the picture did not even belong to him! A fat man who looked like a German brewer did not stop wailing in a lacrymose voice, tears rolling down his cheeks: "Captain! Captain!" And when the captain, his patience at an end, seized him by the scruff of the neck and shouted at him: "Well? I am the captain! What do you want?" the fat man looked abjectly at him and again began moaning: "Captain!"

And yet it was this captain to whom we owe all our lives. First, because he altered our course at the last moment when it was still possible to get to the engine-room. If our ship had gone straight to Lubeck instead of turning sharply towards the shore, she would most certainly have burnt out before reaching harbour. Secondly, because he ordered the sailors to draw their dirks and show no mercy to anyone who attempted to go near one of the two remaining lifeboats—the others had all capsized as a result of the inexperience of the passengers who had tried to lower them into the sea.

The sailors, mostly Danes, with their cold, energetic faces, the blades of their knives reflecting the flames with an almost bloodstained glint, inspired instinctive terror. There was a fairly strong squall, which grew still stronger from the fire which roared in a good third of the ship. I must confess, however my own sex may resent it, that the women showed more courage on this occasion than the men. Deathly pale, the night found them in their beds (instead of clothes only blankets were thrown over them), and however great an unbeliever I already was just then, they seemed to me like angels who had come down from heaven to shame us and give us more courage. But there were men, too, who showed themselves to be without fear. I remember in particular a certain Mr. D—v, our former Russian ambassador in Copenhagen: he had taken off his boots, tie and coat, which he tied by the sleeves over his chest, and sitting astride a thick, taut hawser and swinging his legs, calmly smoked his cigar and looked at each of us in turn with an air of ironic pity. As for myself, I took refuge on an outside ladder and sat down on one of its lower rungs. I looked horror-struck at the ruddy foam that boiled and bubbled beneath me and the spray of which flew up to my face. I kept saying to myself: "So that's where I shall have to die at the age of nineteen!" For I had made up my mind firmly to drown rather than to be roasted alive. The flames rose in an arch above me and I could clearly distinguish their howl from the roar of the waves.

Not far from me on the same ladder sat a little old woman, probably the cook of one of the families travelling to Europe. Hiding her head in her hands, she was whispering prayers. Suddenly she looked up quickly at me and whether it was that she read some sinister resolution in my face or for some other reason, but she seized my arm and said with great emphasis in an imploring voice: "No, sir, none of us is free to do with his life as he likes, and you least of all. As God wills, so it will be. Why, it would mean taking your own life and you'd be punished for that in the next world."

Till that moment the idea of committing sucide never occurred to me, but now because of some desire to show off, which was quite inexplicable in a man in my position, I once or twice pretended to be on the point of carrying out the intention she attributed to me, and each time the poor old woman rushed up to me to prevent what she regarded as a crime. At last I felt ashamed and stopped. Indeed, why indulge in silly histrionics in the presence of death which I thought to be imminent and inevitable at that moment? I had no time to account for my strange feelings nor to admire the absence of egoism (which today would be called altruism) in the poor woman, for at that instant the roar of the flames over our heads redoubled in fury; but at that very moment, too, a voice, ringing like brass (it was the voice of the man who saved us), resounded above us: "What are you doing down there, you poor wretches? You will be done for. Follow me!" And instantaneously, with no idea who was calling or where we had to go, the old woman and I leapt to our feet, as though propelled by a spring, and rushed through the smoke after a sailor in a blue tunic who was climbing up a rope ladder in front of us. Not knowing why, I too climbed the ladder behind him; I can't help thinking that if at that moment he had thrown himself into the water or had done anything else, however extraordinary, I should have followed him blindly. Having climbed up two or three rungs, the sailor jumped heavily down on to the roof of one of the carriages, the lower part of which was already in flames. I jumped after him and heard the old woman jump behind me. From the first carriage the sailor jumped on to a second, then a third and so we eventually arrived at the bow of the ship.

Nearly all the passengers were assembled there. The sailors, under the supervision of the captain, were lowering one of the two undamaged lifeboats, fortunately the largest. Across the other side of the ship I saw a line of steep cliffs, brightly lit by the flames, stretching along the shore towards Lubeck. There was a good mile and a half between us and the cliffs. I could not swim and although the place where we had run aground (we did not even notice how it happened) was in all probability not very deep, the waves were very high. And yet as soon as I caught sight of the cliffs I no longer doubted that I would be saved and, to the astonishment of the people around me, I jumped into the air several times and cried, "Hurrah!" I did not want to go too near the place where the rest of the passesngers were swarming in order to get to the ladder which led to the large lifeboat—there were too many old men, women and children there; besides, from the moment I caught sight of the cliffs I was no longer in a hurry: I was sure I was saved. I noticed with surprise that none of the children showed any fear, that some of them, in fact, fell asleep in their mothers' arms. Not a single child perished.

I noticed a tall general in a group of passengers; his clothes were streaming with water, but he stood motionless, leaning on a bench he had just pulled out and stood upright. I was told that in the first moment of panic he had brutally pushed aside a woman who had wanted to get in front of him and jump into one of the first boats which later overturned through the fault of the passengers themselves. One of the stewards had caught him from behind and flung him back on to the deck. The old soldier, ashamed of his moment of cowardice, swore that he would be the last to leave the ship, after the captain. Very tall, pale, with a red bruise on his forehead, he gazed with a crushed and resigned look upon his face, as though asking for forgiveness.

Meanwhile I made my way to the port side of the ship and caught sight of a little lifeboat bobbing up and down on the waves like a toy. The two sailors in it were signalling to the passengers not to be afraid and jump—but that was not very easy: *Nicholas I* was a very tall ship and one had to drop with great skill not to upset the boat. At last I made up my mind to jump: first I placed myself on the anchor chain which was stretched alongside the ship on the outside of the rail, and was just about to jump when something big, heavy and soft fell on top of me. A woman clutched me round the neck and hung inertly on me. I must confess that my first impulse was to fling her hands over my head and in this way get rid of that heavy mass, but fortunately, I did not yield to it. The impact nearly flung us both into the sea but, luckily, the end of a rope was dangling right in front of my nose (I had no time to see where it was suspended from), and I caught hold of it with such violence with one hand that I grazed the skin off it. . . . Then, looking down, I saw that my burden and I were just over the lifeboat and—we were off! I slid down—the boat cracked in all her seams. . . . "Hurrah!" cried the sailors. I laid down my burden, who had fainted, on the bottom of the boat and at once turned towards the ship where I saw a multitude of heads, especially those of women, pressing feverishly along the side.

"Jump!" I cried, stretching out my arms.

At that moment the success of my bold attempt, the conviction that I was safe from the flames, filled me with quite incredible strength and courage and I caught the only three women who decided to jump into my boat as easily as one catches apples thrown from a tree at harvest time. Everyone of these ladies, let me add, invariably uttered a piercing scream at the moment she jumped off the ship and, finding herself in the boat, immediately fainted. One man, probably losing his reason from panic, nearly killed one of these unhappy creatures by throwing a heavy box which, on falling into our boat, burst open and revealed itself to be a rather expensive dressing-case. Without asking myself whether I had a right to dispose of it, I at once presented it to the two sailors who, too, accepted my present without the slightest embarrassment. We immediately started rowing with all our might towards the shore, accompanied by cries from the ship: "Come back quickly! Send us back the boat!" When, therefore, the water was no more than just over two feet deep we had to climb out. A fine, cold drizzle had been falling for almost an hour, without having the slightest effect on the fire, but it drenched us to the skin.

At last we reached the longed-for shore which turned out to be nothing but a huge pool of liquid, sticky mud, in which we sank up to the knees.

Our boat left rapidly and, like the large lifeboat, began shuttling to and fro between the ship and shore. Only a few passengers were lost, eight in all; one of them fell into the coal hold and another was drowned because he would take all his money with him. This last, whose name I hardly knew, had been playing chess with me most of that day and did it with such passionate abandon that Prince V—, who had been watching our game, could not help exclaiming in the end: "You play as though it were a matter of life and death to you!"

Nearly all our baggage, I am afraid, was lost as well as the carriages.

Among the ladies rescued from the shipwreck was a Mrs. T—,

a very good-looking and charming woman but too much taken up with her four little daughters and their nannies; that was why she had been left deserted on the beach, barefoot, her shoulders scarcely covered. I thought it my duty to play the gallant; this cost me my coat which I had managed to preserve as well as my necktie and even my boots. Furthermore the peasant with a cart, drawn by two horses, whom I had found on the top of the cliffs and sent on for the ladies, did not think it necessary to wait for me and drove off to Lubeck with all my companions, so that I was left alone, half naked, soaked to the skin, in sight of the sea where our ship was slowly burning itself out. I say "burning itself out" deliberately, for I could never have believed that such a "leviathan" could be destroyed so quickly. It was now no more than a large blazing patch of fire, motionless on the surface of the sea, furrowed with black outlines of funnels and masts, with seagulls flying round and round it in a circle—slowly and impassively. Soon it was just an enormous mound of ash, shot through and through with tiny sparks and then falling apart in large curves upon the no longer turbulent waves. "And is this all?" I thought. "Is our whole life nothing but a handful of ashes scattered by the wind?"

Fortunately for the philosopher whose teeth had begun to chatter violently, another carter picked me up. He charged me two ducats for this, but he did wrap me in his thick cloak and sang two or three Mecklenburg songs which I rather liked. I reached Lubeck at dawn. There I met my fellow-castaways and we left for Hamburg, where we found twenty thousand silver roubles which Emperor Nicholas, who had happened to be passing through Berlin just then, sent us by his A.D.C. The men met and decided unanimously to offer this money to the ladies. We could do this all the more easily since in those days any Russian travelling in Germany enjoyed unlimited credit. Now this is no longer so.

The sailor to whom I had promised a vast sum of money in my mother's name, came to demand that I should carry out my promise. But as I was not absolutely certain whether he really was the same sailor and, moreover, since he had done absolutely nothing to save me, I offered him a thaler which he was only too pleased to accept.

As for the poor old cook who had been so concerned about the salvation of my soul, I never saw her again, but of her it can certainly be said that whether she was roasted or drowned, she had a place reserved for her in heaven.

Bougival, June 17, 1883.

IVAN R. DEE PAPERBACKS

Literature, Arts, and Letters
Roger Angell, *Once More Around the Park*
Walter Bagehot, *Physics and Politics*
Stephen Vincent Benét, *John Brown's Body*
Isaiah Berlin, *The Hedgehog and the Fox*
F. Bordewijk, *Character*
Robert Brustein, *Cultural Calisthenics*
Robert Brustein, *Dumbocracy in America*
Anthony Burgess, *Shakespeare*
Philip Callow, *From Noon to Starry Night*
Philip Callow, *Son and Lover: The Young D. H. Lawrence*
Philip Callow, *Vincent Van Gogh*
Anton Chekhov, *The Comic Stories*
Bruce Cole, *The Informed Eye*
James Gould Cozzens, *Castaway*
James Gould Cozzens, *Men and Brethren*
Clarence Darrow, *Verdicts Out of Court*
Floyd Dell, *Intellectual Vagabondage*
Theodore Dreiser, *Best Short Stories*
Joseph Epstein, *Ambition*
André Gide, *Madeleine*
Gerald Graff, *Literature Against Itself*
John Gross, *The Rise and Fall of the Man of Letters*
Olivia Gude and Jeff Huebner, *Urban Art Chicago*
Irving Howe, *William Faulkner*
Aldous Huxley, *After Many a Summer Dies the Swan*
Aldous Huxley, *Ape and Essence*
Aldous Huxley, *Collected Short Stories*
Roger Kimball, *Tenured Radicals*
Hilton Kramer, *The Twilight of the Intellectuals*
Hilton Kramer and Roger Kimball, eds., *Against the Grain*
F. R. Leavis, *Revaluation*
F. R. Leavis, *The Living Principle*
F. R. Leavis, *The Critic as Anti-Philosopher*
Marie-Anne Lescourret, *Rubens: A Double Life*
Sinclair Lewis, *Selected Short Stories*

William L. O'Neill, ed., *Echoes of Revolt: The Masses, 1911–1917*
Budd Schulberg, *The Harder They Fall*
Ramón J. Sender, *Seven Red Sundays*
Peter Shaw, *Recovering American Literature*
James B. Simpson, ed., *Veil and Cowl*
Tess Slesinger, *On Being Told That Her Second Husband Has Taken His First Lover, and Other Stories*
Donald Thomas, *Swinburne*
B. Traven, *The Bridge in the Jungle*
B. Traven, *The Carreta*
B. Traven, *The Cotton-Pickers*
B. Traven, *General from the Jungle*
B. Traven, *Government*
B. Traven, *March to the Montería*
B. Traven, *The Night Visitor and Other Stories*
B. Traven, *The Rebellion of the Hanged*
B. Traven, *Trozas*
Anthony Trollope, *Trollope the Traveller*
Rex Warner, *The Aerodrome*
Rebecca West, *A Train of Powder*
Thomas Wolfe, *The Hills Beyond*
Wilhelm Worringer, *Abstraction and Empathy*
The Shakespeare Handbooks by Alistair McCallum
Hamlet
King Lear
Macbeth
Romeo and Juliet

American History and American Studies
Stephen Vincent Benét, *John Brown's Body*
Henry W. Berger, ed., *A William Appleman Williams Reader*
Andrew Bergman, *We're in the Money*
Paul Boyer, ed., *Reagan as President*
William Brashler, *Josh Gibson*
Robert V. Bruce, *1877: Year of Violence*
Douglas Bukowski, *Navy Pier*
Philip Callow, *From Noon to Starry Night*

Laurie Winn Carlson, *A Fever in Salem*

Kendrick A. Clements, *Woodrow Wilson*

Richard E. Cohen, *Rostenkowski*

David Cowan and John Kuenster, *To Sleep with the Angels*

George Dangerfield, *The Era of Good Feelings*

Clarence Darrow, *Verdicts Out of Court*

Allen F. Davis, *American Heroine*

Floyd Dell, *Intellectual Vagabondage*

Elisha P. Douglass, *Rebels and Democrats*

Theodore Draper, *The Roots of American Communism*

Edward Jay Epstein, *News from Nowhere*

Joseph Epstein, *Ambition*

Peter G. Filene, *In the Arms of Others*

Richard Fried, ed., *Bruce Barton's The Man Nobody Knows*

Lloyd C. Gardner, *Pay Any Price*

Lloyd C. Gardner, *Spheres of Influence*

Paul W. Glad, *McKinley, Bryan, and the People*

Eric F. Goldman, *Rendezvous with Destiny*

Sarah H. Gordon, *Passage to Union*

Daniel Horowitz, *The Morality of Spending*

Kenneth T. Jackson, *The Ku Klux Klan in the City, 1915–1930*

Edward Chase Kirkland, *Dream and Thought in the Business Community, 1860–1900*

Herbert S Klein, *Slavery in the Americas*

Aileen S. Kraditor, *Means and Ends in American Abolitionism*

Hilton Kramer, *The Twilight of the Intellectuals*

Hilton Kramer and Roger Kimball, eds., *The Betrayal of Liberalism*

Irving Kristol, *Neoconservatism*

Leonard W. Levy, *Jefferson and Civil Liberties: The Darker Side*

Leonard W. Levy, *Original Intent and the Framers' Constitution*

Leonard W. Levy, *Origins of the Fifth Amendment*

Leonard W. Levy, *The Palladium of Justice*

Seymour J. Mandelbaum, *Boss Tweed's New York*

Thomas J. McCormick, *China Market*

John Harmon McElroy, *American Beliefs*

Gerald W. McFarland, *A Scattered People*

Walter Millis, *The Martial Spirit*

Nicolaus Mills, ed., *Culture in an Age of Money*

Nicolaus Mills, *Like a Holy Crusade*

Roderick Nash, *The Nervous Generation*

Keith Newlin, ed., *American Plays of the New Woman*

William L. O'Neill, ed., *Echoes of Revolt: The Masses, 1911–1917*

Gilbert Osofsky, *Harlem: The Making of a Ghetto*

Edward Pessen, *Losing Our Souls*

Glenn Porter and Harold C. Livesay, *Merchants and Manufacturers*

John Prados, *The Hidden History of the Vietnam War*

John Prados, *Presidents' Secret Wars*

Patrick Renshaw, *The Wobblies*

Edward Reynolds, *Stand the Storm*

Louis Rosen, *The South Side*

Richard Schickel, *The Disney Version*

Richard Schickel, *Intimate Strangers*

Richard Schickel, *Matinee Idylls*

Richard Schickel, *The Men Who Made the Movies*

Edward A. Shils, *The Torment of Secrecy*

Geoffrey S. Smith, *To Save a Nation*

Robert W. Snyder, *The Voice of the City*

Bernard Sternsher, ed., *Hitting Home: The Great Depression in Town and Country*

Bernard Sternsher, ed., *Hope Restored: How the New Deal Worked in Town and Country*

Bernard Sternsher and Judith Sealander, eds., *Women of Valor*

Athan Theoharis, *From the Secret Files of J. Edgar Hoover*

Nicholas von Hoffman, *We Are the People Our Parents Warned Us Against*

Norman Ware, *The Industrial Worker, 1840–1860*
Tom Wicker, *JFK and LBJ: The Influence of Personality upon Politics*
Robert H. Wiebe, *Businessmen and Reform*
T. Harry Williams, *McClellan, Sherman and Grant*
Miles Wolff, *Lunch at the 5 & 10*
Randall B. Woods and Howard Jones, *Dawning of the Cold War*
American Ways Series:
    John A. Andrew III, *Lyndon Johnson and the Great Society*
    Roger Daniels, *Not Like Us*
    J. Matthew Gallman, *The North Fights the Civil War: The Home Front*
    Lewis L. Gould, *1968: The Election That Changed America*
    John Earl Haynes, *Red Scare or Red Menace?*
    D. Clayton James and Anne Sharp Wells, *From Pearl Harbor to V-J Day*
    John W. Jeffries, *Wartime America*
    Curtis D. Johnson, *Redeeming America*
    Maury Klein, *The Flowering of the Third America*
    Larry M. Logue, *To Appomattox and Beyond*
    Jean V. Matthews, *Women's Struggle for Equality*
    Iwan W. Morgan, *Deficit Government*
    Robert Muccigrosso, *Celebrating the New World*
    Daniel Nelson, *Shifting Fortunes*
    Thomas R. Pegram, *Battling Demon Rum*
    Burton W. Peretti, *Jazz in American Culture*
    Hal K. Rothman, *Saving the Planet*
    John A. Salmond, *"My Mind Set on Freedom"*
    William Earl Weeks, *Building the Continental Empire*
    Mark J. White, *Missiles in Cuba*

Philosophy
Philosophers in 90 Minutes by Paul Strathern
    Thomas Aquinas in 90 Minutes
    Aristotle in 90 Minutes
    St. Augustine in 90 Minutes
    Berkeley in 90 Minutes
    Confucius in 90 Minutes
    Derrida in 90 Minutes
    Descartes in 90 Minutes
    Foucault in 90 Minutes
    Hegel in 90 Minutes
    Hume in 90 Minutes
    Kant in 90 Minutes
    Kierkegaard in 90 Minutes
    Leibniz in 90 Minutes
    Locke in 90 Minutes
    Machiavelli in 90 Minutes
    Marx in 90 Minutes
    Nietzsche in 90 Minutes
    Plato in 90 Minutes
    Bertrand Russell in 90 Minutes
    Sartre in 90 Minutes
    Schopenhauer in 90 Minutes
    Socrates in 90 Minutes
    Spinoza in 90 Minutes
    Wittgenstein in 90 Minutes

Theatre and Drama
Linda Apperson, *Stage Managing and Theatre Etiquette*
Robert Brustein, *Cultural Calisthenics*
Robert Brustein, *Dumbocracy in America*
Robert Brustein, *Reimagining American Theatre*
Robert Brustein, *The Theatre of Revolt*
Stephen Citron, *The Musical from the Inside Out*
Irina and Igor Levin, *Working on the Play and the Role*
Keith Newlin, ed., *American Plays of the New Woman*
Louis Rosen, *The South Side*
David Wood, with Janet Grant, *Theatre for Children*
Plays for Performance:
    Aristophanes, *Lysistrata*

Pierre Augustin de Beaumarchais, *The Barber of Seville*
Pierre Augustin de Beaumarchais, *The Marriage of Figaro*
Anton Chekhov, *The Cherry Orchard*
Anton Chekhov, *The Seagull*
Euripides, *The Bacchae*
Euripides, *Iphigenia in Aulis*
Euripides, *Iphigenia Among the Taurians*
Euripides, *Medea*
Euripides, *The Trojan Women*
Georges Feydeau, *Paradise Hotel*
Henrik Ibsen, *A Doll's House*
Henrik Ibsen, *Ghosts*
Henrik Ibsen, *Hedda Gabler*
Henrik Ibsen, *The Master Builder*
Henrik Ibsen, *When We Dead Awaken*
Henrik Ibsen, *The Wild Duck*
Heinrich von Kleist, *The Prince of Homburg*
Christopher Marlowe, *Doctor Faustus*
Molière, *The Bourgeois Gentleman*
The Mysteries: Creation
The Mysteries: The Passion
Luigi Pirandello, *Six Characters in Search of an Author*
Budd Schulberg, with Stan Silverman, *On the Waterfront* (the play)
Sophocles, *Antigone*
Sophocles, *Electra*
Sophocles, *Oedipus the King*
August Strindberg, *The Father*
August Strindberg, *Miss Julie*
The Shakespeare Handbooks by Alistair McCallum
Hamlet
King Lear
Macbeth
Romeo and Juliet

European and World History
John Charmley, *Chamberlain and the Lost Peace*
Lee Feigon, *China Rising*
Lee Feigon, *Demystifying Tibet*
Mark Frankland, *The Patriots' Revolution*
Lloyd C. Gardner, *Spheres of Influence*
David Gilmour, *Cities of Spain*
Raul Hilberg, et al., eds., *The Warsaw Diary of Adam Czerniakow*
Gertrude Himmelfarb, *Darwin and the Darwinian Revolution*
Gertrude Himmelfarb, *Marriage and Morals Among the Victorians*
Gertrude Himmelfarb, *Victorian Minds*
Thomas A. Idinopulos, *Jerusalem*
Thomas A. Idinopulos, *Weathered by Miracles*
Allan Janik and Stephen Toulmin, *Wittgenstein's Vienna*
Hilton Kramer and Roger Kimball, eds., *The Betrayal of Liberalism*
Ronnie S. Landau, *The Nazi Holocaust*
Filip Müller, *Eyewitness Auschwitz*
Clive Ponting, *1940: Myth and Reality*
A.L. Rowse, *The Elizabethan Renaissance: The Life of the Society*
A.L. Rowse, *The Elizabethan Renaissance: The Cultural Achievement*
Scott Shane, *Dismantling Utopia*
Alexis de Tocqueville, *Memoir on Pauperism*
Paul Webster, *Petain's Crime*
John Weiss, *Ideology of Death*